A Democratic Mind

A Democratic Mind

Psychology and Psychiatry with Fewer Meds and More Soul

I. W. Charny

With a Foreword by
Allen Frances, M.D., editor of DSM-IV

LEXINGTON BOOKS
Lanham • Boulder • New York • London

Published by Lexington Books
An imprint of The Rowman & Littlefield Publishing Group, Inc.
4501 Forbes Boulevard, Suite 200, Lanham, Maryland 20706
www.rowman.com

Unit A, Whitacre Mews, 26-34 Stannary Street, London SE11 4AB

British Library Cataloguing in Publication Information Available

Library of Congress Cataloging-in-Publication Data Available

ISBN 978-1-4985-6139-6 (cloth : alk. paper)
ISBN 978-1-4985-6140-2 (electronic)

™ The paper used in this publication meets the minimum requirements of American National Standard for Information Sciences—Permanence of Paper for Printed Library Materials, ANSI/NISO Z39.48-1992.

Printed in the United States of America

I have a dear close friend in my life, my wife, Judy.
And we have 6 children, and from them
13 beautiful grandchildren.
Children: Adam; Rena; Anna; Michelle; David; and Aviv
Grandchildren: Zachary; Yuval; Tal; Maayan; Matan;
Hallel; Ori; Roni; Tamar; Shira; Lia; Anna; and Nathan
With much love is this book about life
dedicated to each of your lives.
Your husband-friend/father or stepfather/grandfather or
stepgrandfather ("Sababa"),
Israel W. Charny

Contents

Foreword

An Appreciation along with a Debate with the Author

Allen Frances, MD, Editor of *DSM-IV*

This is a fascinating book, expressing noble and spectacularly ambitious aims. Dr. Charny is an idealist. At times I found myself thinking of him as a kind of Don Quixote come to rescue mental health practice. He hopes to perfect humanity and improve society by reducing our inborn tendency to dogmatic, selfish, authoritarian thinking. His premise is that our species is limited by a fairly primitive mental apparatus that needs a "software upgrade" to provide us with the tools to live more at peace with ourselves and with each other.

To accomplish this, Dr. Charny would widely expand the purview of psychiatric diagnosis and treatment. Whenever possible, psychotherapy is given the new and grand purpose of promoting a "free and nonviolent Democratic Mind that enters into basically respectful and egalitarian relations with others." No longer should therapists be satisfied with helping patients reduce symptoms and mental suffering; they should now also identify and remediate the hurtful and even evil tendencies that cause suffering in others. Diagnosis and treatment must also extend beyond the individual to encompass relational problems at the family and societal level. We must not be satisfied with treating pathology; instead, we must strive to create goodness where once there was evil. Dr. Charny's original contribution to diagnosing mental health problems is his proposal that all psychiatric diagnosis revolve around the two sides of a human being's functioning, a person's disabilities and whether they are doing harm to their lives, and whether a person is doing harm to the lives of others.

The author is an expert not only in integrative psychotherapy and family therapy, but also a leader in Holocaust and genocide studies and a close student of all human disasters. Having plumbed the depths of human misery and evil, he remains convinced that many of us can be redeemed and find the good. Now in the twilight of his productive life, Dr. Charny provides a moral legacy, and offers to lead us toward a higher level of living and loving. Dr. Charny is also an unusually brave and honest man who invited me to write this Foreword, with full knowledge that I would disagree with many of his assumptions and conclusions. Few writers are so eager to invite challenge and engage in spirited debate, wherever the chips may fall. I salute him, even as I present a much more pessimistic view of the flexibility of human nature and describe the constraining limitations of diagnosis and therapy in trying to change it.

Let's count the ways Dr. Charny and I differ. Dr. Charny is a hopeful optimist; I am a skeptical pessimist. He shoots for the stars; my feet are firmly stuck in the ground. He hopes for a thoroughgoing reform of human nature; I find this an impossible dream and am happy enough if patients can achieve less distress and better functioning. He hopes that psychotherapy can cure evil; I doubt we have any useful role to play in containing it. He is very dissatisfied with current diagnostic categories and hopes to develop a new system with greatly expanded scope. I am equally unhappy with the current diagnostic system (and know its limitations perhaps better than anyone), but also see the risks and unintended consequences of untested proposals for change. We have both promoted integrative psychotherapy, but he hopes that it can achieve much more in the future than it has in the past. I am a great believer that psychotherapy can reduce suffering and improve relationships, but an equally great doubter that it can change human nature, cure evil, or perfect society. He believes that therapy can at least help people identify evil that is coming at them from others and thus to be less naive and more effective in coping with the stress. And he believes that many of us who really want to be decent people can learn about the harm we are doing to others and correct ourselves. We both oppose the massive misuse of medication resulting from the medicalization of psychological, social, and existential problems, but I am equally worried that we are also under-medicating those with severe mental illness who have no access to care. We both agree that humans are born with chimp morality, but I doubt his claims that human exceptionalism allows many of us to rise much above ourselves. My temperament precludes utopian dreams of human or societal reform. Experience suggests that the one thing we learn from history is that we don't learn from history and that utopian dreams generally turn into dystopian nightmares.

Our differences will become clearer if we use *DSM* as an example. Of course, as the Editor of *DSM-IV*, I am still basically identified with what we were attempting to achieve. And at the same time I welcome constructive critiques and creative suggestions. Dr. Charny is strongly critical of *DSM* because it does so little and leaves out so much. I am accepting of *DSM* because what little it does is much better than nothing and also better than adopting impractical alternatives whose reach exceeds our possible grasp. The work on *DSM-III* began in the mid-1970s, both the best and worst of times for psychiatry. Best because the field was benefiting from interesting ideas, new models of treatment, and the exciting research tools of neuroscience and genetics. Worst because the credibility of psychiatry had recently been put very much in doubt by two damning studies—one that documented the unreliability of psychiatric diagnosis and another showing that prolonged psychiatric hospitalizations occurred even when they were clearly unnecessary. *DSM-III* had as its primary goal restoring the credibility of psychiatric diagnosis by showing it could be done reliably. This would facilitate clinical communication, make research possible, and provide a framework for treatment guidelines. There was no pretense that the diagnoses selected, and the criteria chosen to define them, were based on validated research or that this was the only, or best, way of slicing the pie. *DSM* was meant to be no more than a guide to be used with clinical judgment and to be revised in an iterative process as more knowledge was acquired.

The prevailing model before *DSM-III* was biopsychosocial—a rounded and three-dimensional view of mental disorders and the people who suffer from them. The wide range of treatments included the then new medications, psychodynamic psychotherapy, cognitive behavioral approaches, and a wide variety of family and group treatments. Community psychiatry was in its heyday and systems theory was informing all the different types of therapeutic intervention. The competition among schools of thought was restrained and healthy, because most everyone realized that none held a monopoly on truth or effectiveness. *DSM-III* made the claim that it would provide a theoretical diagnostic tool applicable in all psychiatric work and be neutral to the needs of the various treatment approaches.

I and others predicted that this could not possibly be true. In order to achieve its primary goal of reliability, *DSM-III* had to be based on simple defining criteria that tapped only the most superficial of symptoms and behaviors—those that could easily be agreed upon by different observers. Psychodynamic constructs require inferences about unconscious motivation that are fascinating and often accurate, but are inherently inferential and impossible to reduce to the superficial level of defining items necessary to achieve inter-rater reliability. I was *DSM-III* liaison to the psychoanalytic associations, charged with the unpleasant task of explaining to them why the new diagnostic system could not accommodate time-honored but impossible to assess constructs. *DSM-III* was also explicitly a system meant to be applied only to individuals, not to larger units of possible interest such as families and groups. Family and group therapies were progressively frozen out as more and more people obtained medical insurance that required a *DSM* diagnosis to confirm eligibility. Cognitive therapy and medication management were the only two approaches to evaluation and treatment that were completely compatible with the symptom-driven *DSM* approach. Both thrived at the regrettable expense of their competitors, thus much narrowing the range of effective treatments and their scope.

DSM also had other undesirable, unintended consequences. Hippocrates had said: "It is more important to know the patient who has the disease than the disease the patient has." *DSM* criteria were meant to guide only the diagnostic portion of the assessment, not to totally dominate it. But soon many clinicians lost touch with the complex beauty of the doctor/patient relationship and became rote gatherers of checklist information. *DSM* thus encouraged a biological reductionism that minimized the psychological and social contributions to psychopathology and to its treatment. And, unwittingly, this gave Pharma an opening to disease monger mental disorders as a way of pushing its pills. While working on *DSM-III*, we discussed trying to right the imbalance by publishing a companion volume that would summarize the kind of additional psychosocial information beyond symptom checklists that would help inform treatment with chapters on assessment based on psychodynamic, cognitive/behavioral, interpersonal, family systems, and group principles. But this would have been very difficult, perhaps impossible, to accomplish, and everyone had by then run out of steam—and the project never got done. Everything since *DSM-III* has been just a footnote and the world would be as well off, perhaps better, if *DSM-IV* and *DSM-5* had never been done.

So far Dr. Charny and I mostly agree on the problems created by the *DSM*s, but here we part company. Dr. Charny sees little value in the *DSM* system and blames it for many of the ills that afflict mental health practice and, in a larger sense, even the world. He has a far-reaching idea about replacing it with a much expanded new system that would emphasize the harm one is doing to others along with the harm to one's own self and one's disabilities. While I respect his effort intellectually, I have also learned to be distrustful of ambitious claims. Despite all its well-known limitations, I believe *DSM* still to be useful clinically and that this is all we can expect of any diagnostic system. I don't trust those clinicians who rely exclusively on *DSM*, but I equally distrust those clinicians who use it not at all.

Dr. Charny is so critical of *DSM* because he expects far too much from it. *DSM* is no more, but no less, than a simple guide to diagnostic decision making. It is not a "bible" of psychiatry or a societal manifesto. It is more the result of the forces shaping its times than an independent force shaping those times. Had there been no *DSM*, there would still be biological reductionism driven by the neuroscience revolution and drug company greed. *DSM* contributed to our current unfortunate reductionism, but only as a bit player. *DSM* has been misused, but it is not responsible for all the problems of the world, and there is no diagnostic system likely to materially improve the world.

Freud described his goal as turning neurotic misery into ordinary human unhappiness. Dr. Charny would turn neurotic misery and even some aspects of human evil into a new, utopian, egalitarian mind-set. Would it were possible, but I fear it isn't. I believe in human happiness, but not in human perfectibility. But let the reader decide between Dr. Charny's hopes and my doubts. I hope he is right.

Preface and Acknowledgments

ONESELF AND/OR OTHERS

The following are key aims of this book:

- Upset the applecart of a "symptom-cataloging psychiatry" (which then sells meds)
- Look at disorders that are nowhere in *DSM*, because *DSM* is so busy with classic symptoms and doesn't get the real underlying process of escapes from Being.
- Use the lens of a "democratic mind" to see mental disorders as well as relationship disorders as akin to and deriving from the same kind of "fascist thinking" that makes for terrifying destruction on the societal level
- Propose a basic diagnostic test for mental and relationship disorders: the extent to which people are doing harm to themselves *and* the harm they are doing to others—the common denominator is how one is harming Life
- Seek first and foremost possibilities of inspiration, relearning, and coaching in individual and family psychotherapy (with meds assisting on a selective basis)

This is an original pacesetting work that calls on the fields of psychology and psychiatry to diagnose all cases on the basis of how well or poorly a person is treating both himself or herself and others. Beyond treating symptoms of mental pain and disorder, this work calls for psychotherapy that also treats human evil and cultivates a free and democratic mind that embraces life and does no harm to others.

We expand traditional presentations of psychopathology and psychotherapy to include:

- diagnosis of all mental health conditions based *both* on how a person is suffering and doing harm to *his or her own life*, and how a person is causing or enabling suffering and doing harm to *other persons' lives*;
- a formulation of psychotherapy that goes beyond symptom relief and removal to cultivating a free and nonviolent Democratic Mind that enters into basically respectful and egalitarian relationships with others;
- studying relationship disorders (such as marital or parent-child problems) and bona fide psychiatric conditions as cut from the same cloth of principles of promoting healthy life for oneself and others;
- new concepts for the psychotherapy of *Job* (as in the Bible)-like victims of catastrophic losses, intervening in the heat of emotion-based violence (not criminal or ideological), and how to approach treating common and widespread disorders of evil in life that are normally excluded from our models of psychology and psychotherapy.

In this work, we also make an effort to make the profession of mental health more relevant to our ongoing lives in this world by going beyond concern for how people live out their own personal lives to look at political behaviors that contribute to major destruction of human life as psychological and behavioral roles and not only political choices. We break to a large extent with professional tradition by seeking to construct a bridge between traditional concepts of psychopathology and the politics of fascism, terrorism, and genocide. These subjects are referred to as huge extensions of the everyday psychological issues of how a person treats LIFE.

The book includes concrete suggestions for psychotherapy and case examples of psychotherapy that are based *both* on caring and taking good care of oneself but then also taking good care of other human beings in their chance at life. Psychotherapy is presented as an opportunity to learn truths about oneself and make corrections in one's character, lifestyle, and relationships to other people. It is about our ability to *choose* a better future both for ourselves to enjoy life more meaningfully, and to support other people in the life opportunities they have. The limitations of psychiatric medications are discussed critically but respectfully, and there is special consideration of the overall question of how much we can treat the Mind through the Body.

The basic principle applied to the understanding and treatment of psychopathology and relationship disorders is that features of fascist or totalitarian thinking are at work both on a societal level and in people's personal spaces. There is a considerable parallel between the use of totalitarian thinking in the organization of human experience by the individual and the phenomenon of fascism we know so well and too often on the level of society.

The subject matter of this book is at one and the same time traditional psychopathology and relationship disorders in marriage, parenting, and family life; the two subjects are not segregated into separate books as if they were the provinces of different professions.

In sum, we propose that the optimal goal of psychotherapy lies in the cultivation of a free mind with integrity that will seek not to do major harm to one's own life or to the lives of others. We call it a "Democratic Mind." It is authentic. It includes all that we know as "good" with a basic acceptance even of one's "bad" impulses as emotions and thoughts but not in destructive actions. Democratic Mind is ethical and spiritual in applying feelings and thoughts to furthering life constructively. It is open to truthful information about existential realities and truths about ourselves, our relationships with others, and the collective groups in which we participate.

The prime source of psychiatric and societal health is commitment to a love of life—both for oneself and for others.

ACKNOWLEDGMENTS

Three really good friends-colleagues "walked with me in the forest" of producing this book that I have long dreamt of doing.

The first is my very dear wife, who is also a meaningful professional colleague (to whom, along with our children and grandchildren, I dedicate this book), Judy Katz-Charny, MSW.

My second acknowledgment and professional appreciation is to an information specialist, Marc I. Sherman, MLS, who, in addition to calling me regularly to check if the Old Man is still kicking, accompanies me all the way in seeking and collecting information that I seek and has done the kindness of reviewing and editing the notes of the book and the index.

Finally, my enormous thanks go to my professional assistant, Karen Wolberger, MPH, who has accompanied and assisted me at every stage of this work, and with whom it is a privilege to work and enjoy working.

I am also deeply grateful to Allen Frances, MD, for agreeing to write his complimentary but also (democratically!) critical foreword to this book, needless to say after he had read everything I have to say about psychiatric medications and about the *DSM.*

Along with Dr. Frances, I have thanks for my additional colleagues who wrote such warm endorsements of the book, David Scharff, MD, Michael Berenbaum, PhD, and Susan McDaniel, PhD. Any well-versed mental health professional will recognize in all these colleagues outstanding leaders in the field. To me it's clear that all four have gone beyond conventional professional courtesy about what a "fine and interesting book" it is, and have written with genuine enthusiasm that the book is a wonderful read and that its conception is a game-changer for psychology and psychotherapy. Personally and professionally I am warmed and grateful.

THE CASE HISTORIES IN THIS BOOK

There are clinical illustrations in this book preceded by a diamond symbol and are set off in indented extracts. Needless to say, no identifying information is given about the people in these cases. The clinical illustrations presented have been purposely chosen also to include cases where the treatment was *not* helpful or worse had a bad outcome. I have always felt uncomfortable as well as critical of a kind of hucksterism in the many books which present testimonials only to successes in psychotherapy. *It ain't so*, no matter what wonderful technique of therapy is used, and no matter how capable the therapist.

I love psychotherapy and take joy in the fact that we help many, many people, but it is far from a cure-all, and there are regrettably many poor outcomes. Certainly this book, which is about not pandering to certainties and does not suppress information that is disagreeable, needs to project relatively authentic pictures of people and of the outcomes of therapy. Besides, failed cases of therapy, like many of the mistakes we make in our own lives and the failures we all rack up, also are opportunities for much constructive learning.

Introduction

COMING BACK HOME FROM THE STUDY OF GENOCIDE TO EVERYDAY PSYCHOPATHOLOGY AND PSYCHOTHERAPY

Many of my friends naturally have asked me what the title of the book is that I've been writing these last two years. When I tell them, many of them smile with appreciation for the concept of a "free democratic mind," but no few of them also proceed to ask me: Just what is a democratic mind? Some also go on to ask, "Does this mean that there is no therapy for fascist minds? Is there no help for them?"

The explanation that we are aiming at free minds that do no harm goes pretty easily. Just about everybody recognizes his or her own self when I describe embracing the wide range of feelings and thoughts that come up in us, including the so-called "bad" aggressive feelings and fantasies toward all sorts of people in our lives, as well as a range of sexual feelings and fantasies. Some people are surprised at first, but basically a majority like the idea of accepting what is really coming up in their minds, so long as the preoccupation is done in moderation and is understood to be completely separate from decisions to act on their impulses. People also have no trouble understanding the concept of striving to do no harm to oneself and striving to do no harm to other people's lives.

The tougher concept for many of my friends has been the broader understanding of what a democratic mind means, and how this too is in the province of psychology and psychotherapy and not simply people's rights to their political viewpoints—right or wrong. Now we are entering somehow deeper inner worlds of contradictions, dilemmas, and difficult choices in our hearts and minds that come up about so much of life and toward just about everybody in our lives.

It is to grasp that a democratic mind does not seek total and immediate comforts but tolerates complexity and even tension and anxiety as normal parts of life that also spur on healing and creativity. It is a mind that is tolerant both of oneself and others and does not impose fascist sanctions or use violence against the self or against other persons if they don't behave as we desire. It is both a freer life and a more responsible way of life, both to oneself and to others.

Psychotherapy for a democratic and free mind means working with people on how they are really living and whether they are giving themselves as good a break as can be in this life, and it also means looking at how they are really living with other people and what impact they are having on their lives. It means that asking for psychiatric or psychological help when one feels upset, rattled, or downright crazy should not mean automatically getting flooded by chemicals, submitting to electric shock, or even undergoing quite effective symptom-altering psychotherapy without a real good look at how one is using life's opportunities and affecting other people for better and for worse. Psychotherapy means greater candor with oneself about one's emotions, thoughts, and behaviors and fewer fictions, rationalizations, and escapes from the truth. It means accepting and working with the inevitable contradictions in one's heart and mind toward just about everything and just about everybody.

Can fascists also be treated? *Whew!* If they would only come for therapy. In some situations some do come, usually because they are being forced to face possible dissolution of their marriage and/or family. In contrast to empathy and kindness, we need techniques for confronting them; limiting them; and, *yes*, beating them down, as opposed to naive efforts at traditional psychotherapy that characteristically end in failure. It is a form of what has come to be known as "tough love," and it also involves therapists and mental health agencies calling in the legal system to limit outright exploitation and abuse, such as parents who are sexually abusing their children or using violence toward family members. In *some* of these cases, thwarting the continuation of evil activities will lead to a person and/or family unit being ready to proceed to more traditional treatment to reconstruct their lives. Thus, there are some mental health agencies that also work with people who are actually in jail but are released by the authorities to join in family therapy sessions in the community. But, unfortunately, for the most part committed fascists don't come to therapists.

Healthy minds can also contribute to building a better free and democratic society and to opposing fascist modes, including many currently "politically correct" styles of life that conceal totalitarian destructiveness. *Psychotherapy for a democratic mind that does no harm to life takes us from a psychiatry of symptom control to a psychiatry of healthy living for oneself and with other people.*

FROM THE STUDY OF GENOCIDE TO EVERYDAY MENTAL HEALTH

Many years ago, I decided in my ongoing role as a psychologist and psychotherapist that I would try to contribute understanding about how our human mind works to the vital study of the Holocaust and genocide—that is, to our understanding of how everyday, ostensibly ordinary *human* beings can be the rotten destroyers they—we—are.

Now, after many years also as a genocide scholar and during what naturally will be the final years of my life, I return to my continuing home field of psychology with a hope of contributing new understanding about how our human mind works based also on much that I have learned about our species from the study of genocide.

Basically I have come to the conclusion that our human mind, brilliant as it is on the one hand, is so poorly evolved—such a flawed early version of software from the manufacturer, as it were—that it is basically organized around what I am calling a software program of fascist thinking (totalitarian thinking). Continuing with the computer analogy, the default with which we go into the world, until some of us succeed in learning better to utilize the potential in our software for upgrading, is to conduct our thinking along the lines of absolutism and certainty and to suppress any doubts, questions, and contradictory information that might weaken in any way the systems of belief to which we become beholden.

To my understanding, the same kinds of paradigms of certainty that characterize totalitarianism in society—which characteristically lead to grave suffering, a breakdown of equitable social organization, and finally to widespread destruction of human life—are also at work in the construction of psychological and relationship disorders where we do harm to ourselves and/or to others. In the organization of our emotional selves and personal relationships, too, fascist-type thinking leads to grave suffering, breakdowns of the normal organizational ego of the individual and/or relationship systems, and to destruction of the opportunities for life. Just as in society democratic organization is the best alternative to fascism, so too, the workings of "democracy in the mind" present the healthy alternative on a personal level.

A fascist mind compels the person, couple, or family to conform and obey the totalistic dictates of its designated ideology, and any deviation is treated as deserving of punishment manifesting in unforgiving symptoms in the functioning of the self or of the interpersonal system.

Such "fascist paradigms" will be seen at the center of many psychological problems, such as the inner rules that dictate major eating disorders; self-hypnotic suicidal processes; hedonistic insistence on continuous gratifications such as addictions or unending pleasures of extramarital relationships no matter that one's marriage/family is being torn apart; runaway escalating processes of hurting the other and revenge culminating in marital separation and divorce; other patterns of chronic anger and nastiness in intimate relationships; flights from yielding to dependency or tenderness; obsessive-compulsive symptoms; chronic panic or anxiety reactions; or psychosomatic illnesses, including some unconscious decisions to die whose inner paradigmatic language is, "You are unable to perform as demanded, therefore, you shall suffer your failure."

In happy dialectical contrast, a democratic and free mind delights in existence and claims its inherent rights for self-defense against dangers and extremes. But along with the protection of one's own life and embracing the truths of one's impulses, the democratic mind is always committed to deep respect for the rights of others to live and to their joy in the quality of their lives. As in all dialectical processes, there are tensions, as needs for structure and order conflict with needs for processing openness and change. In the democratic mind the various aspects of humanness are encountered, processed, and integrated with one another to create a flowing process that includes contradiction, complexity, and working with natural ambivalences within one's mind and in intimate relations. The ultimate triumph of a democratic mind is formed through choices to adopt values that promote life both for oneself and for others.

In this vein, psychotherapy is to be seen as building a "democratic mindset" where one learns to take good care of oneself and also decent care of others. Learning to achieve such an integration takes time and sets off anxieties. It requires a period of time in which one endures discomfort and learns to enjoy the music and poetry of growing healthier and stronger. *In such therapy, one does not rush to take a cocktail of mind-altering fixer-uppers in order to escape the tension of upgrading one's way of life.*

HUMAN NATURE INCLUDES A GOOD DEAL OF MEANNESS AND READINESS TO HURT ONESELF AND OTHERS

The study of genocide brought home to me, irretrievably, that there is a lot of lousiness in us human beings, and that everyone (as well as groups and societies) makes choices throughout their lives about how much to be on the side of nurturing and protecting life and how much to succumb to or embrace powers of destruction and doing harm to life—to one's own self or to others.

There is hardly any doubt that leaders are constantly arising who adopt policies of excessive power seeking and a readiness if not a lust to harm others. Nor can one doubt that many ordinary people will participate in genocidal destruction of others automatically or readily. In everyday life we see that "simply" the assignment of power brings out dictatorial and harmful aspects in the personalities of many people. Who has not seen it in work situations? Who has not seen it in family life? The psychology of readiness to hurt and, worse, destroy others is complex, but what can be said simply is that many people are drawn, in a sense "innocently," into roles of destroyers by the dynamics of processes in which they find themselves. A quick example would be following the orders of one's military commanders or civilian bosses and leaders that are ordering unthinkable acts of harming unarmed civilians. Of course this understanding cannot be taken as an excuse! (In the post-WWII Nuremberg Trials of high Nazis, the principle was laid down that one cannot do harm to people and then defend oneself as having "just followed orders."

MENTAL HEALTH IS FOR HEALTHY EXPERIENCING AND GROWING AND NOT JUST FOR REDUCING SYMPTOMS

Mental *health* means people living healthfully, experiencing the gift/opportunity of their lives both meaningfully and pleasurably, growing into fulfillment of their natural talents, being friendly and loving in their personal and especially intimate relationships, and generally being decent and ethical people. *Mental health means not doing major harm to ourselves or to others.*

Psychiatry, psychology, and psychotherapy are less about reducing emotional upset, personal discomfort, dysfunctional patterns of living, or even madness than about teaching, counseling, coaching, freeing, and enabling people to launch themselves into more healthy living. Please note unambiguously that the reduction of distress, pain, confusion, and other mental suffering is *not* ignored. I know how painful psychological distress can be. Reducing psychological suffering is valued just as is reducing physical pain in medical management of illnesses, but still the larger goal of therapy is to renew and free peoples' capacity for experiencing life in its richness, their capacity to cope with life's inevitable problems, and their ability to make constructive choices for their lives.

"Treatments" that purposely or inadvertently knock down, reduce, or suppress experiencing and do not strengthen an inner ability to cope with distress are most of the time inherently *wrong*. Thus, psychiatry once hailed lobotomies as the solution to intractable madness, but it should have been obvious from the start that lobotomy destroys the mind and soul. In our times the nostrum is medication, so there is a huge amount of overmedication with mind-altering drugs that weaken responsibility for oneself and personal willpower—as well as, in too many cases, bring on any number of serious side effects. Moreover, there is a good deal of evidence that the drug industry and medical professionals cooperate to suppress the information of serious side effects. In the case of several wide-selling psychiatric drugs for depression, there have been an incredible number of suicides and a notable number of homicides. Medication also teaches patients that they *cannot* rely on themselves. They themselves cannot learn to be mentally healthy. The damages of addictive reliance on meds are less concretely observable than the side effects, but nonetheless can be deeply injurious to the fulfillment of a person's potential. Obviously, it is wonderful that some medications bring relief from agonizing symptoms, but for the long haul, who should own the honor of increased self-confidence, greater calm, or tougher erections—us or our medications. (Is it the me who has grown and makes love to you—or is it my meds?)

Of course the same issues arise without medications in other ways in psychotherapy, especially when patients are relieved prematurely of the challenges to their lives.

- "You can drop out of school."
- "You're not alone in not having a boyfriend, and you're stressing yourself by trying so hard."
- "You are obviously attracted to [a person of your own sex] and you feel much better than when you've been with members of the opposite sex. Today it is perfectly normal to live a gay lifestyle and many more people are adopting this lifestyle and feel good in it."
- "You should get divorced instead of living with such humiliation."

In our fix-it-quick times, too often therapy is designed to comfort a person prematurely by confirming their dropping out from an arena of life in order to spare themselves anxiety. A therapist needs to think clearly when he/she advises dropping out of school rather than seeking solutions to learning anxieties and problems, or when to confirm a frightened decision to give up the quest for a full-blown sexual relationship and love. Common sense tells us that *sometimes* this is wise advice, but obviously not always, and it is a serious decision for a therapist to make. So many therapies in our time are defined as strictly medical-like symptom-correcting and symptom-reducing procedures. How many patients who gain such relief might have *learned* how to overcome their symptoms from resources within themselves and go on to greater successes in the areas in which they were suffering?

Psychotherapy needs to include tools for helping people to meet up with dangerous and ugly parts of themselves (Jungians have a fine word for these negative qualities one is not consciously aware of—our "shadows.") Psychotherapists need to stand up to evil and destructiveness and try, as wisely as possible, to bar the continuation of harming life.

Suicide?
Homicide?
Violence?
Exploitation?
Degradation ?
Sexual abuse?

These—and more—are behaviors that destroy life that must be stopped—first, for one's own welfare because they corrupt a person's inner self markedly, and second, to spare other people who are being seriously harmed.

A therapy that is always "good" to people and accepting will try to make a person feel better so they don't have to harm life. On the other hand, a therapy that is based on more forthright recognition of evil and impending harming of life will look for more direct and powerful ways to stop harmful actions. To date, too few psychotherapists are trained for such. In fact, in many quarters of the mental health society, it is considered even obscene and a virtual betrayal of the values of psychotherapy to view a patient or client critically and to use anything but positive regard and unconditional acceptance as the foundational values of therapeutic technique.

I've learned that genocide must be stopped.

I've also learned that degrading oneself, abusing oneself, damaging one's body, disowning one's potential, and self-destructive behaviors need to be stopped.

I've also learned that humiliating, insulting, degrading, or enslaving others and violence in relationships also need to be stopped.

Do we know enough about how to do any of these corrective and preventive tasks? *No.* But a first step is to know that we need to think about these issues and not simply seduce more decent and suffering people into a therapy that pretends that all can be good and beautiful, while many of those who do harm especially to others simply walk out of our therapy rooms with a sneer that they can't be stopped from being and doing what they want to be and do.

The therapist must choose very carefully whether to assist a person to back off from looming terror versus encouraging a person to take on the battle to climb the mountain. It is a highly sensitive professional choice to be undertaken in deep thought and in humility. This kind of thoughtful processing is very different from the automatic responses of so many modern-day therapists who are blindly committed to therapies that are based on retreat and escape from symptoms and challenges.

So much of modern psychiatry is an escape from the humanness of anxiety, coping, developing oneself, and ethical self-correction. *This book is dedicated to a creative unfolding of old-fashioned dynamic individual and family psychotherapy toward democratic minds—in people's individual lives, relationships, and participation in society.*

A SPECIAL INVITATION TO COGNITIVE-BEHAVIORAL THERAPISTS (CBT)

The prevailing mode of psychotherapy today in the United States is clearly cognitive behavioral therapy (CBT). This is an approach to therapy that attempts, with considerable success, to be anchored in empirical information, and aims, also with considerable success, at relieving symptom distress and reducing the suffering of many patients. But CBT is also accompanied by and linked to a broader philosophy that I believe constitutes the prevailing current politically correct attitude toward emotional and mental disorders: People with virtually all human conditions and differences are to be honored as they are, patients are to be guided to self-acceptance without "tough love" or other deep therapist-patient relationship-touching techniques that aim at elevating functioning and are intended to facilitate meaningfully deep character and relationship changes.

I definitely *do* practice CBT techniques in the therapy I practice. On a typical day this week, I taught a patient how to regain control over her breathing, which had gotten out of whack ("I feel like I can't breathe," she said in panic); taught a patient how to use breathing techniques in order to fall asleep or resume sleeping after waking up in the middle of the night; instructed a couple to schedule units of structured conversation in which each one shares what is going on in his (her) life and then the spouse is to convey his (her) understanding (though not necessarily agreement); and for another patient I designed a daily exercise in which he is to attempt in his fantasy to be angry and even to hate his mother, who devoted all of herself and then more to her "genius son," who ended up so pleasured that he is now deprived of much of his natural vitality and stamina for standing up to life. My beloved psychoanalyst so many years ago would not have offered me any of the above or anything remotely similar in the way of immediate help and direct active techniques for relief of the considerable pain that I suffered.

My own original training was essentially in psychoanalysis, and alternatively in Rogerian non-directive therapy, and then it was with awe and gratitude that I met up with the first works of the great Albert Ellis on "Rational-Emotive Therapy." Ellis gave me new tools for real help in urgent situations, such as for a college kid who was on the edge of psychosis but had to and wanted to go back in a few weeks to his college in another city to begin the fall semester. I also had the pleasure of being in personal contact with Ellis a number of times and indeed referred several of my difficult patients (in Philadelphia) to him (in New York) for his more expert help. So I am hardly a stranger or antagonistic to CBT.

Yet I have adopted another kind of philosophy of treatment where, whenever possible, the therapy aims at fighting off renunciations of power and achievement by patients who are giving up on themselves. These might be, for example, capable people who are looking to stop their education because of learning difficulties; spouses who are heading uncritically to terminate a marriage (and family) with potential for decency and pleasure because they are currently miserable or, conversely, who surrender to deadness in their marriage when they could do better outside it; and even *some* choices of alternative lifestyle by people who, as it becomes clear in therapy, essentially are running away from the pain of intimacy.

For me, many psychotherapies are profound invitations not only to symptom relief but to very meaningful growth of character, spirit, and healthy interactions in relationships. I see no contradiction between the two goals of providing relief and encouraging growth—although of course I am very aware of the significant technical issue that providing relief very quickly can inhibit what might have been a process of deeper engagement of a person with himself or herself. I believe in a therapy that aims as much as possible at egalitarian experiences with others, banishing prejudice against others who are different than we are, eschewing all violence, and basically living a life where one is good to oneself and decent and good to others—and enjoying living for all its inevitable downs.

To my CBT colleagues—therapists, clinics, and departments that have fully adopted an only-CBT approach—I extend an invitation to read this book openly, if possible without rancor, to disagree with me vigorously, but to be open to a possible contribution from my way of thinking and experience.

BASIC DEFINITIONS

What Do We Mean by a Democratic Mind?

Democratic thinking on a societal level is totally clear to all of us. It involves a system of governance that is based on a legally mandated interplay of different aspects of leadership, such as in the leading democracy in the history of the world, the United States, with a legislature, judiciary, and executive.

Most important, it is where each of these branches of government exercises significant checks and balances on the others. Democracies are also characterized by very high degrees of freedom, especially freedom of speech and of religious belief, and by extensive participation of the citizenry in voting for their leaders and occasionally also directly on policy decisions.

Here in developing a concept of a "democratic mind," we are trying to use a concept that is derived from the above for *everyday* ways of living—thinking and feeling—in the minds of ordinary human beings. In an individual person's life we are seeing an open, free, or democratic mind at work when the following occurs:

- The flow of experiencing thoughts and feelings is not rigidly one dimensional, and one is free to cycle through natural sequences that include "bad" feelings, contradictions, ambiguity, and perplexity.
- Reasonable degrees of accompanying tension and anxiety and even guilt are respected as natural and as sources of creativity; love and anger/hate are expressed in constructive ways both in one's own mind and in relationships, and neither one is lacking or excessive.
- There is a basic respect for others and acceptance of one's differences from them.
- Differences, disagreements, and conflicts are processed without undue fear or accusations of disloyalty and treachery.
- One is empowered to make choices for one's life without dictatorial coercion of a required outcome in one's own mind to oneself, or to and by others, or threats of violence for dissension.

A family that embodies and nurtures free democratic minds can be described thus:

- A democratic family is a basically happy group in which members of the family experience being valued and respected in their respective developmental stage of life.
- Leadership is vested in the parents, with *both* mother and father playing significant and overall equal roles in making decisions for the family and organizing the children's lives and their lives with one another.
- Reasonable tension and anxiety—including cycles of fearfulness about being unloved or experiences of hurt and insult—are accepted as natural to our shared human condition, and even understood to be catalysts inviting greater connection and love.
- Anger, conflict, and even hate are of course upsetting and painful and resented, but are not necessarily treated as irreconcilable, and constructive steps are taken toward resolving bad situations.

In collective situations—at work, in groups, in larger society—that embody and nurture free democratic minds:

- Decision making is rooted in the democratic choices of a group, with significant powers to act reserved for executive leaders, but who are subject to the checks and balances of other leadership bodies and to the people at large.
- Free speech is strongly protected, but there are penalties for incitement to violence and there is disqualification of manifestly prejudicial statements, for example, a sign in La Jolla, California, that read—probably into the early 1960s—"No Jews or Dogs Allowed" (the same sign has a history in other communities in North America, including Canada[1]);
- Policy making characteristically weaves a path between the built-in contradictions of life, frequently alternating between them, and also where possible integrating conflicting ideas, for example, combining free market policies and regulated market policies.
- There is a celebration of pluralism where differences between different constituencies in one's collective groups are afforded basic acceptance and respect.
- There is also an overall humanitarian ethos for extending help and support to a constituent group at times of distress or need for assistance.
- Democratic collective life maintains a categorical rejection of physical violence on every level of human life, with the exception of clear-cut self-defense, including in international affairs, with efforts to end and prevent all terrorism, mass killing, and genocide, and—however unrealistically—with a basic antiwar philosophy.

To conclude, democratic mind is attuned to the complexity of many aspects of human experience and reality, including conflicts, contradictions, and dialectical processes that cycle through alternating stages of our experience, as well as the imponderables, unknowns, and mysteries of life. Democratic mind honors reasonable tension and anxiety as accompaniments of the human condition and as catalysts for a welcome creativity. There is respect for diversity and pluralism and a commitment to largely egalitarian experiences both with others and inside of one's own mind—where a relative calm and pleasure in living are sought in the course of enjoying an unimpeded flow of the symphony of experiences.

What Do We Mean by a Fascist or Totalitarian Mind?

Fascist thinking on a societal level is totally clear to all of us. It involves a dictatorial leader and/or ideology that insists on total obeisance and punishes the almighty hell out of any alleged dissidents, often defines whoever and whatever identity, system, or people as mortal enemies of the society's existence, and often enough consigns the latter to the ultimate unrecoverable condition of being killed off. Here in developing a concept of a "fascist mind," we are trying to use a concept that is generated in the above inferno for *everyday* ways of experiencing—thinking and feeling—in ordinary human beings.

What we mean by "a fascist mind" in an individual person's life:

- A single part of a complex process that normally enjoys an interplay of a diversity of complementary and contradictory directions of experience and activity takes over, overwhelms, rules, or locks out other aspects of the process, and because of its dominant role in effect becomes the totalitarian ruler of the process, for example, a rule that one must succeed and never fail.
- There is a driving need to be a winner at whatever without a readiness to lose and without a general acceptance of losses in the games of life as natural and inevitable, and there is no deeper focus on the joy of playing the game that goes beyond an insistence on being a winner.
- A goal is defined as an invariant totality that must be religiously fulfilled at all times, for example, one must show strength and power with no hint of weakness (although note that there can also be the opposite of an invariant structure where weakness is dominant and strength is suppressed).
- Anxiety and panic are made all the worse because of a lack of acceptance and humility that there can be runaway uncontrolled aspects to our lives and fates with which we need to contend as well as possible, and as long as we are alive without giving up our inner hopes and trying to learn how to overcome and cope.
- Dissension, opposition, and noncompliance to a ruling idea, even inside one's own mind, are treated ruthlessly and often violently.

This is a family that embodies and nurtures totalitarian or fascist minds:

- Mounting anger and rage at a member of one's family—for example, at a spouse or child—far beyond what is justified even when the other is in fact unpleasant or draining a disproportionate amount of family resources (whether financially or in being the focus of worries and attention); and without taking steps to release parts of one's anger, such as yelling like hell in a closed car, or, better yet, to have a constructively firm talk with the person at whom one is angry or hates; and without any effort also at understanding and empathizing with the family member's likely inner stress.

- A submissive, dependent position in relationship to another family member—such as a wife to her husband, or increasingly in our times a husband who is *as if* a shadow personality in relation to his wife, or worse, a beaten, abused or tortured family member who does not show an instinct or ability to fight back to redefine for himself or herself a more equal position;
- Violence in family life—clearly there are frequent cases of violence in families between spouses or physical abuse of a child. (Note how basically the *DSM*'s official psychiatric diagnosis leads "simply" to the determination that there is no sign of mental illness in the abusing person, because the *DSM*'ers look only at traditional psychiatric signs of craziness and don't have the slightest idea or interest in subordinate relationships—enslaving or being a slave to someone else though these too are true forms of craziness).

In collective situations—at work, in groups, in larger society—the totalitarian or fascist mind can be seen here:

- The boss who doesn't take crap or accept feedback and differing opinions, who barks his whip-like orders that are to be obeyed immediately; the officious doctor—even if otherwise capably life-saving—who growls superciliously at every colleague, physician, nurse, or surviving patient; the professor in academia who, variously, holds on to a PhD dissertation for a year before reading it, "steals" funds for his department and project that were contributed to someone else's project, or rules colleagues and students with royal disdain. (Is the description too strong? It is an accurate summary of the academic life of one of the historically great professors in my last university. I personally treated [in private psychotherapy] one of the outstanding students of this "great professor," who made the student wait a full year for his PhD thesis to be read by the cruel great man. My patient has since become a well-known academic figure in another country—he was too burned to return to his native home).
- The employee who submits and goes along with whatever rules and regulations, and with whoever is the person in charge, even when the rules are oppressive or insulting, and even when the person in charge is obscenely bossing and pushing people around to satisfy his own needs or whims. (Have you ever had a boss at work who is matches the description? Have you ever been ordered to some kind of a "back of the bus" in your life?) In a full-blown fascist setup like a cruel POW camp, and certainly in a concentration camp, direct resistance often is foolishly self-destructive, but even in these situations there are brave people who succeed in organizing

some extent of personal and collective resistance—these are the movies that we all love to watch in the late nights.

To conclude, fascist mind refers to allowing any one aspect of human experience—after all they are all natural and to some extent all are parts of all of us in a symphonic configuration—to take totalitarian control of the streams of our experience and activity. It may be inside our own mind, where we ourselves are bossed by that part of ourselves, or in our roles in our family or in groups and society. Fascist mind is the death of a system of checks and balances of emotions and thoughts, in contrast to democratic mind, where, seeing and reflecting on the different sides of an experience we try to balance out as well as possible varied and conflicting sides of issues. Fascist mind orders us to follow whatever orders or else.

CONCLUSION

To conclude: I sincerely hope this book leads to further developments of more effective and more humanly meaningful psychotherapy, and I pray it does that little something for some improvement of our so troubled human species.

I.W. Charny
Jerusalem
February 2017

NOTE

1. Even on Toronto's beaches up to the mid-1950s, one could see signs that read "No Dogs or Jews Allowed." http://www.huffingtonpost.ca/bernie-farber/human-rights-canada_b_1510399.html.

Part I

APPLYING THE CONCEPT OF DEMOCRATIC MIND TO TREATING EMOTIONAL DISORDERS, BREAKDOWNS OF RELATIONSHIPS, AND DISORDERS OF EVIL

Chapter One

A Democratic Mind

A Different Lens for Understanding and Treating for Psychological Health

DEMOCRATIC MIND VS. FASCIST MIND

This book advances a different way of understanding a great deal of the psychological problems and psychiatric conditions in the individual and family by utilizing concepts of democracy and fascism we have previously understood only as concepts pertaining to society.

By fascism, I mean totalitarianism in one's thinking and actions. I suppose it is a giveaway of my age that my deep protest has focused on "fascists"—the Nazi nemesis of my childhood both of my America and of my Jewish people. The word "totalitarianism" also says exactly what I mean. It includes Nazism and it includes Communism. It includes religious fundamentalism—no matter what the religious identity. It includes all absolutist utopian ideologies. It certainly includes *all* those who are out to torture and murder masses of people in the name of any cause. (Even mental health would be included if it embarked on a campaign—as one joke goes—of "*Support mental health or I'll kill you.*")

We apply the concepts of fascist mind and democratic mind systematically to understand traditionally defined psychiatric and psychological disturbances.[1] They are also applied to several as yet unnamed forms of disturbed behaviors; to intimacy and relationship disorders and breakdowns in marriage, parenting, and family life; and to a variety of disorders of doing harm to others. Included in the latter are the contemporary scourge of suicide killers and other terrorists, and a new American mode of craziness of killing randomly in schools, shopping centers, and other public places.

We recommend these concepts at least in a beginning way for possible treatment of conditions of mental and relationship problems. My hope and belief is that a goal of democratic thinking opens a new opportunity and constructive frontier for attempting to enlarge our psychotherapeutic reach and effectiveness. I want to decipher a variety of mental and emotional disturbances in a different way that opens up new possibilities for treatment on the basis of what I believe is the single most basic moral or ethical issue that faces us all at different times in our lives, and that is whether to love life (democratic mind) or to destroy life (fascist mind). I propose to use new knowledge of man's capacity for evil, together with developing knowledge for understanding how man can choose not to be evil, to show how choices of democratic mind versus fascist mind are present in many decisions, such as an individual deciding whether or not to commit suicide, or the self-programming of a person who undertakes a crazy anorexia diet that can imperil her or his life, or even a decision of whether or not to go crazy and thus kill any opportunity for normal living and love of life and people.

The prevailing conception of mental health scholars and practitioners, including many who very much care about societal and political injustice and oppression, is that the knowledge we have been gaining about mind is certainly related to societal phenomena, but nonetheless is far-removed to another sphere of life, and at best is analogic and for the most part no more than a metaphoric reminder of parallel phenomena in the organization of society. Instead, I propose that there is a single pattern of rigid organization of thought, emotions, and behaviors. It is a common source of many familiar disorders of the individual psyche and breakdowns in interpersonal relationships and also the conceptual and ideological base from which totalitarian forms of society are developed and to which fascism appeals for inevitably broad support in every society.

Historically, too often mental health scientists have placed themselves to a large extent apart and separate from the great events that sweep over peoples and societies. Genocidally murderous Nazi fascism, Stalinist totalitarianism, Cambodian communism, and nowadays transnational genocidal world terrorism are not just serious societal problems that need to be solved out there while psychology as the science of human behavior retains its own pure existence as an applied clinical profession and an academic research discipline. For the most part, up until now, psychotherapists have looked through the windows of their consulting rooms onto the larger events of real politics in the world and bemoaned the lack of humanism and tolerance in human affairs. Generally caring persons, they nonetheless have been largely limited to simply observing the destructive fascist events of their eras and have not acted very much in the name of their profession to fight the fascism of their times. The more courageous and involved do seek ways to differentiate themselves from the totalitarian forms of their societies and eras, but they do so mainly as individuals, acting out of their own healthy consciences, and less in the name of their professions as therapists.[2]

Even in their consulting rooms, no few therapists perceive themselves as called on to accept *all* the people who come to them, to be understanding and forgiving of human weaknesses to such an extent that when they learn their patients are doing harm not only to themselves but also to others—such as in imperious behaviors towards employees or in exploitative and disloyal behaviors towards their children or spouses—they continue to try to woo the patient by analysis, understanding, and friendliness, while failing to call a spade a spade and failing to do battle against the various forms of tyranny they present.[3]

On a theoretical level, too, the prevailing psychological conception of man's potential for destructive aggression has pretty much remained Freud's original loose formulation of the human mind and civilization failing to overcome, stem, and organize tumultuous unconscious primal forces that are constantly threatening to erupt in violence. War, mass suicide, terrorism, and genocide are phenomena that are seen unendingly day after day on this planet and in the historical record of our human species, but it is not as if psychology can directly address and touch the ways of thinking that are involved. Certainly there is no connection seen between these behaviors and the phenomena of craziness and emotional disturbances and breakdowns of intimate relationships in the everyday lives of people.

In my judgment, many conditions of emotional disturbance in individuals as well as in marriage and family lives are based on people working themselves into rigid, unvarying positions where they believe that a given way of behaving, thinking, or feeling is the only correct way; no variation on this prescribed way of being in the world can be considered, and even tastes of an alternative way of experiencing life are viewed as wrong and unacceptable. For example, always succeed, never fail; always be strong, don't be weak; always be cheerful and positive; never be sad or anxious—and there are many more.

Once the rule is made, the devotee conforms to it in all respects. She or he becomes a devoted follower, who is loyal and unquestioning and conforms, just as in society at large most people tend to conform to whatever law or societal mode is announced as the prevailing one.

The absoluteness and certainty that are attributed to the conception of how life is to be lived are similar to what we have come to know as fascist ways of thinking about political-social issues. Criticism, differences, or serious consideration of any alternative are treated as "politically incorrect," rude, or heretical, and as if requiring punishment and perhaps "annihilation." In the fascist political state, opposition to the government and governors is ruthlessly suppressed in order to protect the well-being of the state. In the emotional lives of people, any opposition to the way things "must be" can also be ruthlessly suppressed by punishing states of mind or emotions.

Fascism is an "I know nothing world"—certainly nothing critical of the established way of life is countenanced. Sadly, in democratic countries too there can be an enormous pressure to be "correct." In our times the current "politically correct" governs most people. Thus, in the United States obesity became an entirely acceptable alternative to a disciplined diet of eating and exercising in part because of an underlying cultural rule that you are certainly never to embarrass others and especially your loved ones with criticism. So one-third of Americans became obese and literally lost many years of their lives while family, friends, and mental health professionals stood by silently or even smiling approval of the happy fat people. So too, underachieving children should be treated with kindness and understanding of their share of the endless pool of weaknesses that are waiting to be diagnosed in just about everyone. They are to be prescribed Ritalin or such, and little attention is to be given to mere old-fashioned discipline and firm expectation or to therapeutic encouragement to do more of their best. So too, the mentally ill should be accepted with great understanding and be protected rather than motivated and challenged to get better. So too, sexual screw-ups and what we once regarded as "perversions" should be tolerated if not celebrated. There are to be no more norms that define desirable mentally healthy behaviors versus mental pathology. "*We just love everybody*" is taken to mean *We leave everybody to be as they are*—without critical thought about what they might be that would be better for them and for others in their lives.

I believe we have every right to expect our mental health professions to address wrong ways of living our lives and not stop at quieting down symptoms—usually by medicines, but also by methods of psychotherapy that beat off symptoms without looking at a person's "soul" and way of life. To me it is intellectually and esthetically pleasurable to expand our understanding of the psychological processes that define psychological health versus psychological disorders. I believe that the concepts of fascist mind and democratic mind can prove to be widely applicable to a considerable range of the traditional psychiatric problems, dysfunctions, and breakdowns of relationships, as well as to evil exercises of power and doing harm to others.

There is also a further possible payoff that comes into the range of our sight and hopes. If we successfully create a linkage between fascist mind and mental disturbances, and a linkage between democratic mind and psychological health, we are led to thinking about the possibilities of new kinds of psychological treatment. The paradigms of fascist thinking versus democratic thinking invite us to create new ways of treating individuals and families in which patients may be helped to unlock over-certainties in which they have imprisoned themselves. A democratic versus fascist mind metaphor suggests *possibilities* of addressing certain rigid aspects of psychopathologies by addressing the inner logic of a person or family's way of thinking as totalitarian and inviting them to replace their fascist ways of thinking with a more democratic orientation to themselves and to their intimates.

Time after time I speak to colleague psychotherapists, among them well-experienced seniors in the field, and when I refer to the dark sides of the mind (say of a patient about whom we are collaborating or in a consultation that I have been asked to give), their faces go blank. They are so busy with the wonders of positive psychology, optimism, good resolve, narrative therapy, desensitizing trauma, resolving anger (which is defined almost always as unnecessary and a sign of frustration and emotional immaturity), forgiveness and reconciliation—much of the above beautiful and wise in their own right for me too—that they want to skip over entirely the experiencing of anger holed up in a person's inner being and how to discharge the anger morally and effectively. If I propose helping the patient to fantasy-imagine being aggressive to their object of anger—when I emphasize very clearly that there not be any *actual* interpersonal expression of anger—they don't know what I am talking about. And if I dare suggest that a given person is too far over the line of evil and unlikely to respond to our time-honored techniques of counseling and therapy (and should be treated according to other principles for addressing evil), they are upset and disbelieving (and sometimes angry at me (so now at least I have helped them come into contact with their own angry feelings).[4]

Democratic mind "follows the feeling trail" to wherever it leads—love and hate, good and bad—and works with those feelings rather than with a mythology of human innocence, goodness and divinity—again for me beautiful aspects of us humans but far from the whole story. Sigmund Freud wrote: "Unexpressed emotions will never die. They are buried alive and will come forth later in uglier ways."[5]

Deirdre Kramer sums up eloquently the underlying process truth that openness to experience is a doorway to psychological health and maturity.[6]

> Wisdom has been conceptualized as: (1) a rare, highly exercised and developed form of cognitive expertise about the domain of human affairs that allows for multiple conduits or (2) a constellation of personal attributes reflecting a high degree of cognitive, affective, and behavioral maturity that allows for an unusual degree of sensitivity, broad-mindedness, and concern for humanity. Openness to experience is the most frequent predictor of wisdom. Wise people are also found to think more dialectically, exhibit generativity and compassionate concern for others, and accept life's limitations. Wise people show less despair and less dissatisfaction by grappling with existential issues and finding purpose and meaning in adverse experiences.

There are many possible applications of the invitation to openness in the mind. For one example, this way of thinking suggests teaching patients with sleep disturbances how to reprogram a healthier use of mind that will enable them to surrender better to sleep by allowing themselves to let their thoughts and emotions stream uninterruptedly through their minds and not be afraid of the disturbing contents in their minds. Obviously this is different from taking a whopper barbiturate. It is also different from rhythmic breathing or trying to meditate to cleanse the mind of thoughts, both of which certainly can be very helpful but miss out on the further dimension of allowing the truths in the mind to come up. Ideally, both quieting oneself *and* making genuine contact with one's unconscious can be alternated and integrated. The technique of inviting a natural "town meeting" of thoughts and feelings circulating in our minds not only can facilitate sleep, but also is an opportunity for us to meet up authentically with the issues that are really concerning our inner selves at this time in our lives, and to meet up with ourselves and how we are coping.

Beyond treating the dynamics of emptiness, feelings of being unloved, and rage in a mental patient—the stocks in trade of traditional individual counseling and psychotherapy—the democracy-fascism metaphor opens new directions for treatment in the way of instructing the patients how they have locked themselves into rigid ways of thinking and become so set on destroying any opposition to their way of thinking that they are not even aware of how they are contributing to bringing on the destruction of their own lives. So too, beyond interrupting negative transactions between a person and his family in serious marital and family breakdowns, the democracy-fascism metaphor teaches patients how to tell family members what they are feeling toward them, and how to discipline themselves to listen to what their loved ones are feeling toward them, including both sides' criticisms, anger, and even hate.[7] All the while, we need to put limits on any outright abusiveness, but with no censorship of true feelings. This orientation is different from a family therapy that invites reconciliation by replacing bad feelings only with forgiveness and good feelings, such as preached by many faith-based therapists and counselors as well as therapists who cling to an innocent romanticism and an idealistic view of human nature.

Of course, like everything else that is good, mind openness also brings on new problems as well. How much openness is desirable versus how much decisiveness and personal leadership? How much of a danger is there that a person can become obsessive and indecisive? To what extent does openness of mind lead to the characteristics of many artists who, for all their charm or artistic achievement, can end up destroying their lives and driving people close to them crazy with their unreliability and the narcissism of their self-gratification? Democratic minds also need structure and organization and coherent values to guide choices in life.

The Promise and Limitations of the Democratic Mind Conception

Let me be very clear: I will not be able to describe treating for a democratic mind for *all* mental conditions. Nor is there any promise whatsoever that, when attempted, treating for a democratic mind will banish or even lessen all disturbances. There will remain many situations where people are too wounded or give up their will to live. Some won't let go of feelings of hatred, superiority, dominance, revenge, and more. And there always remains our basic natural human condition, which is inherently full of complexity, anxiety, uncertainty, and the definitive value choices we must all make that leave any healthy human being—all of us throughout all of our lives—somewhat *disturbed.* Our conception is that this existential complexity can be a wholesome state, and that a democratic mind can develop quite healthy and invigorating coping skills to a point where overall the game of life is more genuinely satisfying.[8] Rollo May, the acknowledged American "father" of existential psychotherapy wrote: "'I do not believe in toning down the daimonic. This gives a sense of false comfort. The real comfort can come only in the relationship of the therapist and the client or patient.' This compassionate, shared, professional yet profoundly personal human relationship provides both the structured, supportive container and potent existential catalyst for therapeutic transformation."[9]

Back to the out-and-out pathologies. In the end there also remain many conditions *I do not know how to treat.* Nonetheless, even in the worst scenarios I can try to contribute concepts of a democratic mind. When the truly great work of Masters and Johnson first appeared, I knew that a great step forward was achieved, and I diligently studied the new treatment techniques that they had innovated.[10] But from the very first, along with my admiration and gratitude for their advancing us, I hated the naïveté and certainty with which they prescribed their treatment results as overwhelmingly successful—they reported 90 percent success and more. I knew it couldn't be true because there is always so much human despair and destructiveness that are here to stay in our human condition. Thus, there is no way that I can hold out a promise that treating for a democratic mind will bring about greater cures, say, of a borderline personality disorder or paranoid psychosis, or change scandalous swindlers into ethical beings or bring home a disloyal spouse. But I can try—in the great tradition of science and in the wonderful history of psychotherapy—to explore new methods based on this promising and meaningful theory. Intriguingly, in psychotherapy the spirit of such exploration of new techniques in itself becomes a meaningful treatment technique that can touch a patient's heart and inspire new hope.

This book will be enjoyed by readers who want to understand more of the perplexities and convolutions of escapes and retreats into mental illness. Our conception here offers a new frame for interpreting many symptoms that are normally seen as discrete phenomena. We understand many mental symptoms as representative of an overall organizing frame of mind that in our proposed language is fascist-minded and anti-democratic.

❖ A young independent businessman around thirty years old, who has some five employees, suffers from nervousness in his work and a good deal of anger at his employees. He feels they do not follow his instructions and orders sufficiently, but he has little awareness that his own style is insultingly demanding because he is "the Boss." He is enraged and wants to take revenge on workers who do not follow his orders to a T, but also is terrified that he will end up with no staff. He has no insight into how he who hated his cold stern father from a young age is now playing the role of a tyrant. The therapy aims to release his anger at his father and to teach him how to give orders and lead workers in more winning ways.

The Key Mental Issue in Psychiatry Is How Mind Chooses to Treasure or to Destroy One's Own Life and/or the Lives of Others

In this book I will propose that *all* mental diagnosis be directed simultaneously to identifying not only how a person is suffering from disabilities, but also the self-harm that person may be doing and/or the harm being done to others. In medicine you start by seeing how the patient looks overall. In psychiatry, I propose that you start by recording observations around two questions:

1. How is the person in trouble and/or limited and how is the person harming his or her own life?
2. Is the person harming the life (lives) of another (others)—and if so, how, and how much?

Of course, there is a basic ethical and moral position at the heart of this position: It is no less wrong to drive other people crazy or force others to lose their lives than it is to choose a path of craziness or suicide or other serious deterioration of one's own functioning.

There is also an important scientific observation at the base of this orientation to the effect that many times destructive attitudes toward oneself and toward others take place simultaneously as well as alternate with each other. They are both aspects of the same basic psychological condition of a readiness to abuse human life versus a commitment to respect, protect, and treasure the gift of life—one's own and others'. What we do to others is the other side of the "DNA" of what we do to ourselves. Just as scientists found that looking at both sides of the biological DNA chain gave a much fuller picture than looking only frontally at it, in psychiatry, looking at the symptoms in the patient's own self gives only a partial picture. There are also other people involved to whom the patient is doing good and bad things that then rebound positively or negatively.

Both medically and philosophically, I argue that the principle of commitment to protecting life needs to be the basic goal of all psychiatric treatment. This point of view opens the door to more effective treatment than only a medical-like goal of symptom reduction for an individual, however justified the quest for relief from personal anxiety, depression, and other dysfunctions

This point of view also opens doors to thinking about new ways of addressing and treating some conditions of evil where people do quite serious harm to others. Treating for a democratic mind gives a clear rationale for invoking power and authority to stop evil. Traditional psychotherapy is largely at a loss with evil people. It often makes the mistake of remaining passive in the face of evil, for example the harm a parent does to a child or a sibling does to a brother or sister. Sometimes therapy even goes too far in "understanding" evil, offering a priest-like medical absolution for harmful behaviors rather than setting very firm limits on them. In my thinking, therapy's goal is to encourage and evoke more constructive impulses, to exercise a moral conscience against harming oneself or other people.

A Basic Position about Humans: They-We Are Good and Bad and Must Choose

My basic psychological position is that *both* a natural desire for self-preservation and for helping other people to stay alive, *and* a capacity for anger and destruction of others are at work in our original instinctive human machinery. (*Kindly address complaints to the manufacturer.*)

Either trend can be naturally evoked in people by others who exert powerful influences on them, including their society at large and various institutions of their societies. Certainly governments or churches can just as easily whip up people to go to war as to stand nobly for peace. Schools can teach—allow—violence to other children. Sports teams can allow or even whip up fans to use racial and personal slurs and worse against competing teams.

I propose that psychotherapists can influence many people, who are culturally open to the influences of therapists, to give up violence and doing harm to others by helping people connect to the other tendency that awaits in us along with the naturalness of violence—that of holding human life as sacred and protected. Among other things, psychotherapy is a process designed to evoke, respect for and love of life and personal integrity.[11]

The subject of evil, and man's capacity and obligation to choose between good and evil, runs through human thought through the centuries. Thus, in the Bible the prophet Isaiah calls out: "Woe to those who call evil good and good evil, who put darkness for light and light for darkness, who put bitter for sweet and sweet for bitter!"[12] Endless cultural greats have remarked on the choice. Thus,

> A Native American elder once described his own inner struggles in this manner: Inside of me there are two dogs. One of the dogs is mean and evil. The other dog is good. The mean dog fights the good dog all the time. When asked which dog wins, he reflected for a moment and replied, The one I feed the most.[13]

Ironically, in psychology and mental health there are a large number of very significant thinkers who have emphasized the profound importance of encountering these choices, yet at the same time, the field of mental health as a whole has almost scrupulously avoided adopting the subject as a key aspect of psychotherapy. Au contraire: many times a mere reference to good and evil is enough to disqualify a professional from acceptance in the high society of the field.

Among scholars of psychotherapy who have focused very much on the process as central to human existence will be found Silvano Arieti, Erich Fromm, George Kelly, Rollo May, O. Hobart Mowrer, and many more. In family therapy two outstanding voices focusing on the ethical choices made by people in family relationships have been William Doherty and Ivan Boszormenyi-Nagy.[14]

Hopefully this book will help release some people to make creative leaps from fascist bonds that have imprisoned their minds and relationships. I suggest that for all of us, the single most important overall decision in a person's life is whether or not to devote oneself to protect, support, and enhance life or to be drawn toward participating in doing harm to life. Such a decision is expressed by each of us in endless small and large ways, including many seeming trivialities of life and including major political decisions: thus, whether to brush one's teeth and to do so correctly without causing damage to one's teeth and gums; whether to move one's bowels without overstraining and injuring oneself; whether to devote oneself lovingly and courageously as a parent to those (many) of our children who turn out to be problematic and need special attention and assistance; or as a citizen, whether to oppose and disobey evil directives and orders of one's leaders—religious, military, political—to discriminate and persecute others.

Many decent people have said the same thing. What I am now adding in this book is the idea that the essence of this overriding choice whether to support or harm life will also determine whether one can be a basically sane and emotionally healthy person with relatively decent relationships with other people and one's world. Committing oneself to a love of life and to the protection of life triggers the natural wisdom of the mind against getting lost in itself and breaking down or going crazy, and against being insulting, exploiting, power-hungry, or otherwise hurting others. The decision to love and bless life goes far beyond many other value choices. It is a choice at a basic level of our inner existential beings that affects the hum of one's simplest inner personal experience—minute after minute, hour after hour, and day after day. If one feels in one's heart, "I love and treasure my life, and I will do everything I can to promote healthy life both for myself and others," one's life is far less likely to be depressing, lonesome, disappointing, or overwhelming. We are alive to the privilege of being alive!

Say No to Psychiatric and Psychological Escapes from Humanness, Say No to Quick Fixes and Escapes from "Soul"

We will return over and over again to the question of what the goal of psychological and psychiatric treatment is. Is it first and foremost to relieve people of oppressive symptoms? And when that purpose is achieved, is it still important to take a good look at what brought about the symptoms and to treat the underlying causal process?

A great deal of everyday medical practice very much involves relief of pain and suffering and dysfunction, but it is also understood in medicine that in many cases the physician and the patient need to see clearly where these symptoms originated and in many cases to treat the underlying conditions.

In psychiatry a considerable pressure has developed to reduce what were and are in too many cases interminably long treatment processes, but in the process a notion has developed that short-term treatment—there are even serious advocates of single-session treatments—is the only justifiable type of treatment.

My long-standing sense of myself as a therapist is that I accept the responsibility, first of all, to help people reduce runaway pain and distress so they can go on as much as possible with normal living. For example, the therapist is well advised to provide some immediate relief for a person who is unable to sleep or to guide a person who has been beset by phobia to get back to school or work. But I believe the therapist's role wherever possible is also to continue to a second part of therapy that addresses the emotional and life organization issues that have generated the problem.

There is also another aspect of therapy that I have come to appreciate more and more, and that is accompanying treatment of the causes of a problem with exercises—yes, homework—that the patient should do on their own in between sessions to practice new modes of emotion and behavior. The goal of the exercises is to learn how to manage problematic experiences more successfully. Often it is best to begin the exercises with instructed practice in the treatment sessions in the office, and then patients are directed and encouraged to continue the exercise on their own. For another example, I love rehearsing with adults new forms of address and relating that they can employ with a parent who for years has been intimidating them, and not infrequently I arrange for a "deal changer" in the office where they meet their parent in a session in which they carve out a new and better status for themselves. For another example, it gives me great pleasure to help someone who is dying of fright about giving a talk stand up in front of a mirror and give that talk, and then if still needed also to give that talk (or part of it) to me as in the office.

Following are three examples of psychological conditions that present frequently to mental health professionals where significant help can be given to the patient with respect to reducing quite troubling symptoms, but where underlying issues can remain untouched. The consequences of not addressing the infrastructure is quite obviously a high probability of recurrence of symptoms. Granted, in some cases, the original symptoms will possibly remain under control and no longer trouble the patient, but in these cases, too, it is likely that the underlying emotional functions that are involved will continue to have other impacts on people's lives.

Depression

Depression is symptomatically a tough deal for people, and when it gets really bad it is very much deserving of as immediate relief as possible. *But*, say the reduction of the depression is achieved by medications that work quite well and there is no attention to the psychological issues that brought up the depression in the first place. Has the patient really received a fair deal in the treatment? Factually, there is a known and not at all secondary issue with respect to the number of people who respond quite successfully to medication such as Prozac and other SSRIs but then go on to commit suicide or, in a smaller but still meaningful number of cases, to commit murder.[15] I believe that it is precisely because they feel better and stronger that they are capable of taking these serious life-destroying actions, which they were in fact protected from doing by the very depression they were suffering. But if they and we don't *know* what the depression is about in their hearts, they are hardly going to be in a position to protect themselves against further bad feelings. Meds (medications) can help regulate mechanisms of expression of emotions, but much less so how we feel inside about ourselves and our lives and other people.

Male Premature Ejaculation (as one example of the various sexual dysfunctions)

A good number of patients respond well to Masters and Johnson–type behavior tasks,[16] for example, the squeeze technique for inhibiting ejaculation, or behavioral instructions to pause quietly inside the host vagina after penetration rather than racing on excitedly to climax. How wonderful that the instructions for behavior modification can empower a man to be a more capable lover. But no way do all men respond to these directions, and even for those that do get better it can still be the case that they would benefit from a deeper psychotherapeutic exploration of (1) the extent of their anger at the woman to whom they are making love and/or to women in general; (2) the extent of their passivity in experiencing themselves with their partner; and (3) the extent of their narcissistic involvement with themselves and their own needs, with too little caring and love for their partner. These were the three psychodynamics that pioneering psychoanalyst Karl Abraham described in a virtuoso paper (written way back in 1917!) that still takes my breath away, in which I have found a sound basis for a wider therapy for this symptom.[17]

Anxiety

An experience of anxiety can be rough, and a powerful anxiety attack can throw people hard against the ropes with waves of powerful discomfort. Again it is clear that it is our job as mental health professionals to reduce their panic and suffering. But should the goal be removal of *all* anxiety as soon as possible? Many insurance companies will be very pleased if that is the case, and of course, people who were feeling terrible and now feel quieter will understandably celebrate their relief.

But so often it is the case that anxiety attacks are powerful messages from one's very soul, messages from our inner selves to us that deserve to be heard and can do us a lot of good. First of all, anxiety messages are certainly challenges to managing ourselves under adverse conditions. It is well known that many anxiety states are made worse simply as a result of people being so afraid of being anxious that they only increase the effect. So one possible value of living with some anxiety is the opportunity it gives to learn how to be strong and cope with a degree of feeling bad.[18]

More deeply, anxiety often is a call of anger and rage at somebody important in our lives with whom we have a mounting inner battle that is not getting processed constructively for whatever reason.

And, perhaps most important of all, anxiety often is a wonderful ringing of bells from inside that are singing a message and song of our desires to expand ourselves and fulfill wishes and talents that we have not been able to bring to fruition: *I want to write. I want to sing. I want to design. I feel it is time to leave my comfortable guaranteed job and strike out on my own. I want to make a major change in my personal relationships.* Anxiety is frequently a messenger of major new possibilities that call us to the courage to make changes in ourselves and in our lives.[19]

There are many well-meaning people, and that includes a host of mental health counselors, who sincerely want to do away with all the *bad* human traits so that people are gloriously happy and friendly. It's a mistake. The existential philosophy that makes sense to me is that the whole palette (range) of emotions with which we are endowed by nature is precious and needed psychobiologically for healthy living. This means that we should not run away so quickly or try to suppress and drown out all "bad" mental health symptoms. We do look to help people reduce unbearable pain and torment. As therapists we do look to break up symptom configurations that have gotten locked and frozen into states that trap a person from being able to live decently. But most of all, as much as possible we try to get to the real messages of how a person is using his or her mind and organizing his or her life. Democratic mind does not shirk the complexity of unconscious feelings. It processes inner feelings toward the most productive way of life that lies in the patient's reach.

CONCLUSION

The basic tenets of this book are:

1. Say no to psychiatric or psychological cures without a soul.
2. Say no to fixer-uppers that bypass bad feelings without teaching how to live a better life.

Democratic mind goes beyond seeking comfort and ending disturbances to seeking greater fulfillment of one's talents and a greater integrity in human relationships. The goal of psychotherapy as often as possible should be to help the patient live a life of improving his or her ability to cope with stress and growing as a person, more than seeking to be totally comfortable and stress-free.

Many forms of Government have been tried, and will be tried in this world of sin and woe. No one pretends that democracy is perfect or all-wise. Indeed, it has been said that democracy is the worst form of government except all those other forms that have been tried from time to time.

—Winston Churchill[20]

You need never fear that the patient will be harmed by the emotion produced in the entrance of his unconscious into consciousness, for you can theoretically readily understand that the somatic and affective activity of the emotion which became conscious can never become as great as those of the unconscious. For we only control all our emotions by directing upon them our highest psychic activities which are connected with consciousness.

—Sigmund Freud[21]

NOTES

1. Israel W. Charny, *Fascism and Democracy in the Human Mind: A Bridge between Mind and Society* (Lincoln: University of Nebraska Press, 2006). (Awarded Outstanding Academic Book of the Year 2007 by the American Library Association); I. W. Charny, *Psychotherapy for A Democratic Mind: Intimacy, Tragedy, Violence and Evil* (Lanham, MD: Lexington Books, in press).

2. Lynne Shallcross identifies the basic problem of whether psychotherapists allow values to play an explicit role in therapy with regard to social issues in the community and society. She refers not so much to broader issues of terrorism and other violence, but to the underlying issues of social justice within one's community. She cites the work of Rhonda Bryant: "One of the biggest misconceptions counselors have about social justice, Bryant says, is that it has no place in counseling. 'I think this belief is rooted in the idea that counseling is apolitical and value-free,' she says. . . . 'To ignore these realities denies clients' experiences and impedes clients' ability to change their communities through advocacy.'" Lynne Shallcross, "Counselors Taking a Stand," *Counseling Today* (June 15, 2010), retrieved July 18, 2014, http://ct.counseling.org/2010/06/counselors-taking-a-stand/.

See also Etiony Aldarondo, ed., *Advancing Social Justice through Clinical Practice* (Mahwah, NJ: Lawrence Erlbaum, 2007). One reviewer of this book writes: "As one steeped in the culture and values of public health, I must note the long-held public health dictum: No pathological condition has ever been eliminated by intervention with individuals one at a time. In other words, no disease or disorder has ever been treated out of existence. The benefit of working with individuals damaged by the exploitative system is that we learn the nature and causes of injustice that produce toxic social stresses. Then we must move beyond treating individuals to unified efforts to change the system." American Psychological

Association PsycINFO Database Record 2012, retrieved August 28, 2014, http://psycnet.apa.org/psycinfo/2007-06573-000.

3. The foundational concepts that call on therapists to respond to social injustice as part and parcel of psychotherapy are anchored in existential psychotherapy. Angela Highland, a novelist, explains psychotherapy that derives from existential philosophy: "Existential psychotherapy is concerned with more deeply comprehending and alleviating as much as possible (without naively denying reality and *la condition humaine*) pervasive postmodern symptoms such as excessive anxiety, apathy, alienation, nihilism, avoidance, shame, addiction, despair, depression, guilt, anger, rage, resentment, embitterment, purposelessness, madness (psychosis) and violence as well as promoting the meaningful, life-enhancing experiences of relationship, love, caring, commitment, courage, creativity, power, will, presence, spirituality, individuation, self-actualization, authenticity, acceptance, transcendence and awe. . . . Choice, personal and social responsibility, integrity of the personality, courage, and authentically facing rather than escaping existential anxiety, anger and guilt are central features of existential psychotherapy."—Angela Highland, http://www.goodreads.com/author/quotes/6978103

The following are some key classic works on existential psychotherapy: Bugental, James (1956). *The Search for Authenticity.* New York: Holt, Rinehart and Winston; Frankl, Viktor. (1963). *Man's Search for Meaning: An Introduction to Logotherapy.* New York: Pocket Books [New York: Beacon, 2006]; Horney, Karen (1950). *Neurosis and Human Growth.* New York: Norton; May, Rollo (1983/86). *The Discovery of Being: Writings in Existential Psychology.* New York: Norton; Yalom, Irvin D. (1980). *Existential Psychotherapy.* New York: Basic Books.

A 'find' that brings together two of the great classicists is an essay by Rollo May and Irvin Yalom entitled "Existential Psychotherapy" which I found on Internet without a date or other information about the publication at www.cengage.com/resource.../0495097144_81300.do. ("*Cengage Learning*, Inc. is an educational content, technology, and services company for the higher education and K-12, professional and library markets.") Retrieved August 28, 2014.

4. See the section on "Accepting and Containing Anger, Hate and Murderous Feelings" in Charny, *Fascism and Democracy in the Human Mind*, 266–68, including the advice of a Roman philosopher-educator-statesman from the first century! As for recognizing and possibly treating more manifest evils, these are referred to many times in this book.

5. Sigmund Freud, *The Standard Edition of the Complete Psychological Works of Sigmund Freud 1893–1895*, transl. James Strachey London: Hogarth Press, 1961[1923]).

6. Deirdre A. Kramer, Wisdom as a Classical Source of Human Strength: Conceptualization and Empirical Inquiry, *Journal Social and Clinical Psychology* 19, no. 1 (2000): 83–101.

7. An inspiring book about family therapy that is based on helping a family to share a genuine accounting of feelings toward one another is Ivan Boszormenyi-Nagy and Geraldine Spark, *Invisible Loyalties: Reciprocity in Intergenerational Family Therapy* (New York: Brunner/Mazel, 1984); and Ivan Boszormenyi-Nagy, *Foundations of Contextual Therapy: Collected Papers of Ivan Boszormenyi-Nagy, MD*

(New York: Brunner/Mazel, 1987). See also the pioneering work of James Framo on bringing together different generations (e.g., adult children and their parents) in intergenerational family therapy to air their feelings about one another truthfully: James L. Framo, *Family-of-Origin Therapy: An Intergenerational Approach (New York:* Brunner/Mazel, 1992); *James L.* Framo with Timothy Weber and Felise Levine, *Coming Home Again: A Family of Origin Consultation* (New York: Brunner/Routledge, 2003).

8. The concept that anxiety is a fear of not using ourselves and fulfilling ourselves as we are potentially talented to be was the central wise and inspiring message of the classic work by Rollo May, *The Meaning of Anxiety* (New York: W.W. Norton, 1996 [1950]).

9. Cited by Stephen Diamond, "What Is Existential Psychotherapy? Training in Existential Therapy Can Enhance Clinical Treatment Skills," *Evil Deeds: A Forensic Psychologist on Anger, Madness and Destructive Behavior* (blog), *Psychology Today*, retrieved August 28, 2014, http://www.psychologytoday.com/blog/evil-deeds/201101/what-is-existential-psychotherapy. *See also:* Stephen A. Diamond, "What Is Existential Therapy?," In *Encyclopedia of Psychology and Religion*, ed. David A. Leeming, Kathryn Madden and Stanton Marlan (New York: Springer, 2009), 304–5; Stephen A. Diamond, *Anger, Madness, and the Daimonic: The Psychological Genesis of Violence, Evil, and Creativity* (Albany: State University of New York Press, 2007).

10. William H. Masters and Virginia C. Johnson, *Human Sexual Inadequacy* (Boston: Little Brown, 1970). While Master and Johnson's techniques are very beneficial for many people, they do not produce lasting results for many patients.

11. William J. Doherty, *Soul Searching: Why Psychotherapy Must Promote Moral Responsibility* (New York: Basic Books, 1995); See also William J. Doherty, "Value-Sensitive Therapy," in *Theories and Strategies of Family Therapy*, ed. Jon Carlson and Diane Kjos (Boston: Allyn & Bacon, 2001), 98–122; Boszormenyi-Nagy and Spark, *Invisible Loyalties*.

12. Isaiah. 5:20.

13. This parable is cited as "an old Native American legend" by Steven Baum in his excellent book on the psychology of genocide: Steven K. Baum, *The Psychology of Genocide: Perpetrators, Bystanders, and Rescuers* (New York: Cambridge University Press, 2011), 237–38.

14. Silvano Arieti, *Abraham and the Contemporary Mind* (New York: Basic Books, 1981); Silvano Arieti, *The Parnas: A Scene from the Holocaust* (Philadelphia: Paul Dry Books, 2000); Erich Fromm, *Escape from Freedom* (New York: Henry Holt, 1992 [1941]); Erich Fromm, *The Anatomy of Human Destructiveness* (New York: Henry Holt, 1992 [1964]; Rollo May, *Power and Innocence: A Search for the Sources of Violence* (New York: Norton, 1998 [1972]); George Kelly, *A Theory of Personality: The Psychology of Personal Constructs* (New York: Norton, 1963); O. Hobart Mowrer, *The Crisis in Psychiatry and Religion* (London: Forgotten Books, 2013 [1961]; O. Hobart Mowrer, "Integrity Groups: Principles and Procedures," *Counseling Psychologist* 3, no. 2 (1972): 7–33. Doherty, *Soul Searching*; Doherty, "Value-Sensitive Therapy"; Boszormenyi-Nagy and Spark, *Invisible Loyalties*; Boszormenyi-Nagy, *Foundations of Contextual Therapy*.

15. The subject of Prozac and its considerable effectiveness along with its deadly and widespread "side effects," plus the incredible capitalist-system denials of its dangers, will be treated in chapter 4 and again in chapter 5.

16. Masters and Johnson, *Human Sexual Inadequacy*; Helen S. Kaplan, *The New Sex Therapy: Active Treatment of Sexual Dysfunctions* (New York: Brunner/Mazel, 1974). Helen Kaplan, a psychiatrist, argued convincingly that although the Masters and Johnson treatment exercises, which she too continued to use, were a great contribution, they should not be given to a couple until there has been a full clarification of their basic relationship and the meanings of their sexual relationship, and whether any "sexual sabotage" is at play.

17. Karl Abraham, "Ejaculatio Praecox," in *Selected Papers of Karl Abraham* (New York: Basic Books, 1957 [1917]), 280–98.

18. I never forget my indebtedness and gratitude to Albert Ellis for his earliest work on how to cope with anxiety more effectively. Prior to his work the only conception I had was that one must work on the flaws in one's personality and then the anxiety attacks will pass. From Ellis I learned first of all about managing the experience of the anxiety attack itself (it is not the end of the world), as well as some of the underlying cognitive biases of unnecessary anxiety (such as a demand always to be loved), and then one is happily that much better equipped to go on with the psychodynamic work on flaws in one's personality. For me personally Ellis was very helpful both during my psychoanalysis and in my work). Albert Ellis, *Reason and Emotion in Psychotherapy* Secaucus, NJ: Carol Publishing Group, 1994 [1962]).

19. As noted earlier, the concept that anxiety is a fear of not using ourselves and fulfilling ourselves was the central wise and inspiring message of the classic work by Rollo May, *The Meaning of Anxiety*.

20. Winston Churchill, Speech in the House of Commons, November 11, 1947.

21. Sigmund Freud, "On Psychotherapy," in *Selected Papers on Hysteria and Other Psychoneuroses* (New York: The Journal of Nervous and Mental Disease Publishing Company, 1912).

Chapter Two

Understanding Totalitarian Meanings in Relationship Disorders and Psychopathology

PSYCHOPATHOLOGY AND FASCISM ARE LARGELY BEDFELLOWS

This book is intended to aid in the actual everyday therapy of people. Non-mental health professionals may find they are not interested in some sections that contain clinical details about psychiatric and psychological disturbances. However, mental health is obviously a universal concern for all of us, for professionals in other fields and for many laymen who are deeply interested in some of the mental ailments that affect so many of us and in a sense threaten all of us. Non-mental health professionals of course will not pick up all the nuances of how the analyses in this book are different from conventional psychiatry's emphases in our time on biological conditions deriving from a hereditary destiny or from unknown causes of disturbances in brain functioning. But all readers, layman and professionals, are likely to be intrigued by the fact that we describe and explain many (though not all) emotional disorders as deriving from a fascist or totalitarian mind organization of thoughts and experience.

In this book, we will be reinterpreting many psychiatric conditions as based on people organizing themselves in a self-destructive way—a fascist way—by defining and setting for themselves totalitarian rules for the management of their thoughts, feelings, and relationships with others.

The following are some of the major totalitarian rules that are set for the pursuit of absolute goals:

- Over-certainty
- Magical thinking
- Censorship and suppression of a free flow of information in one's mind

- Undue obedience and conformity, beginning with one's own suppressive rules and/or blind conformity to someone else
- Feelings of superiority over others
- Seeking excessive power in relationships
- A readiness to do violence toward oneself or others in retaliation for non-conformity to one's absolute ideas
- Denials of doing harm to oneself and to others

Our point of view is that many mental conditions can be beaten by replacing fascist-mind thinking with more democratic-mind ideas that embrace a search for objective information, greater openness to differences and uncertainty, and even a healthy degree of anxiety, and that are deeply committed to avoiding prejudice and violence against any living creatures—oneself or others. The underlying conception of this model is that many of the ideas that lead an individual into mental and emotional disturbances are similar to the ideas we see being played out on larger scales in too much of the sorry destructive collective organization of world society.

I propose a conceptual bridge between Mind and Society which tells us that the same characteristics we see in fascist societies, which lead to vast destruction of life, are manifested in totalitarian-type thinking in the individual mind where they also lead to destruction of normal life.[1]

The beloved poet Khalil Gibran, recognized the excessive needs people have to control their lives absolutely: "Our anxiety does not come from thinking about the future but from wanting to control it."[2] Former chief of staff of the US Armed Forces and then secretary of state Colin Powell also observed that we must separate ourselves from efforts to get our way absolutely: "Avoid having your ego so close to your position that when your position falls, your ego goes with it."[3] I propose that the fascist characteristics of mind, such as devotion of oneself to an absolute and over-certain way of thinking, take place on an everyday level and are comparable to the fascist processes we recognize on a larger societal level. I believe it is such types of thinking that are influential in the formation of many cases of what we know of as psychiatric disturbances.

Psychiatrist Mordecai Kaffman[4] was very interested in "mind structures." He gave the name *monoideism* to the phenomenon of a patient adopting a single, absolute solution to life's anxieties and problems, where the single idea becomes unresponsive to the corrective information that flows in from reality. Kaffman described how the mental health problems of many patients derive from such a method of organizing life through a thinking style that is rigid, absolute, and unchanging. In a deep sense, it is this style of thinking and living that is the more real or intrinsic psychiatric disorder than the patient's symptoms. Over and over again the same faulty way of thinking and being in the world is repeated through blind ritualistic preservation which derives from one's monoideisim. The patient is unable to correct his or her behavior even in the face of the overwhelming damage that begins to accumulate to his or her mind, health, and life style. Kaffman proposed this concept essentially for understanding paranoid disorders, but in the process he also noted, without detailing more fully, that the concept of monoideism would be useful in understanding a wider range of psychiatric disturbances.

Author's Disclosure of Theoretical Beliefs

My understanding of psychiatric conditions is based, first of all, on an acceptance of the *existential* facts of a patient's human condition along with respecting the patient's personal narrative of his or her life, and also on traditional *psychoanalytic-psychodynamic* understanding, which to this day I find, overall, provides an extremely rich and useful description of what goes on inside a patient's mind and how symptoms are constructed. This understanding is then supplemented by *behavioral-cognitive* interpretations of how people get into guiding images, beliefs, and mind-sets that dictate to them wrong ways for organizing their experiences. For example, a severe reaction to rejection or to a socially humiliating experience may occur because one has made no provision for expecting to be hurt in life and has not readied oneself to survive such experiences. Next, the combination of psychodynamic and cognitive understanding is expanded further to bring in another level of observation, which derives from *systemic or family therapy* understanding of patterns of intimate and interpersonal relationships that characterize the disturbance. Altogether each component process is looked at for what it is contributing to the overall reality of the patient in his or her way of life.

I believe that together the combination of psychodynamic, cognitive, and systemic understanding within an integrative existential view offers a fruitful approach to understanding mental illness that does not categorize mental and emotional disorders as mysterious "illnesses" of unknown origin or ascribe them to quite unproven supposed biological causes. I believe that many cases of mental disorders do show psychosomatic features, but in many cases they too are derived from basic emotional and thinking errors—which are the primary original causes of the disturbance and the triggers of many physiological processes—rather than the other way around, where the physiological process is assigned the role of the *cause* of the disturbance. When further organized by a democratic mind vs. fascist mind metaphor, emotional problems and mental illnesses make a whole lot of sense as human disturbances, as our common sense has always told us.

When mental illnesses are conceived of as illnesses that befall people from unknown sources, or as illnesses that are triggered by genetic programs over which the person has very little control, these ways of understanding psychiatric conditions remove and absolve people from responsibility for themselves. But also, what is far more important, they distance people from much of the *possibility for healing themselves*. On the other hand, if one sees mental illness to a large extent as an outgrowth of wrong choices at critical junctures in one's life that are made by the individual on the basis of free will, then the conception of psychiatry changes to one where the individual can be in a position to contribute a great deal to his or her own cure and also to the prevention of future mental disturbance.

The concept of *choice* does not exclude understanding the circumstances and influences on a person's life—personally and in the context of their culture, society, and period of history, nor does it exclude the power of one's genetic makeup and the identification of inborn tendencies. Clearly much of the development of any and all of us is determined by a mysterious all-powerful program of genetics, and so much also is determined by the personal and cultural experiences one encounters in life without having chosen them. Moreover, we know that most of us have suffered from an inadvertent lack of knowledge of how to lead a healthier mental life. But the idea that ultimately it is *we ourselves who choose a great deal of what we are* puts us humans at the center of our own lives and futures along with our predetermined fates and destinies.

This is a way of thinking that empowers people to make themselves better and healthier persons during their lives. It is very different than a culture of givens and predetermined fates with consequent mindless pill-popping and brain surgeries or the manipulations of brain functioning that I believe are coming in our 1984-like science fiction world. *I strongly prefer this old-fashioned way of thinking about the human spirit. There is a great deal we can do for our own mental health, and remain freer people.*

How and Why This Book Does Not Use Diagnostic Categories Strictly According to the *DSM*

The framework I use in this book does not overturn or replace most of the nomenclature in the traditional American Psychiatric Association *Diagnostic and Statistical Manual or DSM* classification.[5] However, there are several instances where I use different words—including paradoxically some of the older *DSM* words, which I don't believe ever should have been dropped from *DSM*. More important, there is a major philosophical difference between the way I approach basic psychiatric diagnosis and the way the *DSM* operates.

First, I believe that emotional health or disturbance is largely or mainly a result of how we organize our minds and live our lives with ourselves and other people. Second, in my opinion the purpose of psychiatry and psychology is *not* to help people to function well at *anything* that they want to do without being distressed. It is to help people to function at being better and finer human beings, where the latter—being better and finer people—is both for ourselves and for others in our lives on our shared planet.

Students in conventional professional training programs, and certainly those who are facing an exam in abnormal psychology or psychopathology at any level of the formal worlds of academic or professional accreditation, should *not* use this book as their basis for learning diagnosis, for there are a good number of discrepancies in the language I use for describing symptoms of emotional and mental disturbance versus the official psychiatric *DSM* system, and I don't want them to flunk their exam.

The discrepancies with traditional psychiatry begin with the above-named fact that in a number of cases I call conditions by somewhat different names. But most of all, the intent of many of the descriptions I use is to understand mental and emotional disturbances as well as relationship disturbances as thinking disorders and incorrect use of emotional reactions that lead to unwise programs for organizing life experience, both in respect to the conduct of our own lives and in respect to our ways of conducting relationships with other people. The spirit of naming and classifying that prevails in the *DSM* is much more to create a taxonomy of diseases and conditions that resembles classifications in traditional biological medicine.[6]

One outstanding difference that immediately will be noted is that I continue to use the classic word *neurosis* (the issue will be discussed more fully later).[7] The *DSM* has dropped the word and relates to each of the traditional neurotic conditions as a syndrome of symptoms that constitutes a disturbance pretty much in its own right. There is little note or hint of a possibility that each variant of the neurotic disorders nonetheless shares a basic common quality and function with the other conditions, namely, that we are talking about human beings who are frightened of themselves, and frightened of fulfilling their potential for living, and too insecure to enjoy relationships with other people, who escape their fears in a way of living that generates a configuration of symptoms through which they complain about their lives, so to speak.

Neurosis refers to symptomatic conditions in which a person is suffering anxiety, discomfort, tension, or dysfunction in simple tasks of everyday living because he or she *has gotten stuck in a disturbed and incorrect way of trying to organize their living experiences*. Neurotic lifestyles distance and remove people from the authenticity of vital parts of their humanness, be it their sexuality, loving, caring and friendship, rights to aggression and anger, intelligence and creativity, capacity for healthy conscience or spiritual values, or their capacity for effective organization and administration of themselves. Neurosis also means not knowing how to accept and work with one's weaknesses and limitations along with one's talent. The neurotic is fleeing his or her talents and weaknesses.

In contemporary psychiatry, in most conditions other than obvious traumas, it is as if mysterious disease-like categories descend as curses from the heavens onto hapless people. In a sense, the *illness* becomes more the subject matter of psychiatry than the *person*. In the *DSM*, if you've got the kinds of symptoms that can bring you to a doctor with bona fide complaints of a psychiatric disorder, you are a subject of psychiatry; but if you're *just* "lazy," "fat," "not focused" or can't put together a healthy meaning for your life, go see your minister perhaps, but not your psychiatrist or even psychologist. In contemporary psychiatry there are pills for the symptoms and the illnesses they represent, but less so treatments that are inspirational and corrective lessons for people as to their judgments about how to organize themselves constructively for life.

The psychiatric establishment's removal of the conceptual category of *neurosis* in the *DSM* seemed to me to weaken the concept that neurosis is brought about by a basic error of failing to live well, such as an escape from pleasure and self-fulfillment, or a style of confusion and inability to feel the preciousness of intimate relationships, or excessive anger and hate that are making people feel miserable and/or unable to function well. My point of view is that the ways in which you think about life and organize it come back at you either in a sense of strength and pleasure in your living, or in various degrees of symptomatic malaise. In this view of life, it is one's chosen pattern of living that is of greater importance than the symptoms we suffer—these are signals on our dashboard that a system is out of order.

Another major difference between the presentations of emotional disorders in this book and the traditional *DSM* has to do with conceptualization of the personality disorders. For one thing, I also retain the old-fashioned word *character disorders* as a phrase that I also use along with and in continuation of *personality disorders*. I like it because it suggests that the basic ways in which we use ourselves as human beings very much include our choices of values, meanings, and goals as well as the ways in which we do and don't pursue our goals. I believe that our characters as people make a difference between wholesome basically happy people versus mixed up, miserable, or unstable people who are harming themselves and/or others. In my own thinking I like to organize personality disorders into three categories, where the first category places the focus on the ways in which people primarily do harm to themselves (though not necessarily only to themselves); the second places the focus on the ways people allow themselves to go for excesses of self-gratification and indulgence; and the third refers to an addiction to seeking excessive power where, crazy as it sounds, traditional symptoms of upset may first appear in the *other* persons over whom power is exerted, and yet the primary locus of the psychiatric disturbance which should be identified is in the person who is lording over, exploiting, abusing, or inciting the others. The most common denominator to all the personality disorders is that they represent unforgiving demands for immediate gratification even at the expense of the good health of oneself and/or of others.

Another obvious difference between the traditional language of contemporary psychiatry and my overview of psychiatric disorders has to do with my retention of the word *paranoia*. As will be described later, this fascinating concept simply disappeared between the third and fourth editions of the *DSM*, with no explanation that I have ever seen—and in fact no explanation was forthcoming in response to my specific inquiry to the American Psychiatric Association as to why the concept was dropped (I will recount how I received a reply that simply referred to the page in the *DSM* book that presented the revised nomenclature). *Paranoia* was the word that traditionally described a well-organized system of delusional ideas—meaning hateful, prejudicial, and persecutory suspiciousness and accusations of others, including the dehumanization, scapegoating, and fear and suspicion of people of another religion, ethnicity, nationality, or what have you: *they* will destroy *us*. Since genocide is statistically the leading cause of unnatural death in our world, or as Marc Pilisuk and Lyn Ober suggested, "Public Health Problem No. One,"[8] I can't help but return to the psychiatric-psychological foundations of genocide as a crucial mental health problem as well. I find the category of *paranoia* remarkably meaningful for describing the thinking and political ideology of a good number of the world's most demented leaders, including those who were responsible for the deaths of *millions* of human beings as a consequence of their nutty thinking—Hitler, Stalin, Mao, and many more. I feel strongly that we need words in psychiatry and psychology for these behaviors, and even more that we need concepts that address these phenomena and their causes in our human minds not only on the level of political and social systems.

Our biggest job in mental health is not simply to be guardians over individual mad men and women in our sanitoria and clinics, but to help develop thinking about the nature of our human experience and how to organize the opportunity of being alive in ways that will protect and enhance the lives of all human beings. Our mental health professions need to play a role in inspiring us to do something about reducing the bizarre and terrifying carnage in human life where literally *hundreds of millions* of people have their lives cruelly terminated prematurely by their fellow human beings. If psychiatry and psychology are not about trying to stop such ultimate *craziness*, then I will find our wonderful professions are trivial—and I would rather watch a Charlie Chaplin movie.

In general, my way of thinking about psychopathology (to which I purposely return repeatedly in many discussions in this book) is that I would like mental disturbances to be defined either as disabilities and disturbing one's own life, or causing disturbance to the lives of others, or both. And I would like us to be thinking about mental health as the ways in which people make life good both for themselves and for others.[9]

When one accepts this point of view about psychiatric disturbances, one also has a much more usable frame of reference for thinking about *new* symptoms and forms of mental illness that we have not yet known to describe. It is well known that psychiatric symptoms vary in different cultures, also that they undergo fascinating changes from generation to generation within the same culture, so that there are new symptoms and syndromes that will be appearing with new frequencies in future time frames in our civilization.[10] In psychiatric illness the issue should be far less a given cluster of symptoms that an approach to the way one lives with oneself and the way one impacts one's fellow human beings.

There is a whole variety of unrecognized bedeviling syndromes of mental disturbance that have not earned any recognition in the official lexicon of psychiatry. These include quite serious conditions, including several where the price paid is literally in murders of innocent human beings—where the symptoms have absolutely no reference base in contemporary psychiatric diagnosis because the kind of thinking that is needed to make these diagnoses is missing in a psychiatry that focuses on symptoms and over-biologizes everything. Also included is the perplexing, so-enraging and so-saddening contemporary problem of terrorist suicide bombers, surely not only a grave political problem, but a thorny psychological and psychiatric one as to how people can and do choose to do themselves in and kill so many other innocent people! Everyday people often react to such terrorist events spontaneously with a plain and simple cry, "*Crazy*." They are intuitively right, and it's our field that has to catch up with commonsense understanding.

There are certainly powerful forces including biological conditions acting on human beings that determine a good deal of our behaviors, but ultimately we are talking much more about our *choices* of the guiding ideas for organizing our lives. These choices define what we will and won't allow ourselves to do. Again, I want to emphasize the optimistic payoff of this point of view: This way of thinking gives us hope that we can train ourselves to think in wiser and more effective ways about our lives. We can test our thinking against objective standards of whether given behaviors do or do not enhance human life—our own lives and the lives of others, and how we can do much better for ourselves and for others.

In psychotherapy this way of thinking is a basis for teaching unhappy and disturbed people not to allow themselves to succumb to mind messages that direct them to do major harm either to their own selves or to other people.[11] I think that is the real task of the mental health professions of psychology, psychiatry, and social work. Insofar as mental health adopts this purpose, it joins the finest traditions of human thought in a great variety of fields ranging from education, religion, and medicine in its wonderful goal of saving life, as well as the arts and philosophies and other fields of human thought and creativity that affirm that the truest meaning of life is to protect and enhance the quality of life.[12]

The Diagnosis of Factitious Disorders Deserves to Be Celebrated and Taken as a New Point of View for Many Psychiatric Diagnoses

An intriguing expression of the difference between our thinking about treating for a democratic mind and standard *DSM* thinking is that we embrace the little-known and very fascinating category and concept of factitious disorders that, amazingly, *does* appear in the *DSM.* In my opinion it is a diagnosis not only of a specific kind of disorder where patients make themselves ill or more ill than they really are, but more broadly it is a remarkably revealing point of view about many other psychiatric disorders as well. Sometimes little-noticed ideas carry within them the seeds of tomorrow's major progress. I believe that one such concept in the standard psychiatric manual or *DSM-5* is this concept of factitious disorders.

Factitious disorders are defined in *DSM-5* as follows:

A. Falsification of physical or psychological signs or symptoms, or induction of injury or disease, associated with identified deception.
B. The individual presents himself or herself to others as ill, impaired or injured.
C. The deceptive behavior is evident even in the absence of obvious external rewards
D. The behavior is not better explained by another mental disorder, such as delusional disorder or another psychotic disorder.[13]

In *DSM-IV* the text also listed as an explicit criterion the following statement: "The motivation for the behavior is to assume the sick role." For me, not continuing this criterion in the *DSM-5* listing is another subtle *DSM* weakening of the significance of mind, but the underlying concept of a person making themselves look and feel psychiatrically impaired nonetheless continues even in the somewhat watered-down version. The key to the concept of factitious disorders is precisely that the production of psychological symptoms is apparently under a person's voluntary control. But *"voluntary" does not mean conscious control.*[14]

DSM emphasizes that *factitious disorders* are differentiated from *malingering* in that malingering is intended consciously to gain a specific goal. Without, heaven forbid, using the terrible word ("unconscious"), the *DSM* in effect says that factitious disorders are more *unconscious* psychological maneuvers to act psychiatrically sick because this gives the patient's "soul" or inner mind some kind of pleasure or safe feeling.

The concept of factitious disorder, with its strange name, is intended to solve the problem that there are many conditions in which patients present with significant and even horrid symptoms either of physical illness or of mental illness, and yet on examination doctors feel that the symptoms are not "real" so much as they have been *elected* by the patient to create a condition. Psychiatry says that we will call these conditions psychiatric conditions and treat the patient for needing and choosing to look like they are psychiatrically ill when they really are not. Again it should be emphasized that these are *not* instances of plain old lying and cheating and faking an illness with malice aforethought in order to gain some objective that will be served by being recognized as ill, such as being exempted from army duty or to gain a disability pension. The patients with factitious disorders do not have a full conscious awareness or intentio*n* of creating a fake condition and no conscious intention of manipulating others.

Let us go over once more the fuller meanings of the patient voluntarily taking on symptoms. There is a full-blown contradiction here. Patients with factitious disorders are described by the traditional psychiatric diagnosis as both electing to produce their symptoms voluntarily *and* as being thoroughly unable to stop doing so. The condition is chosen voluntarily, yet the patient is unable to cease the production of these symptoms because the patient is compelled from within to self-inflict the conditions that he or she is presenting. In other words, as we noted earlier, although the venerable word and concept does not appear in the *DSM* description, the real meaning of these conditions is that the patient is *unconsciously* driven to need to be sick, or appear to be sick, in whatever form of physical or mental illness, and the patient's mind wills or elects to simulate or adopt a semblance of illness.

Diagnosing a factitious disorder is a challenge. Many times patients look like they are suffering the real McCoy when it is they themselves who are simulating the mental symptoms and don't fully know it. Insofar as the patient's symptoms do not match accurately whatever clinical manifestations of the physical illnesses and psychiatric conditions that are known to occur commonly, it becomes likely that the patient has *chosen* to appear ill. With the concept of factitious disorders, psychiatry takes advantage of the basic contributions of psychodynamic thought to help understand how people can, in their mind, voluntarily, will upon themselves various states of apparent dysfunction and illness, which then become all too real.

For psychiatry this construction of factitious disorders solves the problem of the patients who don't look "the way they're supposed to" but are evidently disturbed and ill through what they are bringing on themselves. Not surprisingly, *DSM* psychiatric writing "favors" descriptions of those factitious disorders that take more concrete forms, especially where people present for medical treatment unnecessarily as if they are sick. Factitious disorders are also described quite clearly when they fall into the category of a disorder that is imposed on another person such as in the syndrome that used to be called "Factitious Disorder by Proxy" or "Munchausen Syndrome by Proxy" and now, with the endless changes that *DSM* makes, is labeled "Factititous Disorder Imposed on Another." Other concrete symptomatic indicators that are cited in *DSM* include extensive knowledge of hospitals or medical terminology; presence of many surgical scars; presence of symptoms of harming others, such as injuring a baby when the patient is alone or not being observed; and willingness or eagerness to have medical tests, operations, or other procedures.

These are relatively concrete forms of the disorder. Yet even about these more describable conditions, the Cleveland Clinic has written, "There are no reliable statistics regarding the number of people who suffer from Factitious Disorder. Obtaining accurate statistics is difficult because dishonesty is common with this disorder. In addition, people with Factitious Disorders tend to seek treatment at many different health care facilities, resulting in statistics that are misleading. It is estimated that about 1% of those admitted to hospitals are believed to have Factitious Disorder."[15] *DSM* states, "Although it is a rarely reported diagnosis, it often may not be recognized."[16]

But in my opinion, the significance of the concept goes far beyond the more concrete forms of patients creating fake symptoms. I believe that *DSM* itself does not recognize that in this concept it has hit on one of the major sources of many if not most mental conditions. In general, many people are frequently unconsciously happy to be sick, and that includes psychiatric illnesses. As many a patient has discovered in a successful psychotherapy, people often bring on and reinforce and prolong their illnesses and disabilities because they feel safer being troubled than being free people living out unhampered the risks of life. In other words, the symptoms can be essentially real, and yet a driving force in producing the symptoms can be the unconscious desire of the patient to be emotionally ill, and this issue becomes a critical one to address in the course of psychotherapy.

DSM thinking has not had the wisdom to identify and probe the extent to which the inner mind (unconscious) reaches out to create and reinforce many other psychological disturbances, such as anxiety attacks, depression, excessive marital quarreling, feelings of rejection of one's children, failures in school, repeatedly messing up on one's job, and more. The various mental and even relationship disorders are treated more as illnesses or conditions similar to illnesses, deriving, as it were, from their own sources, such as they are in nature, and little to no attention is given to the fact and truth that many a patient also is "making a living"—extracting great satisfaction—from being more disturbed and disabled than they need to be. The quite deep concept of factitious disorders is transformed by *DSM* thinking into sounding more like a medical condition that can be X-rayed, rather than a profound existential choice by the patient.

❖ I have seen one quite brilliant and nice man in intensive psychodynamic psychotherapy for whom I also arranged psychological testing when his therapy hit a serious snag. Both the computerized diagnosis (MMPI) and projective testing (Bender-Gestalt and Rorschach tests) given to him revealed a person who repeatedly chose to make himself appear far more disturbed than he really was.

We went on in his therapy to map relentlessly how and why he did this. Among other things, he learned how he literally smiled broadly and joyfully inside himself when he would choose to stay small and damaged—to continue as he had been. In time he revealed that the image in his mind that most appealed to him at times of stress was that mother was opening her blouse to offer him—the adult son—her breast. It also emerged that his almost conscious (preconscious) goal in the therapy was to celebrate ending therapy with a declaration that it had failed, and indeed he did come close to finishing his therapy successfully, but never did. He dropped out of therapy with the "finish line" in view.

For me, the most important implication of the conceptualization of factitious disorders is that we need methods of therapy that are predicated on the understanding that in many cases the patient is contributing, to various extents, to bringing about the reality of the psychiatric illness; and correspondingly, there is a possibility that the patient might be motivated or directed away from this style of thinking to a better *choice not to be ill*. This is the real point of psychiatric and psychological treatment, not treatment of a "condition" as such, but treatment of the patient's system of *choices*.

One senses that in the construction of the category of factitious disorders, the Establishment Psychiatry of our times has wiggled its way uncomfortably, almost inadvertently, into adopting and using major tenets of psychodynamic thinking about consciousness and unconsciousness because it was forced to solve a problem of widespread psychiatric conditions that look like but admittedly are not "real." I believe that in the process psychiatry has opened a Pandora's box to the possibility that, ultimately, we may also recognize that in many other psychiatric conditions, including those where the symptom process does match the traditional description of the condition, the fuller truth may also be that the patient has chosen to a significant extent to be ill—a choice that is both voluntary in the sense that it issues from a decision actually made in the patient's mind, but at the same time is not subject to conscious control because it is a function of unconscious forces or aspects of the mind with which the patient is not in contact and cannot control.

Personally, my professional experience leads me to believe that this model is truer of *many* psychiatric conditions than many other explanations of emotional and mental disturbances. It does not cancel out other causes, but adds the critical dimension of how many people choose paths of illness in response to the deprivation they suffered in childhood, while many others do not and do overcome the pull toward disability from their own intuitive wisdom or from the help they get in successful psychotherapy.

From the point of view of this book, it can be said that the patient has adopted a wrong solution to his or her existential situation; in other words, a life style that induces emotional or mental disturbance, and holds on rigidly to hidden comforts and gratifications of being disturbed and gratification from being supported by others, such as one's family or the psychiatric and social welfare systems, for being ill and dysfunctional.

Again I will emphasize that the most important implication of this conceptualization is that therapy of these conditions must then be predicated on the understanding that just as the patient is bringing about the reality that s/he is living out, there is a possibility that the patient could be motivated or directed away from this style of thinking to a better choice *not* to be ill. This is the real point of the psychiatric and psychological treatment that is needed, not treatment of the "condition" as such, for after all it is not a "real" condition, but treatment of the patient's system of *choices*.

The concept of democratic mind leads to a proposal that instead of giving in to feeling chronically bad, one should try, as much as possible, different strategies for overcoming one's emotional disturbances and needs such as—

- Identifying and clearing away major hatreds
- Correcting ways of expression of emotions in one's mind and in relationships (see especially constructive handling of anger)
- Resting and resolving to get better and stronger

- Resolving to pay less attention to symptoms and treating them more as passing aspects of being human
- Getting help from decent people—whether professionals or not—who will encourage one's spirit to fight against one's disturbance
- Going to work and doing one's best to do a good job even though one is upset
- Trying to identify and clear up the ideas and feelings that are pushing one down
- Cultivating the best possibilities one has for being with other people in friendship, intimacy and love

Good things don't just happen to lucky people. In most cases one has to work at winning the good outcome. In other words, a democratic mind-set suggests to people that they give up the safety of the certainty of their emotional disability and re-embrace the process of life in its complexity and diversity.

❖ By the age of twenty-three, he had been hospitalized in four different psychiatric hospitals and had made one relatively serious suicide attempt. The unquestioned diagnosis was schizophrenia based on the bona fide symptoms of hallucinations and disorientation that had been evidenced during the acute phases of his illness.

His parents succeeded in arranging for private outpatient treatment, where a series of rules were laid down by me, his therapist, including that the patient had to be gainfully employed or there would be no therapy. Over a period of several years of family therapy and individual therapy, many aspects of the patient's "love affair" with being mentally ill were revealed. We reconstructed the great glee with which he would watch his family and others around him react to his episodes of mental illness. Inwardly he would literally celebrate when a psychiatric ambulance would be called to take him away to the hospital. From his point of view, the mental health aides who came to take him away proved his omnipotent power to make his environment respond to his will. For him, making himself nuts and the ward of society were his ways of confirming himself.

I also learned that this creative young man had written a book describing his mental illness and experiences that would have made a respectable addition to this genre of literature. In this book he made it clear how happy and superior to others he felt in his chosen role as a psychotic. As his therapist, I read the book manuscript and congratulated him for his fine writing, but then over the patient's vociferous protests I refused to return the beloved manuscript to him! *Did he ever protest! And I told him he was absolutely right but still wouldn't budge.* The symbolism of my dastardly behavior was clear.

At this writing, twenty-five years later, the manuscript remains in my hands and the patient has never been rehospitalized. (I have been the recipient of vigorous criticism for this caper as violating the integrity of the patient. Obviously the criticism has justification, but I think the help the patient received from my metaphoric actions justifies it. In later years I have received holiday greetings from this former patient, but he has never repeated his request for the manuscript—which I think says something).

In all fairness, it should be noted that the patient's combined family and individual psychotherapy was also accompanied by psychiatric medication, though of course he had received such medication to no avail from the beginning of his diagnosed illness and through all of his hospitalizations. Was it a new medication that finally did the trick? *Your choice*. To me, it seemed clear that major changes were taking place in his choices of life style.

Who knows how many mental illnesses are a result not of chemical disorders, or not only of chemical disturbances, but result largely from wrong ways of thinking about organizing reality in the patient's mind? The very basic contradiction in the conceptualization of factitious disorders, that the patient is compelled to think and act the way he does but *also* is willingly and voluntarily bringing on the symptoms with which he suffers, is an extraordinarily helpful concept and perspective that can lead to our thinking much more creatively about treating many mental illnesses more vigorously and hopefully. It means that professionals and patients' families need to exercise courage to identify patients' participation in choosing to be ill, including defining knowledgeably and realistically the extent to which renewed choice remains available to the patients, versus the degree to which the capacity for choice and change for all practical purposes has been put out of commission. Sickness and distorted lifestyles do take their tolls after all, and not everything is reversible.

On Violence and Doing Harm to Oneself and Others in the Fascist Mind

As the daily news in every community confirms, an enormous amount of violence is going on in family life, let alone in human society. Violence to spouses and violent child abuse are frequent in family life—even in religiously devout communities. Incest in families and sexual exploitation is pandemic, and there are clinical observations that this may even be more pronounced in religious communities or settings of undue cultural taboos on happy sexuality.

Nonetheless, the larger picture in our knowledge of psychopathology has always been that there is surprisingly *little* violence on the part of openly crazy people. In most cases of the recognized psychopathologies, we do *not* find the manifest violence that is otherwise common in everyday family life and society. Even most "passionate murders" are found to be the acts of so-called "normal" people. In fact, it has been suggested that psychodynamically, one of the major purposes of some mental illnesses is to drain off and neutralize the violent emotions that have been building dangerously in a person's feelings in order *to prevent and protect one from becoming overtly harmful and violent to others*.[17] In many cases the people who become actively mentally disturbed are by inclination good people who very much want *not* to be destructive. They prefer to sacrifice themselves to a form of mental disturbance rather than take a risk of acting out harmfully the anger, hate, and rage they *do* feel toward someone in their life.[18]

Strangely, what seems to have happened in the field of psychiatry is that so long as the people committing violence do not appear crazy, out of contact with reality, or otherwise seriously emotionally unstable, psychiatry does not seem to know how to deal with these disturbances in its worldview of mental phenomena. Absurdly, a great deal of violence has been ruled out of traditional mental health diagnosis when it was found that many of the violent people do not show other signs of traditional mental disturbance. The violence remains as political choices and/or criminal choices outside the sphere of psychiatry. For example, when it was found that child abuse is more often than not committed by *normal* people in the language of existing traditional diagnosis, child abuse was ruled not to be a psychiatric phenomenon! One obvious reason for this is that the basic medical model on which psychiatry bases itself and prides itself involves a person being ill in his/her own right and does not so much concern harming *other* people and making *others* dysfunctional (although it may be said that in medicine issues of contagion and transmission of illness to others do have an important place and might have served as a conceptual model for concepts of transmission of psychiatric disorders to others, but psychiatry did not choose to cultivate this notion[19]).

Violence, clearly, is an expression of a totalitarian conviction that one can punish and retaliate against others and injure them violently. Fascist states do this to their own citizens promiscuously. Many relationship disorders and psychological conditions involve being consumed with hostile destructive wishes toward someone in the person's life that they do not know how to discharge effectively and healthily. And so does the human mind to itself—people punish themselves for failing to meet some absolute demand and command they have issued to themselves, such as, "Don't show weakness," or "Be number one, better than all the others (in whatever area of life)." A democratic philosophy accepts and encourages expression of anger—first, in one's own mind where just about everything can be "said," and second, in well-chosen powerful interactive confrontations and clarifications with the people who are angering us. Totalitarianism is sloppily violent; democratic mind thinking is disciplined, practical, and problem solving, and never forgets the principle of protecting human life—even when one is "crazy killer mad." Violence is a single-minded demand for control over the other. Granted, in many situations it is born out of the deepest frustration, hurt, and insult, but even then, in most cases violence screams absolutisms: "I won't let you get away with it" and "You must do it my way." In the many cases where violence is a regular way of life of a person who controls, punishes, or terrorizes others, the fascist mind theme of absolute control over others is even more evident.

Traditional psychiatric concepts do address abusive persons as problematic and disturbed to some extent. Several of the personality disorders such as narcissistic personality disorders and antisocial personality disorders refer to some qualities of contempt, domination, and abuse of family members and/or others. Yet the traditional definitions of symptoms show a greater interest in proving that these personality characteristics cause the patient himself or herself distress and discomfort than in explaining the transactions between the abusive person and the victimized others and showing the impact on them. The interpersonal, relational, and ethical meanings even of abuse fade into a secondary position if related to at all.

In family therapy, as compared to traditional individual therapy, the situation is different. Abuses done to others in a family are more likely to be treated as disturbed actions and to be defined as the focus of treatment. Also, the focus of treatment is generally defined in systemic terms that include both victimizer and victim in interlocking roles. Without erasing the clear differences between abusers and victims, it is recognized that all the parties to the abuse, perpetrators and victims alike, are being victimized by a disturbance in the quality and integrity of the relationship.

Unfortunately, even within its own ranks, family therapy has failed to produce a systematic classificatory system for diagnosing disturbed and harmful relationships, and within the larger mental health community, family therapy has not enjoyed a genuinely serious status as a source of diagnostic characterizations of mental and emotional disturbances and personality disorders.[20] The result is that overall in the mental health system, the bona fide "patients" have continued largely to be those who themselves are the suffering victims, and far less those who drive others *meshuga* (crazy) or to drink or to whatever breakdown and misery, who should also be defined as mentally disturbed people *because* they do such harm to the lives of others.

In part, one exception in recent years has been a growing awareness of the widespread incidence of sexual abuse, obviously cases of doing harm to others but the sexual abuser too has not been entered fully into *DSM*-diagnosis. *DSM* manages to get the victims and to a small extent even the perpetrators of sexual abuse listed in the Holy Manual, but only after two convoluted definitional tricks that in effect say "We are listing you because the people who come knocking on psychiatry's door with these problems are forcing us to do so, but you really do not have a psychiatric problem." *DSM* does this by listing these behaviors in a section entitled, "Other Conditions That May Be a Focus of Clinical Attention" introduced by an explicit statement: "*The conditions and problems listed in this chapter are not mental disorders*"[21] (italics mine).

To add a further nonsensical defense against the condition being seen as a real problem in its own right, even the names given to these problems carry a further emphasis that they are being recognized because people insist on coming to ask for help about them. Thus, the victim of apparent sexual abuse (remember it is not a mental disorder!) is given a diagnosis which is in *DSM* as follows: "Encounter for mental health service for the victim of child sexual abuse by parent."[22] And the perpetrator is defined thus: "Encounter for mental health services for perpetrator of parental sexual abuse."[23]

The larger issue is that psychiatry has to make a great paradigm change toward adopting the basic principle that one needs to look for many different forms of causing mental and emotional harm to *others*. So far, no such paradigm shift has taken hold in psychiatry despite growing attention to many dramatic cases of sexual abuse.

Another source of avoidance of issues of abuse has emerged in family therapy, paradoxically, from the very laudable intent to develop systemic thinking that looks at all parties. Systemic thinking is a great leap forward to seeing how people conspire, as it were, to share in creating patterns of behavior with one another. But understanding abuses in systemic terms as a function of an interactive *codependency* of victim and victimizer has been taken by many family therapist thinkers as a basis for avoiding defining in clear-cut terms the individual perpetrator's behavioral and moral *responsibility* for the execution of the abuse, as if the abuse now derives only from a unified field of forces and responsibility and can no longer be assigned to the single party who is the actual perpetrator of the actual abuse.[24] Understanding systems that include the dynamics of a victim's participation in inviting the violence cannot dilute the unambiguous responsibility of the perpetrator of violence.

Avoiding defining perpetration of evil as a disturbance in its own right reached a bizarre extreme in the classic literature on violent abusers of children. According to long-standing definitions in the field, the majority of parents who abuse their children violently are *not* emotionally disturbed. This incorrect conclusion is used as a basis for telling the parents that their unfortunate behaviors are obviously deriving from some human weakness or are a repetition of their own violent upbringing, but since they are not mentally or emotionally disturbed, it will not be that difficult to teach them how to overcome this weakness. This removal of blaming may *possibly* be a helpful strategy for teaching some people how to stop an abusive behavior chain, but at what price of reason and truth? While a good cause may be served for approaching the violent parent, it is utter nonsense to ignore the fact that anyone who seriously abuses his/her child is, in fact, obviously seriously *disturbed.* One might still try to reach the perpetrator parent respectfully and helpfully but without distorting reality. Injuring a child violently is violently pathological in any commonsense understanding.

Doing harm to others is disturbed behavior. This includes situations where a person influences another to do harm to himself, or a situation where a person, say a parent, accepts and allows the other to cause self-harm without efforts to block and correct it. Thus, in a couple where one becomes obese, the other not standing up against the spouse's committing self-injury thereby becomes a party to a collusive "agreement" to allow and maintain the obesity. Both are indeed involved, though of course the mate who becomes obese carries the greater weight (hah) of responsibility for self-harming behavior. Similarly in respect of violence, the victim may be playing a role in enabling, inviting, or reinforcing the violence, and it is of great importance to flesh this out and treat it, but the overriding fact is that he or she who perpetrates the harms is always *fully* responsible for injuring the other.

For me, there is no doubt that doing harm to life is disturbed. In fact, this is what I have proposed be considered the major basis for the diagnosis of all mental disturbances: The essence of all psychiatric disturbance is unnecessarily harming any human life—whether one's own life or another person's life, and certainly when both are harmed.

Surprise! Surprise! Suicide and Suicidality Are Not Included in the *DSM*!

Believe it or not, another major form of doing harm to life that is nowhere to be found in the *DSM* is suicide. Nor is suicidality—the state of intention or being drawn to committing suicide. Go look for suicidality in the almighty *DSM*, and what do you find? *Nothing*. It is as if one announces: Harken ye normal people everywhere, here is another behavior to keep in your list of apparently normal options in life! Once again, this is a situation where everyday people spontaneously react very often with a plain and simple word, "Crazy." To me, as a mental health professional, it is almost insane that suicide and suicidality do not earn coverage in the *DSM* but are swallowed up in references to a symptom of depression, as if that explains the terrifying choice of a human being to put an end to his or her life.

Indeed, many psychopathologists have insisted that in the absence of florid signs of manifest mental illness, suicide is *not* a sign of psychiatric disturbance![25] I willingly agree that suicide as a philosophical choice under severe duress, say of a terminal illness or being placed in a death camp or concentration camp by a totalitarian regime, need not be considered a psychiatric disturbance, but it seems to me common sense that suicide as giving up on a life that could have been continued honorably or courageously is by definition very much a psychiatric condition.

I confess that to my own amazement it was only after many years in the field that I realized that *suicide is not listed as a psychiatric condition in the DSM*! I suppose the stated reason might be that suicide is supposedly only a symptom and not a full-blown condition in its own right, and that in many cases it derives from another recognized condition of a psychiatric disturbance that is in the *DSM*—especially depression, of course. But common sense has it that most suicides in their own right are the craziest and saddest thing people can do to themselves. Common sense also has it that when a person is looking suicidal or expressing an intention or desire, or a fear, of committing suicide, a mental health specialist should be called to help manage and treat the suicidality as such. *Suicidality is a condition in its own right* over and above a state of depression, which may or may not be present. In fact, a not insignificant number of people who commit suicide are not in a state of depression if by that you mean sadness and emotional paralysis. They may be at the end of their wits or hopes or sense of options. They may be yearning for an escape from life to an eternal rest, or to a magic of dying and being reborn. They may be crazy with revengeful anger and the suicide may be more a way of punishing someone they leave behind. A further bad joke is that many non-psychiatric mental health practitioners (psychologists, social workers, and others) tend to panic in the face of suicidal danger and feel (I believe often incorrectly because at that moment it conveys a fear and a lack of confidence about helping the person overcome suicidality) that they must call in a psychiatrist. But the joke is that the danger of such suicide doesn't appear in the list of disorders to be treated by psychiatrists, so we have the absurdity of a practitioner being asked to heal a condition that is not on their list.

In truth, the existential state of suicidality or being suicidal and developing, harboring, and acting on a suicidal plan in itself is a profoundly disturbed mind process that often develops over a considerable period of time. Obviously, thinking about and deciding to act on destroying the gift of life has to be a bona fide psychiatric condition in its own right. As every professional in mental health knows, an inclination to suicide very much requires skilled treatment in its own terms as a decision-making process, and not only treatment of the depression or mood disturbance from which the suicidality often but not always springs.[26] Frequently enough, the therapy needed includes freeing the patient from a sense of absolute necessity for something or other, be it success, rest, or revenge. Often enough, too, the person needs help not to feel obligated or required to bring the suicidal thoughts and plan he has been harboring to its ultimate completion. The suicide is to be a final compliance with the demands of whatever totalitarian thinking.

The genuine larger issue is that any and all violence, either to oneself or to other people, is inherently fascist. It needs to be defined as an intrusion on the human capacity to enjoy and function in life, and therefore is a psychiatric disturbance. Again I note that I propose that psychiatry concern itself with the combination of conditions of doing harm to oneself and doing harm to others. Doing harm to the lives or the quality of lives of *others* should be seen as the other side of the same coin of a person doing self-harm. Both types of conditions alternate with one another and are transformed into one another more frequently than we have often recognized. Moreover, both conditions are essentially solutions to the *same* existential anxiety—a dread of nothingness and death with which all of us human beings must cope in our lives.

The concept of a fascist paradigm in our thinking enlarges the base of our understanding of both types of harm to life. Violence can be the punishment done either to oneself or to others for failing to exercise blind unquestioning compliance to ideas that are laid down as certainties never to be questioned. The fascist way of thinking begins in the minds of men with an insistence on a definite and unchanging way of being, absolute truth, over-certainty, obedience, and conformity, and not necessarily in a quest for violence as such, but the need to protect the fascist principle can easily lead to violence on its behalf. For example, setting rules in one's mind not to have angry thoughts or never to be second best or never to have real joy or sexual pleasure can be accompanied in one's mind by injunctions that require one to punish oneself if and when one violates the rule. Similarly, rules about relationships such as jealous demands that no spouse dare look with any interest and desire at another sexual object, or that a spouse must submit to one's demands, or that children must be devoted and obey their parents' demands unquestioningly can be accompanied by built-in rituals of punishment of the one who dares break the rule.

In fascist-mind thinking barriers are set up to make heretical any opposition to the defined certainty. The chosen truth is defended at all costs against any and all who might be enemies of the certainty. Any alternative information is unwelcome, and even newly developed scientific demonstrations of contradictory truths must be suppressed. Violent retaliation against dissent can be directed against the self, for example, torturing obsessions as punishment for hostile thoughts, or disabling hysterical fits of fainting and weakness for daring to think of separating from a parent who lays heavy emotional claims on a son or daughter's life as if in perpetual servitude. Or the retaliation can be against others who defy the mandated rules, for example, a lover or spouse who has upset the applecart of one's security to a point where they "must be punished," such as by not speaking to the person for days, being financially or sexually or emotionally disloyal to, or exercising violence against the betrayer. In many situations of criticism and protest, the intent of the behaviors at first may not be to destroy the opposition, but often it develops that the believers become convinced that they must stop those who oppose their one-and-only solution and are standing in their way.

Those who seek perfect solutions are naturally driven to polarize and delegitimize the opponents of their certainty. They also are naturally inclined to invoke other fascist-mind characteristics of power, superiority over others, and too often full-blown violence.

It is all fairly obvious on the level of society, of course, where ways of silencing and eliminating opponents and enemies are common in too many political cultures. In actual fascist societies, approved modes for getting rid of those who stand in one's way will easily include brutal measures to silence and destroy the opposition and can lead all the way to elimination of many dissenters. In a society that is avowedly dictatorial and totalitarian and does not have democratic safeguards, state-organized disappearances, torture, imprisonment, concentration camps, and execution are normative. In partial or "posed" democratic societies, such as today's Russia under Putin or in economically flourishing but thought-controlling China, the retaliatory violence can be disguised as bona fide police actions and judicial rulings—or unfortunate "accidents."

But there should be no false belief that violence does not take place in democracies too. There are also serious dangers of mobilization of institutional and legal powers against dissenting individuals and groups in democratic societies. Periods like the McCarthy era in the United States or the policy of random beatings of innocent Arab civilians in Israel in 1988–1989 (a serious failure of the later-to-be-great hero of seeking peace, Yitzhak Rabin, when he issued a horrible power-wielding call to "break their bones") bring out the extent to which horrible persecutory processes can develop even in democratic societies, although clearly there are many more safeguards against the more devastating forms of violence in democracies than in non-democracies.[27]

Once processes of destroying others are set in motion, they also set off powerful psychological processes of collective excitement, satisfaction, even orgiastic pleasure, rationalizations ("they must be doing something wrong or they wouldn't be punished"), and dynamics of "cognitive dissonance" that require one to go on doing more of what one has been doing in order to feel consistent and at home with oneself.[28]

Nonetheless, even in avowedly totalitarian societies, the original intention frequently is the achievement of the perfect solution rather than a wish to be violent and destructive, and it is in the service of insuring the perfect outcome that there develops a momentum of destroying those who are perceived as one's enemies. It is this kind of destruction that does *not* stem from hostile impulses and compulsions that has probably been the most puzzling for would-be psychological diagnosticians who would like to know in advance which people will prove to be murderous under whatever group or societal conditions (e.g., the Milgram experiments and Zimbardo experiments).[29] What we have learned is that the *mindset* induced by a structure that authorizes and invites people to operate in the name of authority is certainly capable of taking *most* people captive. *Milgram, Zimbardo, and others in effect prove that only a minority of people are able to fight off successfully seductions to be fascists.* To this day we do not know how to identify in advance personalities who will go the route of becoming persecutors. This is partly because so many people originally do not intend or seek to be fascists, and so it is harder to identify them in advance. We need to learn to identify people who are the more likely to be drawn into fascism when it seeks them out, so to speak.[30] The dynamics of violence derive not only from prior ideological commitments to be violent and destructive to others, but also from the pull of "normal dynamics" or structural and process laws that draw an individual into doing things s/he never intended to do such as pressures to find absolutely "correct" solutions and to perform "100%" as expected. The quest for certainty impels many people to protect their vaunted belief system from interference by using violence against the dissenter.

Disorders of Pseudo-competence, Invulnerability, and Doing Harm to Others

Traditionally mental health concepts have focused largely on self-imposed dysfunctions or victims of congenital weaknesses or hurts imposed by others, for example, having been neglected or unloved by one's parents. The sufferer is unable to make an effective adjustment to reality or to find pleasure in the reality of life, and the emotional or mental disturbance tends to take on "a life of its own" as a pathology.

There are other types of behaviors that have been examined by psychiatry where people are affecting the lives of *others* in a disturbing way, but with a closer look we will see over and over again that much of the meaning and justification for the psychiatric diagnoses given to people whose disturbing behaviors are hurting others are derived more from focusing on the suffering that the person is causing his/her *own self* as a result of what the person is doing to the other. Rarely has the focus in psychiatry been on the harm being done to others as such, with a clear-cut statement that it is disturbed *because* it is destructive to the life of another human being.

Thus many situations in which harm is done to others are subsumed in traditional psychiatric diagnosis under the category of personality disorders. The general diagnostic criteria for a personality disorder in *DSM* specifies that "the enduring pattern leads to clinically significant distress or impairment in social, occupational, or other important areas of functioning."[31] The overriding emphasis in traditional psychiatric diagnosis is on how the life of the doer—the perpetrator—is damaged; only thereby does the person "earn" a diagnosis of psychiatric disorder.

In an effort to create a new framework for diagnosis of psychopathology as both doing harm to oneself and/or to others,[32] I have proposed a framework for diagnosis of two types of disorders: This first group, which covers most existing psychiatric disturbances, is called *Disorders of Incompetence, Vulnerability, and Personality Weakness*. In the face of life's challenges, and the anxiety they produce, exaggerated weakness and disavowals of potential competence, strength, and mastery can reach a point where the person is unable to function well enough and is designated as "emotionally disturbed" or "mentally ill."

I further suggest that when the same range of familiar psychiatric conditions takes the form of burdens inflicted on *other* human beings, interfering with their well-being, the conditions can be seen as a second group called *Disorders of Pseudocompetence, Invulnerability and Doing Harm to Others*. Incompetence, vulnerability, and weakness are immediately understandable and familiar to us as the commonsense meanings of psychiatric disturbance—they involve persons who cannot function adequately for themselves. Pseudocompetence and invulnerability are also entirely familiar to us in everyday life, but are not associated by us with traditional descriptions and definitions of psychiatric disturbances. These behaviors refer to many different qualities of bravado, pomposity, excessive toughness, denials of vulnerability, and denials of needing the support and caring of others. People who organize themselves in these ways may appear enviably confident of themselves under stress, but they are in fact often prone to poor functioning because they are so out of touch with their normal vulnerability. Thus, studies have shown that more effective soldiers are normally afraid and overcome their fears; and studies of more effective students have shown that they do experience tension and fear of examinations and overcome them.

Moreover, there is a natural connection between disconnecting oneself from normal vulnerability and being arrogant, hurtful, abusive, and cruel to others. Ernest Becker[33] has written eloquently on how much human evil derives from denials of one's own mortality, and by extension all weaknesses. The need to overemphasize one's toughness invites projections of contempt to others and projective exploitation of others to be the sufferers/victims of what one fears might happen to oneself. As I described in the original article in a psychiatric journal where I first presented the concept.

> Disorders of Pseudocompetence represent reactions to universal anxiety about life and death through disavowals of one's weaknesses and demonstrations of one's pseudomastery at the expense of other people. The dread of normal human weakness and needs is repressed through various degrees of overstriving, an inflated sense of oneself, claims of power over others, exploitation and manipulation of others, denials of others' human rights and lives, abuses, cruelty, and actual destruction.[34]

Note that adding the second category of *disorders of pseudo-competence* to traditional *disorders of incompetence does not require any change at all in traditional definitions of psychopathology*. I am *adding* a dimension to existing theory without proposing any changes in the present existing classification. The addition of this dimension is accomplished by a "simple" structural device of rotating conventional definitions of disturbances to *oneself* on their axis toward the counterpart statements of a person inducing or forcing the same degree of disturbance on *others*. This is an addition that seems to make simple good sense, and it is not unlike other theoretical advances in science where an existing known principle has proven to yield hidden extended meanings when turned over or reversed. Thus, a traditional diagnosis of a neruotic condition is based on various manifestations of nervousness, irritability, fearfulness, and chronic unhappiness in a person. The additional basis for diagnosis we are making involves situations where one person is demonstrably triggering and reinforcing such states of nervousness and chronic distress in *another* person—a husband or wife, for example—driving the other up a wall, or a parent inducing chronic sadness and misery in a child, or vice versa (even though the behavior of the child also has to be recognized as reflecting the parental influences on them). No longer is it only the victim who is to be diagnosed, it is also the person doing the harm to the other.

❖ He had come for therapy troubled and puzzled that for all his apparent success as a junior manager he felt unable to progress further or to feel genuinely masterful. He also had trouble standing up to negative positions taken by his wife, such as her repeated refusals to have sexual relations. After two years of therapy, he finally saw clearly how each and both of his parents had conveyed deeply to him (and to his siblings too) their expectation that he be supposedly successful but really a weak and limited person in his functioning. He puzzled especially over how they had brainwashed him into believing they were giving him love and support. He recognized that both of his siblings had emerged damaged and might never achieve normal self-competence, and he was resolved that he would overcome the curse of mediocrity that had been sneak-messaged to him.

It was not only that he was disturbed, but he was discovering that his ostensibly undisturbed parents were the original "causes." It was they who unconsciously wanted to have all their children defective and inadequate.

CONCLUSION

I suggest that a framework for mental health treatment which makes more sense than addressing medical-sounding conditions and disabilities in persons only for themselves is one which calls for integrity and decency both to oneself and to others. Psychiatric diagnosis then becomes a matter of identifying how people are treating either themselves and others or both themselves and others in lousy ways. To me this makes a lot of common sense. Mental disturbances are ways of being bad to people—oneself or others. Mental health is being good to living people—oneself and others. Jackie Robinson, who broke historic ground as the first Black player in the major league baseball, summed up clearly our relationship to other people: "A life isn't significant except for its impact on other lives."[35]

> Power tends to corrupt, and absolute power corrupts absolutely. Great men are almost always bad men.
>
> —Lord Acton[36]

Unlimited power is apt to corrupt the minds of those who possess it.

—William Pitt[37]

NOTES

1. Israel W. Charny, *Fascism and Democracy in the Human Mind: A Bridge between Mind and Society* (Lincoln: University of Nebraska Press, 2006).
2. Kahlil Gibran, *The Prophet* (New York: Alfred A. Knopf, 1923).
3. Colin Powell, "My *Thirteen Rules," in It Worked for Me: In Life and Leadership* (New York: HarperCollins).
4. Mordecai Kaffman, "Monoideism in Psychiatry: Theoretical and Clinical Implications," *American Journal Psychotherapy* 35, no. 2 (1981): 235–43; Mordecai Kaffman, "Inflexible Belief-Constructs in Families of Paranoid Patient," *International Journal Family Therapy* 3, no. 4 (1983): 487–500; Mordecai Kaffman, "Paranoid Disorders: The Core of Truth Behind the Delusional System," *International Journal Family Therapy* 4, no. 6 (1984): 220–32; Mordecai Kaffman and Tovah Sadeh, "Anorexia Nervosa in the Kibbutz: Factors Influencing the Development of a Monoideistic Fixation," *International Journal Eating Disorders* 8, no. 1 (1989): 33–53.
5. The basic reference of *DSM*-Psychiatry is the current *DSM* manual: American Psychiatric Association, *Diagnostic and Statistical Manual of Mental Disorders: DSM-5*, fifth edition revised (Washington, DC: American Psychiatric Association, 2013), referred to more briefly as *DSM-5*. Many of our references and citations are to the brief edition: American Psychiatric Association, *Desk Reference to the Diagnostic Criteria from DSM-5* Washington, DC: American Psychiatric Association. 2013, referred to more briefly as *DSM-5, Desk Reference*. Previous full editions of the *DSM* were *DSM-IV* (1994) and *DSM-III* (1980).
6. See later in this chapter the section, "The Fascist Paradigm and Factitious Disorders: The Welcome Wisdom of the Diagnostic Category of Factitious Disorders for Psychiatry"; and then a fuller discussion of the differences between the diagnostic concepts used in this book and the current politically correct *DSM*. See also in chapter 4: "The *DSM* and the Human Condition" the section "The Roles of the Unconscious, Human Relationships and Basic Value Choices in Psychiatric Disturbances and Psychological Health."
7. See in a later chapter "Neurosis—A Word and a Conception of the Unconscious That Have Been Exiled from Contemporary Psychiatry." See also about the disappearance of the category of paranoia: "Paranoia—A Category That Might Have Helped Develop a Psychiatry for the Hitlers and Bin Ladens—That Has Been Made to Disappear."
8. Marc Pilisuk, and Lyn Ober, "Torture and Genocide as Public Health Problems," *American Journal Orthopsychiatry* 46, no. 3 (1976): 388–92.
9. The original main presentation of the concept that all psychiatric diagnoses combine the harm a person is doing to themselves along with the harm they may be doing to others was developed at some length in my earlier presentation in the psychiatric literature, Israel W. Charny, "Genocide and Mass Destruction: Doing Harm

to Others as a Missing Dimension in Psychopathology," *Psychiatry* 49, no. 2 (1986): 144–57. Subsequent major presentations include Israel W. Charny, "Evil in Human Personality," in *Handbook of Relational Diagnosis and Dysfunctional Family Patterns*, ed. Florence Kaslow, Florence (New York: Wiley, 1996), 477–95; and Israel W. Charny, "A Personality Disorder of Excessive Power Strivings," *Israel Journal of Psychiatry* 34, no. 1 (1997): 3–17.

10. See Silvano Arieti and Johannes M. Meth, "Rare, Unclassified, Collective and Exotic Psychiatric Syndromes," in *American Handbook of Psychiatry*, vol. 1 (New York: Basic Books, 1959), 144–57. A related issue to which we will refer periodically in this book is the way psychiatric medications and physical treatments work. So many studies show a considerable suggestive effect—at levels that in other areas of medicine often would disqualify a medication from being taken seriously. Even the popular press of our times reports these placebo results frequently. For example, a 31 percent improvement of depression on a placebo is reported versus 41 percent improvement on real medication (of a Prozac-type). See Marcia Angell, "The Epidemic of Mental Illness: Why?," *New York Review of Books*, June 23, July 28, 2011.

Similarly and even more dramatically, no less improvement was reported in elderly depressed patients who underwent a simulation of an electric shock treatment that included being put to sleep with an anesthetic but then did *not* receive the actual electric shock, compared to the improvement of patients who underwent the actual electric shock. See J. Lambourn and D. Gill, "Controlled Comparison of Simulated and Real ECT." *British Journal Psychiatry* 133, no. 6 (1978): 514–19. (Note this study applies to depressed patients and not to schizophrenia.)

In my opinion, it is perfectly fair to say that the chemical and physical procedures *do* have meaningful effects on some patients; but it is anti-scientific and a kind of rigid "know-nothingness" to ignore the large effects of suggestibility in these procedures. The latter are further proof of how much the mind as a psychological instrument of our experiencing, and even if unknown to ourselves, our minds are choosing and deciding powerfully whether we will be mentally ill or not.

11. A friend-colleague of mine, both professionally and in our both being in the growing-old age group that brings for many of us serious and life-threatening illnesses has handled his bouts of heart disease and surgeries very bravely and energetically. He refers to a choice between "*a die or survive mentality*" for those coping with major illness. I am expanding his wonderful metaphoric conception to include a fuller range of promoting our lives and relationships to promoting the lives of others, so that I make it a combination of choices between "*a die or survive mentality*" and "*a hurt-harm others or help others to live mentality*."

12. One important European philosopher in the twentieth century who "got it" is Emanuel Levinas who taught in the language of philosophy, which at once can be so obscure yet so touching, that the face of the other person(s) in our lives calls on us to take responsibility for the other. Roger Burggraeve, *The Wisdom of Love in the Service of Love: Emmanuel Levinas on Justice, Peace and Human Rights*, transl. Jeffrey Bloechl (Milwaukee: Marquette University Press, 2012); Roger Burggraeve, ed., *The Awakening to the Other: A Provocative Dialogue with Emmanuel Levinas*, (Leuven, Belgium: Peeters, 2008).

13. American Psychiatric Association, "Factitious Disorders," in *DSM-5: Desk Reference to the Diagnostic Criteria from DSM-5*, 165. Readers will also be interested in seeing how this concept was presented in the previous edition, *DSM-IV*, 471–75.

14. *DSM II-III* had the most explicit statement about factitious disorders: that "they are under voluntary control". . . however, the individual is unable to restrain from [the] behavior. These concepts have been toned down somewhat in subsequent editions, but in no way were they repudiated. My hunch is that the *DSM* authors felt they were getting too close to a statement about unconscious behavior—*touch wood.*

15. Cleveland Clinic "An Overview of Factitious Disorders," June 11, 2013, http://my.clevelandclinic.org/disorders/Factitious_Disorders/hic_An_Overview_of_Factitious_Disorders.aspx

16. American Psychiatric Association, *DSM-5*, 11.

17. Harold F. Searles, "The Desire to Become Nonhuman as a Defense against Various Feeling-States," in *The Nonhuman Environment in Normal Development and in Schizophrenia* (New York: International Universities Press, 1960), 223–49.

18. Robert A. Clark, "Friends and Aggression" (mimeographed paper) (Philadelphia: American Friends Service Committee). Robert Clark was a psychiatrist in charge of the acute inpatient service in a Quaker hospital in Philadelphia (Friends Hospital) years ago. In a seminar session that is an unforgettable experience for me, Clark gave a description of how psychiatric breakdown characteristically takes place in believing Quakers who are practicing their well-intended peaceful and nonviolent way of life. The scenario he described was one of mounting unconscious anger and rage in the good Quaker person toward someone or other, but of course the good Quaker is duty bound to deny this anger to himself/herself, and then the perfectly normal sequence in the unconscious mind is for an escalation into death wishes and fantasies of getting rid of the enemy violently. This is the breaking point. Such un-Quaker thoughts are not allowable. It is at this point, Clark explained, that the good Quaker panics and chooses to go crazy as a way of insuring that he or she does not commit any evil act of aggression.

19. It is not that other people are never mentioned in the *DSM*, but they are largely incidental to the juicy descriptions of the disturbance and madness in the identified patient. The fact that a patient upsets or hurts another person may be noted, but it is generally treated as a spillover or add-on to the primary symptoms and evidences of disturbance in the patient himself. If, as happens often enough, there are no manifest psychiatric symptoms in the perpetrator person who is causing disturbance in the other, psychiatry doesn't know what to do and "drops the charges" against the person who is doing the harm. The fact that another person has been hurt and forced into some dysfunctional state in itself is not registered as a profound psychiatric disturbance. Thus, what is the psychiatric diagnosis of a father who forces incest on a daughter? *None, other than as a condition someone might complain about*. And that's really crazy.

20. Florence W. Kaslow, ed., *Handbook of Relational Diagnosis and Dysfunctional Family Patterns* (New York: John Wiley and Sons, 1996). The volume on "relational diagnosis" edited by family therapist Florence Kaslow represented a welcome

thrust toward sorely needed new concepts and frameworks. See further information in chapter 5 of the present book, "The *DSM* and the Human Condition." However, while Kaslow's very fine work presented many valuable new and alternative ideas to diagnosis, it did not result in a coherent consensual proposal of an alternative diagnostic classification to the *DSM*, and it is doubtful that it is having a major impact on the *DSM* process in psychiatry.

21. American Psychiatric Association, *DSM-5, Desk Reference*, 355.

22. Ibid. 360.

23. Ibid., 361.

24. Israel W. Charny, "Psychological and Ethical Responsibility in Systemic Thinking," *The International Connection* [Newsletter of the International Family Therapy Association], 7, no. 1 (1994): 7–8.

25. The first text on abnormal psychology on which I was "brought up" in my professional training insisted explicitly that the majority of people who committed suicide were not mentally ill. See James D. Page, *Abnormal Psychology* (New York: Prentice Hall, 1949). The author was also the professor for my first course on "Abnormal Psychology," and he was obviously "right" that the formal psychiatric criteria for mental disturbance indeed did not apply to a great many of the people who took their lives. But what an absurdity it was to my young eyes to read that suicide was not generally the act of abnormal people. I knew inside of me that this was a blatant contradiction of reality (even as I prepared to answer the instructor's examination question the way he expected on the next test). So many years later the same absurdity continues to prevail.

26. Aaron Beck, H. L. P. Resnick, and Dan Lettier, eds., *The Prediction of Suicide* (Philadelphia: Charles Press Publications, 2015 [1974, 1986]). The text I learned the most from was H. L. P. Resnick, ed., *Suicidal Behaviors: Diagnosis and Management* (Boston: Little, Brown, 1968).

27. Many Americans are concerned in the wake of 9/11 about a hardening of bureaucratic procedures and more intrusive police investigative procedures and powers under umbrellas of counterterrorism procedures. There have been many reports of an increased disregard of basic human rights and mounting degrees even of sadism and cruelty in the handling of people under scrutiny and investigation. One of the interesting aspects of these events is how many officials automatically enforce *procedures* literally to the final letter of the law without an ability to differentiate and make judgments about *people*.

28. Leon Festinger, *A Theory of Cognitive Dissonance* (Evanston, IL: Row-Peterson, 1957).

29. Stanley Milgram, "Some Conditions of Obedience and Disobedience to Authority," *Human Relations* 18 (1965): 57–76; Stanley Milgram, *Obedience* (film) (University Park: Pennsylvania State Audio Visual Services, 1965); Stanley Milgram, *Obedience to Authority: An Experimental View* (New York: Harper & Row, 1974); Philip G. Zimbardo, Craig Haney, W. Curtis Banks, and David Jaffe, "The Psychology of Imprisonment: Privation, Power, and Pathology," in *Doing unto Others: Joining, Melding, Conforming, Helping, Loving*, ed. Zick Rubin (Englewood Cliffs, NJ: Prentice-Hall, 1974), 61–73; Philip G. Zimbardo and Alan Funt, *Candid*

Camera Classics in Social Psychology: Viewer's Guide and Instructor's Manual (New York: McGraw-Hill, 1992); Philip G. Zimbardo, Christina Maslach, and Craig Haney,"Reflections on the Stanford Prison Experiment: Genesis, Transformations, Consequences," in *Obedience to Authority: Current Perspectives on the Milgram Paradigm*, ed. Thomas Blass (Mahwah, NJ: Lawrence Erlbaum, 2000), 193–237; Christina Maslach, "An Outsider's View of the Underside of the Stanford Prison Experiment," "My Role in the Stanford Prison Experiment" (Section in chapter by Zimbardo, Maslach, and Haney), in Blass, *Obedience to Authority*, 214–20. Note that *both* marvelous classic experiments, Milgram's and Zimbardo's, are being looked at years later in the informative and even charming book by Thomas Blass even though the title refers only to Milgram.

30. I have addressed this issue more explicitly in a textbook I wrote for the course cluster on genocide at the Open University of Israel in a pioneering series of books in Hebrew entitled "Genocide," edited by Yair Auron for the Open University of Israel: Israel W. Charny, "*And You Shall Destroy the Evil Within You": We Are the Human Beings Who Commit Holocaust and Genocide* (Hebrew). An English translation has been published: *The Genocide Contagion: How We Commit and Can Prevent Holocaust and Genocide* (Lanham, MD: Rowman & Littlefield, 2016).A noteworthy feature of the book in both languages is that, as far as I know, for the first time, they include exercises for the readers to meet up with themselves and their potential for playing roles in a future genocidal event. In general, the aim of this book is to look at the core psychosocial processes at work in a person's mind long before the time comes that history/society call on a person to execute or participate in genocide. This is a period when men and women who are going to be perpetrators or accomplices themselves have no idea they will be killing or assisting the killing of others. Until the time comes, many of them can be seen smiling and well-dressed, hard at work in perfectly normal occupations, and loving parents to their children.

31. American Psychiatric Association, *DSM-5, Desk Reference*, 321.

32. Charny, "Genocide and Mass Destruction."

33. Ernest Becker, *The Denial of Death* (New York: Free Press, 1973).

34. Charny, "Genocide and Mass Destruction," 146–47.

35. Jackie Robinson with Alfred Duckett, *I Never Had It Made: An Autobiography of Jackie Robinson* (New York: Putnam, 1972).

36. Lord Acton (1834–1902), in a letter to Bishop Mandell Creighton in 1887.

37. William Pitt the Elder, Earl of Chatham and British Prime Minister from 1766 to 1778, in a speech to the House of Lords in 1770.

Part II

PSYCHOLOGICAL HEALTH, THE WOES OF DSM, AND MULTIPLE SCHOOLS OF THERAPY

Chapter Three

Psychological Health

Protecting and Improving the Quality Of Life—My Own Life and the Lives of Others

RESPECT FOR HUMAN LIFE—RESPECTING ONE'S OWN AND THE LIVES OF OTHERS AS THE ORGANIZING PRINCIPLE FOR PSYCHIATRIC DIAGNOSIS

Psychological and psychiatric diagnosis should provide a rounded picture of how well a person is functioning in this world and not only describe what problems or symptoms they suffer. Of course good diagnosis must also address the weaknesses and failings of a person including existing, predetermined, and emerging defects and limitations (God knows that my own list is not a short one, but I think this is in no small part true of most of us human beings—it is part of what we call the "human condition"). Mental health diagnosis also necessarily should include a great deal of information on medical conditions and processes that in themselves can set off significant psychosomatic processes (to be more precise psychosomatic and somatopsychic processes) in their impact on various levels of a person's functioning, whether cognitively, emotionally, or in behavior.

But even as a complete psychological diagnosis of a person involves many aspects of life, the larger issue—the one that goes to the deeper heart of who we are and how psychologically healthy and sick we are—is how a person is working with what they have, and this is why I emphasize for psychological and psychiatric diagnosis above all else *how a person is treating the opportunity of life.*

Once again I repeat the "game-changing proposal" that two main questions or ways of organizing information for examining mental health by mental health and health professionals should center on one's relationship to life itself and whether a person is doing harm to life. The two key questions are about the person's treatment of himself/herself and about a person's treatment or impact on other human beings:

1. Is the person suffering or doing significant self-harm in his or her basic style of living?
2. Is the person doing significant harm to other human beings and damaging their lives?

Examining these questions might be compared to a physician asking how the patient feels—or in the case of infants how the baby looks. I have heard many times from doctors that the way a patient looks to them is a very important diagnostic sign—sometimes even more important than other diagnostic information. Moreover, along with making the critical overall assessment, the psychologist or psychiatrist can also go on to assemble many specific pieces of information about how a person is functioning, including the two cardinal principles of a relative ability to work and love that were laid down wisely by Sigmund Freud.

Traditionally, it is a literary error to be repetitive, but I repeat these two basic criteria emphatically all through this book because they go to the heart of what I am trying to contribute, and because we know it will take a strong battle to get the psychiatric establishment to add concern for others to its "delicious lists" of individuals' symptoms.

A century ago a wise American psychologist, Urie Bronfenbrenner, grappled with the question of merging the wisdom of the West about individualism with the wisdom of other cultures including the Soviet (despite the fascist horrors of Soviet communism) and Eastern philosophies about collective good.[1] Many people have criticized psychiatric thinking, I think correctly, for being too involved in how an individual patient is faring without sufficient attention to what the patient is doing to others. In general, many thinkers have criticized the Western world for its "me-ness" or advancing personal security, comfort, and gains at the expense of not looking at the well-being of a broader collective.

Famed social psychologist, Marie Jahoda, wrote:

> "Absence of disease" . . . is rejected as a criterion [of mental health], not only because of the difficulty in circumscribing disease but also because common usage of the term "mental health" now includes something more than the mere absence of a negative value.[2]

Erich Fromm described mental health to a large extent in terms of the individual's relationship with a larger social universe. (Any comparison of Fromm's definition with the *DSM* would indeed be purely coincidental.)

In fact, Fromm relates his concept of a mentally healthy human being to a "concept of a universal human nature rather than on the values of particular cultures or societies."[3] He says:

> The mentally healthy person is the productive and unalienated person; the person who relates himself to the world lovingly, and who uses his reason to grasp reality objectively; who experiences himself as a unique individual entity, and at the same time feels one with his fellow man; who is not subject to irrational authority, and accepts willingly the rational authority of conscience and reason; who is in the process of being born as long as he is alive, and considers the gift of life the most precious chance he has.[4]

Already years ago in the *International Encyclopedia of Social Sciences* (from which we cited both Jahoda and Fromm), we find the wisdom that "for the mental health enthusiast . . . the mental health idea implies a new conception of moral and social progress in the form of self-correctability, self-perfectibility, inner growth, personal fulfillment, and inward and outward harmony, or the like."[5] I am happy to say that in the present book that we too have joined the mental health enthusiasts.

Long ago, a wise rabbi, Hillel (110 BCE–10 CE) in Jerusalem taught: "If I am not for myself, who is for me? [But] if I am only for myself, what am I?"[6] The two basic questions I pose speak to both the world of the self and of others.

The question of harming oneself in effect refers to a great many of the traditional mental health diagnoses of dysfunctions and difficulties in carrying on a successful "normal" life. The question of harming others pertains to all personal relationships, certainly to family relationships—between spouses and between parents and children (in both directions), and to work relationships such as between a supervisor, manager, or employer to the workers (and back again too). It also extends to one's relationships with one's community and society, such as whether a person is engaging in prejudice, discrimination, or persecution of whomever and whichever group of people.

Of course one has to add to the concept of 'harming oneself' conditions, where a person really is *unable* to function satisfactorily and very much deserves our understanding, sympathy, and therapeutic help as to how best to manage the problem. In truth, the first question I am asking is a larger one that combines the extent to which a person is suffering harmful damages, weaknesses, failures, or disabilities and/or to what extent the person is the source of or the enabler of the harm to himself or herself? In many cases it is very hard to track the dividing points in the flow between the givens of problems that are "landed" on a person and the person's own role in shaping and managing his or her life incorrectly. Moreover, there is a whole range of opinions and differences of opinion between professionals as to how much people are or are not responsible sources of the different psychiatric conditions. Many psychiatrists in particular promote a disease-from-unknown-source kind of model, while other clinicians, like myself, lean (undoubtedly sometimes in error) to the power of the patient to initiate, maintain, or exacerbate a problem, and correspondingly to a far greater potential of the patient to reduce and heal the problem. So I am allowing for a kind of broad poetic meaning when I ask both what harms are going on inside one and what harm one is doing to oneself. Yet, even in situations of disability, we note that there are those who do an admirable and sometimes even stunning "Stephen Hawking mobilization" of all the functioning they can manage to live a life of meaning, while others go down, down, down with their limitations and disabilities. In other words, even when there are built-in weaknesses, there remains a considerable role to the spirit. What we are interested in is what people are doing with their potential for life, such as it is, even as we take serious note of all objective illness, defects, and built-in limitations. Thus, being blind is indeed a condition, but it is not a mental condition; yet the blind person who sits home and does not reach out to create a satisfying life is suffering a mental problem.

I knew a brilliant young man of about twenty who lost his sight in a war, but went on to get his PhD, became a full professor, married a beautiful woman, and fathered several children (at least one of whom I met as a practicing psychologist).

I ask questions that explore in detail and depth the quality of treatment of oneself and the integrity of relationships to others. How well does a person take care of himself? How capable is a person of making her life a growth experience? In their everyday ways of living, is a person seeking to take power over others to an extent that seeking power is a central driving force in the person's experience, or to an extent that leads to emotional indignities against other people?

> ❖ His wife had left him. He came to ask for therapy and said that he knew he had been bossily dominant, self-centered, and unresponsive to his wife's emotional experiences. We gathered several of the adult children (genuinely fine people) together with their father in a family session that was intended to clarify why the mother had taken such an extreme step and whether there should be any hope of restoring the marriage. There was a uniform consensus that the father was a good person who had meant no harm, but that he had centered the whole world around himself to a point where, according to the oldest daughter, her mother felt she could die if she didn't get to live her own life.

No *DSM* would come close to picking up this disturbance, but a diagnostic scheme that gives equal weight to what a person is doing to others would have picked the issue up years before the sad breakdown.

It is true that my way of diagnosing good and ill mental health can widen the net of identified psychiatric disturbances considerably, but I think that I am bringing up on screen truths about our human lives that most of us experience intuitively and naturally every day. A majority of human beings don't know how to love and protect both themselves and others, and don't know how to make this a sane planet without so much violence, crime, prejudice, drugs, suicide, homicide, terrorism, genocide or wars—and that isn't healthy psychiatrically or in any way. Isn't it better for us to have a mental health diagnostic map that tells it more like it is, and tells it earlier rather than after the fact about whether a person loves life or is destructive of life?

We have seen how the common trap in defining mental health or normality is that it is often restricted to demonstrating an absence of prominent symptoms of maladjustment—such as neurosis, psychosis, and personality disorders; or, on a more concrete level, mental health is defined as an absence of distressing experiences such as anxiety, depression, incompetence in aspects of functioning, signs of bona fide madness, or various kinds of inability to tow the line of social norms—including succumbing to addictions or engaging in violence and criminal behaviors.

Two outstanding psychologists, David Rosenhan and Martin Seligman, grope toward something bigger than an individual's adjustment for his or her own self with references also to a person's impact on the well-being of society and to a person's moral standards. In their book on abnormal psychology they say that abnormality is to be seen largely as a failure to function adequately as defined by suffering, maladaptiveness either on the level of individual well-being or the well-being of society, rare and undesirable behavior and unconventionality, loss of control, and "violation of moral and ideal standards."[7]

Our view is both simpler, beginning with the two global questions about whether a person is harming his or her own life and/or the lives of others, but at the same time broader in that we inquire whether a person is "living" fully, meaning as an all around person who is—

- not only not plagued by symptoms, but enjoying being alive, vibrant, appropriate, responsible and productive
- not only not violating social norms in a demonstrable way, but is committed to decent values for protecting and advancing life, one's own and the lives of others, including in a kind of progression: one's family, neighbors and work colleagues, community, nation, and people, and humanity as a whole as well as our planet

- sociable and social
- empathic
- egalitarian
- productively on a path of fulfilling goals and ambitions
- able to work effectively through traumas, pain, losses, stresses—all inevitable in human life
- capable of responding constructively to the challenges and tests of life

Good mental health is an ongoing experience of positive living, including self-love, self-respect, and a basic friendliness and relationship to others of hope and respect though without being naive about evil people and behaviors. At the same time, a concept of psychological health also needs lots and lots of room for the endless *normal* suffering that all of us experience in our lives, and to the fact that all of us are deficient and incompetent in some number of areas of our functioning, but these human experiences do *not* qualify us as mentally troubled. How we address and cope with our human downs and limitations is so important. I can hardly diagnose a twentyish young man as emotionally disturbed if he suffers, variously, troubling anxiety about his new job, fears of public speaking, premature ejaculation, or shyness about finding a girl to whom he can commit. He is in his twenties, and those are normal life tasks and challenges.[8] This does not mean that the young man should not ask for professional psychological help any more than he should not go to his dentist with pain in a tooth. In both cases a diagnosis of a health problem is obviously justified, but hardly a global diagnosis of a category of a more serious sickness, disease, or disability. In fact, intrinsically he may or may not be very healthy.

Paradoxically, we know that in the long run it is the seemingly totally successful performers who are more certainly at bigger risk because being a healthy human means rolling with and growing from the endless challenges and stresses of life, which the all-too successful people are not learning how to do. I put my money more on copers, overcomers, and growing people—even if at any given time they fall short of the total winners and "got it all" stars (who so often are going to burn out) .

In contrast, conventional psychiatric thinking tends to label upset too often as a psychiatric illness, often a serious one, and frequently with a kind of implication that the condition will be chronic (and thereby lays the groundwork for whatever pills). It also does not celebrate good coping with stress as a quintessence of good mental health, and certainly doesn't recognize the "supermen" and "superwomen" as people at risk of collapse if only because if and when they do fall they haven't learned how to come back "even taller." Moreover, conventional psychiatric diagnosis does not understand that an absence of joy, friends, productivity, and balance in one's life is by definition mental disturbance even if a person is not experiencing suffering and does not stand out as strange or ne'er do well but is "just" gray and joyless.

In its concern with all things abnormal, traditional psychiatry tends to leave out looking at everything that is good in a person's life. The concept of a democratic mind clearly aims toward quality human living rather than being restricted to the presence or absence of signs of disturbance in functioning.[9] Thus, a sourpuss, an overly shy or fearful person, an overly loud, smugly confident, overpowering person don't appear anywhere in formal psychiatric definitions of abnormality, but from our point of view they are *not* desirable for a quality life. Psychological illness includes unhealthy personalities who are "give-uppers" in whatever major parts of life, the gray, spiritless ones who though they are not clinically depressed are not really living. Psychological disturbance also includes the "never-give-uppers" who can't bear to lose or acknowledge their weaknesses, errors, or unfairness. They too don't appear anywhere in the official psychiatric nomenclature, which is devoted to people who are not functioning well, but they too are hardly expressions of a quality life experience.

Establishment psychiatry and psychology get stuck on definitions of abnormality on the basis of symptoms more than on the basis of the *processes* of life experiencing. A desirable definition of a psychologically health personality is as broad and expansive as the range of potential skillfulness, beauty, decency, and creativity of the human mind and spirit. Obviously all of us vary immensely in these and other characteristics, just as we vary immensely in our physical makeup and health. What is desirable is for one to live a continuously developing and self-fulfilling life in which one reaches toward the better that lies available in the natural range of one's potential talent. I have always taught students in abnormal psychology that the great artists who nonetheless burn themselves out self-destructively with rotten ways of life—that in too many cases even lead to their early deaths—are *not* to be admired, and certainly not to be thought of as desirable models for ways of living for the rest of us, no matter how much some of us may want to be notable artists.

Hardly anything of the above formulation is really new. Wise thinkers have said such things over the centuries, and the great folklores of many peoples have eloquent statements of this way of thinking.[10]

Much of the above clearly fits universal man's common sense. A good life is one of basic joy and a joy of coping, even with heavy difficulties, and not a problem-free existence. Too often we lose contact with the courage of coping with the natural stresses of life, and the beauty of such competence. I think that the best overall way to sum up the healthy human personality is to say it enjoys a deep *respect for life*—one's own life and the lives of others.

HOW MUCH UNCERTAINTY, EMOTIONAL WEAKNESS, ANXIETY, AND SUFFERING ARE TO BE EXPECTED AND EVEN WELCOMED FOR PSYCHOLOGICALLY HEALTHY PEOPLE?

A lot! This is a key difference between our concept of psychological health and those definitions of psychological normality and health that see every lapse into uncertainty, unsteadiness, and emotional distress as ranging from utterly unattractive to disastrous failure. This is the way the pill-pusher custodians of contemporary mental health insist that people be free of discomfort, sadness, and nervousness. Note the parallels to how most "totalistic" ideologies—of all sorts—promise their faithful totally happy and good living.

Horwitz and Wakefield have described how two major aspects of human experience, anxiety and sadness, have both been "transformed" into mental disorders by contemporary psychiatry and are not respected as natural experiences that recur periodically in our lives.[11] They argue that the result is a social trend that teaches people to be afraid of natural feelings. The further result, obviously, is that people rush and are rushed by their doctors to take medicines to get rid of such feelings too quickly, without allowing these feelings to play out their natural roles and contributions to our being human, and to our getting stronger over the course of our lives in being able to handle the inevitable anxieties and sadness that come up quite naturally. (It is exciting to see in the reviews of the books by these authors a wide-ranging number of psychiatrists, psychologists, and sociologists confirming powerfully the understanding that psychiatry has been mislabeling these reactions as disorders.)

My own position then goes a step further with regard to treatment of such conditions as I argue that even when the extent of anxiety clearly constitutes a diagnosable anxiety attack—which I have had the "pleasure" of experiencing, and in fact went into psychoanalysis for the first of two times when I was twenty-one years old when I was flooded regularly with anxiety attacks—and even when the extent of sadness justifies calling the experience a depression, the treatments of choice still are best built around going with the underlying feelings rather than suppressing them.

There is a great deal of evidence, let alone a philosophical attractiveness, for the understanding that all of us are faced in the course of our lives with endless disappointments, dilemmas, scary challenges, profound losses, and personal failures. Alan Watts has touched poignantly on a core difficulty that is inherent in trying always to feel good and safe:

> If . . . we cannot live happily without an assured future we are certainly not adapted to living in a finite world where, to spite the best plans, accidents will

happen and where death comes at the end. There is a contradiction in wanting to be perfectly secure in a universe whose very nature is momentariness and fluidity. If I want to be secure, that is, protected from the flux of life, I am wanting to be separate from life. Yet it is this very sense of separateness which makes me feel insecure.[12]

If you look for people who avoid uncomfortable experiences adamantly and suppress them as soon as they raise their heads, you will find a great variety of ideological zealots, including religious extremists and political extremists, as well as people engaged in extreme overdoing and over-identification with any number of areas of life, whether the too much is at:

- work (you can even die from it)
- sports (the body pays a price when it is too much)
- good old sex (you can get plain drained, or you can lose your very taste for this delicacy or for the relationship you're in)
- endless pursuit of money and the rich things money can buy (Saddam Hussein had something like fifty villas, and many of us are protesting the grotesque greed in the top echelon of capitalist societies even as middle-class people are struggling as never before)

The least that can be said is that the lives of those who are into a "too-much" mode obviously lack a certain kind of balance that common sense tells us is needed for body and soul. There are any number of intriguing high profile cases of very successful people who kill themselves when they run into a problem that for them destroys their "perfection," and they leave people around them aghast without comprehension of how such a winning person could do himself in.

You will also find those who seemingly escape from all stress, who escape from life into a chemical Valhalla that even will kill them prematurely after killing off their potential ability to achieve their talents (the drunk and addicted). The too-much extremes are like other extremist systems of certainty that progressively take on qualities of totalitarianism with a likely inevitability of some forms of destructiveness.

These states of excess are different from living out with courage core human experiences of anxiety and discomfort. We refer several times in this book to the brilliant definition of anxiety that famed psychologist Rollo May offered years ago, that the experience of anxiety is a call from within our best selves of a potential and talent that are "dying" to be expressed.[13] Anxiety, we learn from May, is a message and an invitation to forge ahead and become the more of ourselves that we really want to be and can be. *It is great stuff*—although of course it should be kept from being agonizing or debilitating.

New York Times columnist, David Brooks, has written eloquently about the potential value of suffering in human lives:

> People in the midst of difficulty begin to feel a call. They are not masters of the situation, but neither are they helpless. They can't determine the course of their pain, but they can participate in responding to it. The right response to this sort of pain is not pleasure. It's holiness. . . . It means seeing life as a moral drama, trying to redeem something bad by turning it into something sacred. . . . When people are thrust down into these deeper zones, they are forced to confront the fact they can't determine what goes on there.[14]

Genuine and more lasting emotional strength includes the ability to live and lose and endure degrees of pain and uncertainty within a context of seeking to find solutions and to be creative in one's life. To have all the answers, experience no tension, and never fall on your face is most often and by definition, pseudo-strength.

The choice between a hedonistic escape from stress and a more balanced living out of the human condition is played out both in individual people's lives and in the collective culture processes of people in different eras. A longtime editor of the *New Republic*, Leon Wieseltier, sees in America the trend of avoiding unhappiness increasing and merging with a "giddy" emphasis on technology, speed, efficiency, and comfort. He observes that a major casualty is the deliberation of the basics of good and evil—forget them, what counts is what works. Another casualty is critical judgment—just do whatever works.

> If there is no criticism, then the praise isn't worth anything either. People are now ignoring critical judgment, and this is a cultural disaster. . . . No one wants to gain enemies. Everyone is "liking," and "friending," and it distorts. Everyone wants to be liked and therefore all of this praise is worthless, inconsequential.[15]

HOW DO WE APPLY OUR CONCEPTION OF PSYCHOLOGICAL HEALTH TO ACTUAL TREATMENT?

If psychological health is defined by us as the absence of all distressing experiences, then the logical and necessary purpose of treatment is to remove or reduce these symptoms and make everyday life more bearable for the suffering patient. Even here, however, I add with a strong conviction the stipulation that therapy for removal of symptoms should include not only relief for the patient but also a focus on the roles the patient may be playing in imposing suffering on others. The purpose of treatment for a democratic mind is to help people to live better in themselves and for themselves, but also to guide people and to insist that they stop doing serious harm to others.

If psychological health is defined as living meaningfully, developing oneself, reaching toward the best of one's potential to be alive and vibrant mentally and emotionally, being committed to decent values for oneself and others, and coping as well as possible with the inevitable stresses and losses of life, then the purpose of treatment, logically and hopefully, is also to develop one's capacity and shape one's ways of living to achieve these wonderful parts of being alive. Treatment is not for killing symptoms but for "growing life." Of course, symptoms that get in the way of such living and growing do need to be reduced and overcome, but the fuller goal of psychological treatment is to help and facilitate becoming more alive inside and outside and to be decent people. (See how this is also a very healthy way of defining a desirable goal for parenting our children,[16] and it is a great way to define a really good marriage such as the achievement of a "co-creative marriage."[17])

In other words, we have two levels of definition of psychological health, and thereby two levels of goals for mental health treatment. The first level is summed up as overcoming undue distress and symptoms. The second level can be summed up as growing as a person to fulfill oneself and to be decent to other people in our life journey.

Realistically and unfortunately, in a great number of cases we are unable in therapy to reach for the second richer level. We have more than enough on our hands to make progress on the first level of putting out fires and stopping explosions of suffering and craziness and doing manifest harm to others. Moreover, even when goals of reducing suffering are achieved quite well, there are many patients who show little interest in continuing treatment toward the larger expanded goals of living more fully.

❖ My own very beloved psychoanalyst, with whom I worked (oh, did I ever!), twice and more a week for four years, later went on to become the psychiatric director of a clinic in a very poor crime-laden heavily ethnic neighborhood. My therapist's meritorious personal goal was to contribute to the broader community need and not only to treat more cultured and able-to-pay patients like myself. But before long, he too was into dispensing lots of psychiatric medications for symptom control and relief (he had absolutely refused to prescribe anything for me during a horrible period of insomnia.) In most cases, therapy for overcoming symptoms psychologically and therapy for growth was an unreachable ideal.

Again I will acknowledge that as a practicing psychotherapist, I recognize and accept that my first job is to reduce unbearable suffering and restriction of functioning, but when that process is meaningfully on the way I personally love much more going on to what I call in my heart the real therapy. I can't say that I don't like the first part of the job. It is quite fascinating in its own right—for example, helping people to wind down their psychological contributions to major psychosomatic illnesses such as colitis, high blood pressure, and asthma, even to reduce epileptic convulsions; or bring an end to violence in a family, especially in psychotherapy that is aimed at experiencing anger and expressing it, but never in violence, or helping a person not to commit suicide. I know that as a doctor of clinical psychology I do address agony and relieve distress, and I can't say that I don't enjoy this work. Nonetheless, I know that I literally breathe more deeply and feel warm waves going through me when I am able to get into working on better ways of living, see a person developing to be so much more of themselves, and see the growth of relationships to be so much warmer and more authentic.

Again it is only fair to take note of what are the resources that are and are not available to enable people to go for broader treatment. If therapy is private, it means a lot more sessions and a lot more money. If therapy is in a public venue, it means a lot more sessions and a lot more money from the public till. Personally, I was blessed to undergo an earlier psychoanalysis at the university hospital where I was studying for my doctor's degree in clinical psychology at a fee of fifty cents an hour (which even then was a huge bargain)! After graduating and moving to another city, I went to a second analyst about whom I just wrote, and had to spend almost all of our young couple income for several years. But I never regretted the expense, and in plain economic terms I am sure that the wonderful career I have enjoyed from which I've earned a healthy income was enabled by the therapy I had. Still, you can't get angry at people for not having money, and you can't get angry at public institutions that have to allocate their budgets carefully and in many cases must restrict the number of sessions and length of treatment that can be given. Even so, I believe that unlike much of the specific symptom-reducing therapy prescribed today in public venues and by the blessed insurance companies (in the Bible "blessing" has two possible meanings—so you figure it), one can purposefully put into brief therapy protocols some time also for reviewing basic lifestyles. notwithstanding the fact that it will not be possible to access deeper unconscious issues. I can only urge as many people who can to take big risks and try in every way to gather the necessary resources for the fuller kind of treatment—the results of which they are likely to enjoy in many aspects for the rest of their lives.

Beyond the reality of resources, therapists also have huge roles in determining the definitions of goals in each treatment. Guiding the treatment work of every clinician is a conscious or unconscious assessment of the potential of the patient. It makes a huge difference whether one thinks that one's patient is or is not capable of changing a wrong way of thinking or living for the better, or more "simply" needs to be quieted or cleansed of crazy thoughts and reorganized. It also makes a big difference if one not only looks at the patient's errors in thinking and living in the areas of poor functioning and subjective complaints and discomforts, but also offers treatment that is intended to touch on and free as much as possible further expression of a better and more creative self.

You will find that when the goal of therapy is to control and alleviate symptoms, there will be many more times when a therapist will also advise the patient to learn to live with it. Of course, this is not such bad advice for all of us as we hit the "I can'ts" of our bodies and minds and fates. But it's patronizing and possibly seriously destructive advice when given to a person who *could* try to reach higher levels.

Thus, compare these contrasting advices:

It takes a lot of courage and effort to keep going, but I want to encourage you because I feel you can make it.	You don't have to finish school if it's taking so much out of you.
You are very unhappy in your marriage, but do you think you still want to work hard at changing it?	You are so unhappy in your marriage that you ought to end it.

What a difference! One choice is likely to make you feel immediately relieved and quieter. The other choice will keep up a great deal of tension even if you're inspired to try, and you may not succeed, but what if you do!

I have a gifted family doctor who never fails to encourage me to do whatever I want to do but am unsure that I can handle physically. Obviously, someday he's going to be dead wrong, but I sure am grateful for the many years until then.

WHAT CAN WE LEARN FROM PSYCHIATRIC DIAGNOSTIC SYSTEMS SINCE TIME IMMEMORIAL?

Karl Menninger and his colleague psychologists, Martin Mayman and Paul Pruyser at the famed Menninger Clinic provide in their book *The Vital Balance* a brilliant, lengthy, detailed appendix of the endless history of psychiatric definitional systems over the centuries.[18] Their real point is that the overly detailed psychiatric nosologies are nonsense. What matters is patterning the degree of mental disorganization. Symptom manifestations can change over time and in different cultures, but it is the basic process of adjustment and failure to adjust that tells the real story. Interestingly the authors note that they originally proposed to call their book, "The Return to the Unitary Concept of Mental Illness."

The authors assemble the information about the history of mental diagnoses respectfully, yet also with some delicious tongue in cheek ("Our immediate ancestors were human beings like ourselves, with nerves and brains like ours, desires and disappointments like ours"). Their history begins with primitive psychiatric classifications going back to 2600 BC–500 BC. This is how they invite the reader to see the history of psychiatric classifications:

> Don't go, please. We have something yet to show you. It is a collection of precious documents, a review of the psychiatric nosologies of all times. Each of them represents the labors of a lifetime—the dedicated, loving efforts of a scientist, or even a whole school of them, to record what he saw and believed.
>
> Gaze kindly upon them, dear reader; they are a noble heritage. From them grew the concepts of today. Leaf the pages and observe for yourself what the trend has been. These are not mere words arranged in columns; these are thoughts, these are views of mental illness projected by our predecessors. Each had its day, its friends, its users. Each received from those that preceded, and contributed to those that followed.[19]

Menninger and his colleagues' conclusion seems only too true today as well:

> And so we are still in an era of nosological upheavals, confusion, and uncertainty. Were it not for the pressure of statistical reporting to public health agencies, and hospitals, practicing psychiatrists would have a wide choice of classifications from which to choose in line with their own beliefs and leanings. . . . The duties of reporting to official health boards often force their users to engage in a double system of bookkeeping, as it were, one in which to state one's beliefs, the other in which to conform.[20]

The authors themselves are interested in the degree of a patient's disturbance and especially how it is organized more than in its contents. They create a model of five levels or "orders of dysfunction." Note also their strong emphasis in the earlier levels on the improper use of aggressive feelings.

- *Disorganization of a First Order*: In common parlance this is "nervousness" or an increase in tension. "The ego recognizes a greater than average upsurge of anger, of fear, or of other emotions betraying the arousal of aggressive impulses."[21]

- *Second Order of Dyscontrol*: The "Neurotic" Syndromes and Personalities: This is a degree of dyscontrol or disorganization represented by the traditional clinical syndromes of the neuroses. "Some increment of aggression escapes in various forms less well neutralized than the ego would like. Some of the elements of normal living and normal productivity are sacrificed."[22]
- *Third Order of Dyscontrol*: "Naked Aggression": Now there is an "escape of more or less directed undisguised aggression" appearing in two syndromes, the first chronic repetition of milder though still serious aggression, the second explosive outbursts of "very serious aggressions."[23] "The restraining control of the ego has been lessened when we see a person strikes out at his wife, his child, his acquaintances, or even complete strangers… the facade of social conformity has been demolished and the hateful murderousness which the ego has been trying to control has been exposed in action."[24] Gathering resentments, suspiciousness, paranoid thinking, up to and including delusional paranoid states, are extreme forms of this dyscontrol.
- *Dysfunction of a Fourth and Fifth Order*: "Extreme states of disorganization, regression, and reality repudiation which constitute the classical picture of severe mental illness—so called psychoses" are the fourth order. More than interestingly, the authors note that fourth order cases "are well advanced, but all tend to recover!"[25] I must say that this report of 100 percent good outcome is not quite understandable to me although I deeply appreciate its optimism and definitely know it is true for *some* cases. This is not so for the fifth order cases. Fifth order disorganization is described as "malignant anxiety and depression eventuating in death, often by suicide."[26]

By now it is very clear that this is a group of a psychiatrist and psychologists who do not stand in awe of symptoms as is so much the case in *DSM* psychiatry today, although they certainly recognize that psychiatric symptoms can be deadly severe. For them "a symptom has more than merely a distress-signal meaning." Symptoms are not recorded seemingly joyfully to prove that psychiatric help is needed. They are respected and an effort is made first of all to understand them in their contributions to the patient's life. Symptoms, say the Menninger team, are "devices employed by the ego to deal with emergencies, disturbed equilibrium and threatened dyscontrol"[27] and that help is needed.[28] Symptoms are not descriptors of a disease entity; they occur in human beings who are losing their ability to organize their lives constructively and normally and are calling out for help. The symptoms are temporarily helpful in organizing people, but in the long run the symptoms create difficulties as "they may become permanent boarders, established as habitual techniques of living."[29]

In overwhelming contrast to the *DSM* thinking that seemingly celebrates symptoms as entries into psychiatric treatment—that in most cases of course calls for medication to suppress the symptoms—these authors recognize that in many to most cases at least the less severe forms of anxiety and dyscontrol may very well be signals of achievable wishes and potential for growth! In other words, the patient who is currently feeling lousy and scared may very well be on the edge of fulfilling urges and talents for growth that are pushing to come up from inside their current less developed and more immature self. The authors quote other writings of one of them, Martin Mayman, who wrote in an earlier publication:

> Inner unrest, even turmoil, need not signify the illness, it may signal incipient change for the better. Not all disequilibria are unhealthy; instability may indicate a condition still in flux whose direction of change may remain uncertain until a new integration is reached. . . .[30]
>
> Certainly, unrest holds out at least the prospect of a change for the better unlike the stagnation which often characterizes those patients who seem to have settled into a state of illness. . . . A relatively healthy ego often welcomes (even invites) disturbance in its equilibrium.[31]

In a cautionary statement that I wish could be turned into a mandatory wall plaque in every psychiatric clinic, the Menninger team concludes, "Positive striving may be mistaken for wasteful inner strife."[32]

CONCLUSION

Allen Frances is a distinguished psychiatrist who was no less than the editor of *DSM-IV*. In recent years, he has become a profound critic of psychiatric medications.[33] This is some of what he has to say about psychotropic drugs:

> *About research of psychiatric drugs:* "The data are proprietary and closely guarded; negative results are routinely buried; tiny, trivial, or chance positive findings are hailed as the second coming; investigators are corrupted; and sometimes scientific papers are ghostwritten by company hacks."[34]
>
> *About the distribution between psychotherapy and medication:* "Too Little Psychotherapy—there is no organized psychotherapy industry to mount a concerted competitive push-back against the excessive use of drugs."[35]
>
> *About the terrible toll of overprescribing psychiatric medications:* "Diagnostic inflation and polypharmacy go hand in hand and can be a lethal combination.

How remarkable that so little is being done to stop this almost completely preventable cause of death and disability—especially since there is an easy technical fix to end the glut of dangerous over-prescription."[36]

In the coming chapter we go on to look further at the basic issue of how much can we try to cure the mind through the body. In the process, we will meet up with several horrendous treatments in the history of psychiatry which are not only important stories in their own right, but illustrate how painfully far medicine can go wrong once it takes off on a basic paradigm that human experiences and feelings lie more in their physiological expressions than in the hearts and minds of humans in their actual lives.

> When he took the time to help the man up the mountain, lo, he scaled it himself.
>
> —Tibetan Proverb[37]

NOTES

1. Urie Bronfenbrenner, *Two Worlds of Childhood* (New York: Simon and Schuster, 1970).
2. Marie Jahoda, as cited by Morris S. Schwartz, and Charlotte Green Schwartz, "Mental Health," in *International Encyclopedia of the Social Sciences*, ed. David L Sills and Robert K. Merson (New York: MacMillan, 1968), http://www.encyclopedia.com/topic/Mental_health.aspx.
3. Erich Fromm, as cited by Schwartz, and Schwartz, *International Encyclopedia of the Social Sciences.*
4. Erich Fromm, *The Sane Society* (New York: Reinhardt & Co., 1955), 275. See also Erich Fromm, *The Heart of Man: Its Genius for Good and Evil* (New York: Harper & Row, 1964).
5. Schwartz, and Schwartz, *International Encyclopedia of the Social Sciences.*
6. Many times I have taught students that Hillel deserves to be called a great psychologist and also a great sexologist—think of yourself and the other in making love! Hillel also taught a Golden Rule: "That which is hateful to you, do not do to your fellow," and instructed further, "That is the Whole Torah, the rest is the explanation."
7. David L. Rosenhan, and Martin E. P. Seligman, *Abnormal Psychology* (New York: Norton, 1984), see 5–11 (quotation p. 11).
8. Gail Sheehy, *Passages: Predictable Crises of Adult Life* (New York: E.P. Dutton, 1976).
9. Roberto Assagioli, *Psychosynthesis: A Manual of Principles and Techniques* (London: Turnstone Books, 1965); Roberto Assagioli, *The Act of Will* (Baltimore: Penguin, 1973); Erich Neumann, *Depth Psychology and a New Ethic* (New York: G.P. Putnam, 1969 1949]).

10. Sharon Louden, *Living and Sustaining a Creative Life: Essays by 40 Working Artists* (Chicago: Intellect, University of Chicago Press, 2013).

11. Allan V. Horwitz and Jerome C. Wakefield, *All We Have to Fear: Psychiatry's Transformation of Natural Anxieties into Mental Disorders* (New York: Oxford University Press, 2012); Allan, V. Horwitz and Jerome C. Wakefield, *The Loss of Sadness: How Psychiatry Transformed Normal Sorrow into Depressive Disorder* (New York: Oxford University Press, 2014).

12. Alan W. Watts, *The Wisdom of Insecurity: A Message for an Age of Anxiety* (New York: Vintage, 2011 [1951] (quotation retrieved from Maria Popova at http://theattentivesoul.me/2014/01/13/the-age-of-anxiety/)

13. Rollo May, *The Meaning of Anxiety* (New York: W.W. Norton, 1996 [1950]).

14. David Brooks, "What Suffering Does," *International New York Times,* April 9, 2014. David Brooks goes on to say: The theologian Paul Tillich wrote that people who endure suffering are taken beneath the routines of life and find they are not who they believed themselves to be. . . . Suffering gives people a more accurate sense of their own limitations, what they can control and cannot control.

15. Maya Sela, "The Title I Answer to Is Intellectual," *Haaretz English Edition,* June 14, 2013.

16. Edward Z. Tronic, "'Of Course All Relationships Are Unique': How Co-creative Processes Generate Unique Mother–Infant and Patient–Therapist Relationships and Change Other Relationships" *Psychoanalytic Inquiry* 23, no. 3: 473–91.

17. Israel W. Charny, "Marriage as Effective 'Therapy,'" in *Existential/Dialectical Marital Therapy: Breaking the Secret Code of Marriage* (New York: Brunner/Mazel, 1992), 42–49.

18. Karl Menninger, Markus Mayman, and Paul Pruyser, *The Vital Balance: The Life Process in Mental Health and Illness* (New York: Viking Press, 1963). The survey of diagnoses is offered as "Appendix: Attest and Exhibits," 419–89

19. Ibid., 419.

20. Ibid., 489.

21. Ibid., 163.

22. Ibid., 174.

23. Ibid., 213.

24. Ibid., 221.

25. Ibid., 262.

26. Ibid., 250.

27. Ib .id. 164.

28. Ibid., 169.

29. Ibid. 171.

30. Ibid., 413–14, with citation to Martin Mayman, "Ego Strength and the Potential for Recovery from Mental Illness," in *Festschrift for Gardner Murphy* (New York: Harper, 1960).

31. Ibid., 414.

32. Ibid.

33. Allen Frances, *Saving Normal: An Insider's Revolt against Out-of-Control Psychiatric Diagnosis: DSM-5, Big Pharma, and the Medicalization of Ordinary*

Life New York: William Morrow, 2013). See also the author's proposal for a better diagnostic system in Frances Allen, *Essentials of Psychiatric Diagnosis* (New York: Guilford Press, 2013).

34. Allen Frances, *Saving Normal*, 90.
35. Ibid., 108.
36. Ibid., 214.
37. Widely cited anonymous Tibetan proverb.

Chapter Four

A Basic Question for Psychiatry and Psychology

How Much Can We Try to Cure the Mind through the Body?

In the previous chapter we have given our conception of mental health, but there is also a "ghost" hanging around of the crazy reality that *most* treatment in psychiatry today is medical and hardly focuses on whether a person respects his own life and the lives of others. Basically the medical procedures are designed to remove the symptoms of distress and incompetent functions that a given patient suffers. So before we end our formulation of what is mental health, it seems appropriate for us to look at the medical approach and to give our evaluation of this way of thinking.

In my opinion, the really basic question is how much can we cure mind problems through treatments of our bodies? The question is a huge one, and we won't attempt a full history of such efforts, or to provide in-depth evaluations of all the various specific treatments, for example, electric shock (ECT) for depression and for psychosis, Ritalin for attention deficit hyperactive disorder (ADHD), let alone for more simple cases of ADD without hyperactivity, tranquilizers for anxiety, antidepressant medications, or antipsychotic medication (see in various places in the book references to the damages that can be caused by SSRIs). There is a lot to say in each case, which we can't possibly cover, but this book is a place to develop an overall *perspective* about physical treatments of mind problems.

In order to do so, we will look at some opinions about the proliferation of psychiatric medications and at the hair-raising stories of two major "psychiatric surgeries" that reigned as saviors in the past. We will also look briefly at mental hospitals insofar as the majority of these institutions represent very strongly organic conceptions of mental disorders and promote the use of medications and organic procedures to "cure" mental problems.

The issue is both a scientific and a basic philosophical one—an epistemological question of whether one is closer to the truth of human experience through the avenue of the mind or through body functions. In our time, any such discussion immediately becomes also a position statement on the overall field of psychiatry in our era. For many years psychiatry gave us giants of psychotherapy, but now in our times it has obviously turned toward medical concepts of diagnoses and treatment. For me psychiatry has turned to a false god and has plunged into a Dark Age. I believe medicalized psychiatry is an escape from experiencing a more whole humanness to a robotization of people.

After such a strong statement, perhaps I should also make it clear that "some of my best friends" have been and in a few cases still are psychiatrists. In general, the field of psychiatry was something of a mentor to my newer field of clinical psychology, and I read and studied the works of so many wonderful psychiatrist pioneers of psychotherapy, including Karl Menninger whom I cite a lot in this book, and William Menninger, Karen Horney, Franz Alexander, Leon Saul, Carl Whitaker, Ivan Boszormenyi-Nagy, and many others—several of whom I had the pleasure of knowing personally. My own beloved psychoanalyst was a psychiatrist. My chosen mentor in family therapy and the teacher who taught me the most about how to get out of the box to respond to patients from a more creative and authentic self was a psychiatrist. My superb teacher of child psychiatry, who taught me how to help children and all people to be alive for themselves and not for someone else was a psychiatrist. I have the deepest respect and even love for the professional discipline—that was, but now (with some exceptions, of course) is no more.

My main argument with treating the body in order to repair an ailing mind is that you don't simply cure broken hearts or raging emotions of longing, jealousy, anger, or revenge by erasing them from the brain or by manipulating endocrinological and neurological expressions of emotions. And yet my readers will be surprised that I answer the basic question, "*Can physiological tools help in the treatment of mental distress?*" with a *Yes*. Sleepy under-functioning response systems can be turned on, and runaway excessive psychophysiological responses can be slowed and rechanneled by different medications. A wise patient and a wise doctor will make use of some medications quite honorably—for example, a tranquilizer to quiet down a roar of anxiety or to help one have precious sleep after being ensnared in discomforting insomnia, or a stimulant to help a distracted student who is scared about failing. But how much? How often? Meds mechanically given and taken without human caring and encouragement? Meds to solve the issue without really looking at a person's real feelings and experiences?

There is a logic that flows from defining an issue of mental distress as essentially psychological—in the mind—versus ascribing it to a large extent to physiological causes. The logic is that management of one's mind-release of emotions and the redefinition of mental attitudes are better treated *in the mind.* Thus, heavy grief over the death of a loved one, terrible haunting flashbacks of a trauma such as in combat, despair over a failing marriage *might* be reduced and perhaps ended with medications, but is that wise?

My own rule of thumb in most cases is that medication is a gift for reducing unbearable distress, but should not be prescribed in heavy doses or too often or regularly insofar as counseling and psychotherapy are available options. Almost always medication should be accompanied by a genuine psychotherapy and not just "How are you?" conversations with a caring psychiatrist.

"AFTER DECADES OF TRYING TO PROVE IT, RESEARCHERS HAVE STILL COME UP EMPTY HANDED"

Marcia Angell has written a marvelously comprehensive review essay on the state of contemporary psychiatry.[1] Angell brings together reviews of three important books on psychiatry, drugs, and what she defines as an "epidemic" of diagnosing mental illness on the basis of *DSM*-type checklists.

> Nowadays treatment by medical doctors nearly always means psychoactive drugs, that is, drugs that affect the mental state. In fact, most psychiatrists treat only with drugs, and refer patients to psychologists or social workers if they believe psychotherapy is also warranted. The shift from "talk therapy" to drugs as the dominant mode of treatment coincides with the emergence over the past four decades of the theory that mental illness is caused primarily by chemical imbalances in the brain that can be corrected by specific drugs.

The three books are *The Emperor's New Drugs: Exploding the Antidepressant Myth* by Irving Kirsch[2]; *Unhinged: The Trouble with Psychiatry—A Doctor's Revelations about a Profession in Crisis* by Daniel Carlat; and *Anatomy of an Epidemic: Magic Bullets, Psychiatric Drugs, and the Astonishing Rise of Mental Illness in America* by Robert Whitaker. Irving Kirsch is a psychologist at the University of Hull in the UK. His work includes a fifteen-year scientific study to answer a question about whether antidepressants work. "Kirsch found that placebos were three times as effective as no treatment . . . and placebos were 75 percent as effective as antidepressants."[3] Robert Whitaker is a journalist and previously the author of a history of the treatment of mental illness called *Mad in America.* Whitaker takes on the entire spectrum of mental illness and asks whether psychoactive drugs create worse problems than they solve. Daniel Carlat is a psychiatrist in Boston. He writes more in sorrow and "looks mainly at how his profession has allied itself with, and is manipulated by, the pharmaceutical industry. . . . All three authors are in remarkable agreement," says Angell, who summarizes the key points on which they agree so clearly:

> First, they agree on the disturbing extent to which the companies that sell psychoactive drugs—through various forms of marketing, both legal and illegal, and what many people would describe as bribery—have come to determine what constitutes a mental illness and how the disorders should be diagnosed and treated. . . .
>
> Second, none of the three authors subscribes to the popular theory that mental illness is caused by a chemical imbalance in the brain. . . .
>
> Instead of developing a drug to treat an abnormality, an abnormality was postulated to fit a drug. . . .
>
> It was entirely possible that drugs that affected neurotransmitter levels could relieve symptoms even if neurotransmitters had nothing to do with the illness in the first place (and even possible that they relieved symptoms through some other mode of action entirely). As Carlat puts it, "By this same logic one could argue that the cause of all pain conditions is a deficiency of opiates, since narcotic pain medications activate opiate receptors in the brain." Or similarly, one could argue that fevers are caused by too little aspirin.
>
> But the main problem with the theory is that after decades of trying to prove it, researchers have still come up empty-handed. . . . Carlat refers to the chemical imbalance theory as a "myth."[4]

Interestingly, adopting a medical conception of psychiatric problems has also been found to invite less empathy for people in their suffering. In an intriguing article in the *New York Times*, a journalist who specializes in writing about psychiatry and social psychology concluded that research showed that those who adopt biological-medical conceptions of mental illness generally wanted "less contact with the mentally ill and thought of them as more dangerous and unpredictable. Even when it is spirits and gods who are conceived of as the source causes of mental illness, there is much more to be done in the way of treatment that addresses the mind causes of the illness and there is much more of a readiness to interact with the mentally ill."[5]

THERE HAVE BEEN TOO MANY MISTAKEN AND EVEN CRIMINAL PSYCHIATRIC TREATMENTS OF THE BODY

Another or second perspective on the issue of medical treatment for mental conditions is caveat emptor. Medical treatments for mental conditions are known to have caused unbearable and irreversible damages that go beyond an acceptable range of the dangers of the "side effects" that accompany virtually all medicines and medical treatments. Take the condition of tardive dyskinesia, for example tremors of the mouth or limbs that result from many psychiatric medications that are not always a function of the dosage and too often are incurable even after the medication is stopped. Another example to which we refer a number of times in this book are the suicidal and homicidal outcomes of Prozac-type (SSRI) medications, and how these medications have been disallowed in the UK for children and adolescents but continue to be big-capital winners in the United States.

There is a further frightening issue that goes far beyond the damages that medication and other medical procedures can cause some people while helping others. At its core, the issue flows from the overall conception of whether we should try to treat the mind issues through the body. If it were only medications—especially those that have fewer and less serious side effects—there would be less reason for concern. But in addition to the facts that many medications are heavily overdosed and that many do serious damages, it turns out that the license medicine has to penetrate our bodies too often has proven an invitation to absolutely *meshuga* (nutty) ideas that have destroyed people's minds, individualities, and spirits. There have never been well-thought-out checks and balances on medical power and on the unbearably far-reaching consequences of many medical procedures, such as brain damage—loss of memory—from ECT (electric shock), or the wipeout of individualism and initiative from lobotomies. I fear that new manipulations of our brains are going to come out of the current rage of (fascinating) brain science. We have definitely not seen the last of robotizing/brainwashing totalitarianism à la the prescient *1984*.

Strange as it may seem, some of the truly nutty destructive treatments win memorably long periods of acclaim before they are exposed. I will discuss two such case studies here—there are many more. Both originated within the great American democracy. In openly fascist countries there are histories of psychiatric hospitalizations as coercive and torturing (such as in the Soviet Union), or "eugenic" (supposed improvement of the race!), where mental handicap was a basis for "euthanasic" murder (such as in Nazi Germany). But, unbelievably, democratic nations and cultures also have their share of histories of psychiatric fascism and sadism. Thus, French mental hospitals participated like German hospitals in the Nazi killing of children defined as mentally disabled or psychiatric cases;[6] and there were thousands of forced sterilizations of people defined as defective in the United States.[7]

The two rotten "treatments" that we will review here were authored and executed by America's finest professionals and were literally applauded as pacesetting solutions to the curse of serious mental illness. Both are twentieth-century sagas that are still within the living memories of many of us. Obviously each saga of a murderous "wonderful new medical treatment" is a scandal in its own right—including the way in which in their eras of glory such treatments became politically correct, and woe was there unto clinicians who challenged them during these years. In my opinion, the larger meaning is that the basic wrong conception that psychological programs are to be cured by tinkering with body functions instead of being cured by corrections of mind program is what brings on bizarrely harmful treatments for the mental and emotionally ill.

Of course the history of medicine is full of mistaken treatments, but I would further differentiate between those that were based on incorrect notions that nonetheless flowed from sensible ideas versus those that, on the very surface of it, were clearly based on nonsensical ideas and obviously carried a serious potential of being destructive of bodies and minds. I will say about myself that I sometimes go "crazy" when I am stuck and can't move my bowels, but the solution both to my GI blockage and to my craziness is hardly removing my intestines. So too I sometimes get way too agitated with emotions, but the solution is hardly in cutting out my physiological machinery for experiencing emotions.

The following are two cases from the early and mid-twentieth century. The stories are in their own right engrossing reading, so much so that they are almost fun, and it is easy to forget that they exemplify the stupidity and evil that are highly probable in medical procedures that are out to do the impossible of resolving human distress and problems in living by major brain/mind/body altering procedures rather than addressing human experiences and hungers for connection and meaning.

Extractions and Amputations—for Your Mental Health, of Course

Back in 1907, Dr. Henry Cotton, the director of one of the large mental hospitals in the United States, in New Jersey, came to the conviction that mental illness is caused by various infections of the teeth, tonsils, or large intestine. Therefore, the treatments that followed for many years were extractions and amputations of these parts of the body from many patients—even the cervix and the seminal vesicles were sometimes removed. The gripping story of these fallacious and destructive treatments is told by Andrew Scull in *Madhouse: A Tragic Tale of Megalomania in Modern Medicine*.[8]

One reviewer, Robert Darby, who is identified as an independent scholar in Australia, has written: "Like a medieval priest or tribal sorcerer casting out demons, an astounding number of modern physicians, all boasting of their scientific credentials, seem to have worked on the assumption that the human body is its own worst enemy, and thus to have concluded that the road to health lay through the extraction or amputation of whatever body part could be held responsible for the dysfunction.[9] Amazingly, Cotton was reporting to the health authorities an 85 percent success rate.

Cotton published his findings in the respected medical journals of the time, and was supported generously by leading psychiatrists and politicians. "Hundreds of patients streamed to the hospital in Trenton to receive treatment," and among other recognition and honors Cotton was received with royal acclaim in England.[10] Not that there weren't various professional examinations of what was going on at Cotton's hospital. Unbelievably, in the reviews and investigations by other professionals there was a report of a 50 percent death rate from operations on the large intestine, and also reports of "fabricated results, biased statistics, abuses of patients, mistreatment in surgical procedures performed against the will of the patients or their families."[11]

This bizarre but terribly real scenario was being played out during a period when the leader in the field of psychiatry in the United States was the very respected professor, Adolph Meyer—many of whose quite humane conceptions of how to treat serious mental patients remain valid and usable to this day. Meyer himself subscribed to the theory that mental illness was caused by centers of infection. Meyer did send a researcher—a young woman psychiatrist who later became a well-known psychoanalyst, Dr. Phyllis Greenacre—and she came up with much of the truth about the terrible results of Cotton's treatment, but Meyer, who was "a great admirer of Cotton, did not give his approval to the publication of the incriminating findings."[12] Another researcher reached similar conclusions and showed the death rate was even higher and that there was no improvement whatsoever in the mental health of the survivors, but here too the results were squashed.

Finally, there came a point where Cotton was investigated by the State of New Jersey. It is reported that one day when Cotton was leaving the court house in bad weather without proper clothing "he lost his sanity."[13] Continuing the unbelievable, it is then reported that the staff and the administration of the hospital hid the doctor until he returned to direct the hospital once again and continued its killing surgeries for another fifteen years.

Even after the death of Cotton, his students continued to extract teeth and to remove tonsils until 1960. Remarking on the similarity of this frightening story to the story of lobotomies, Joel Donchin, a professor of medicine in anesthesiology and director of the Patient Safety Center at Hebrew University's Hadassah Hospital, writes:

> Even the inception of a treatment that was thought to be innovative at the time—lobotomy, the surgical removal of part of the brain's frontal lobe by inserting an ice pick into it, which was supposed to replace other treatments—did not lead to the end of the amputations and other surgery. The studies that pointed to the

> danger and stupidity of Cotton's methods were buried in the archives of Johns Hopkins and the management of the hospital in New Jersey.[14]

Donchin adds: "One must ask himself: Is it possible [in our time] that political power combined with the dominance and arrogance of the medical profession could lead to patients receiving an ineffective (or harmful) medication, or that a reputable surgeon could perform experiments and distort the results? To my regret, the answer is in the affirmative."[15]

Reviewer Robert Darby summarizes the Scull book as "at once a gripping, narrative, a muckraking expose of medical fraud and professional vanity, and a sobering cautionary tale for our own times."[16] The same reviewer also makes a further linkage to the advent of lobotomies (which will be our next subject) in that Adolf Meyer, who we just said played a role in suppressing the damning critical report on Cotton, later "did much to win acceptance for lobotomies in the 1950's."[17] The largest moral of the story, writes Darby, is its "embodiment of a deep-seated trend in the medical profession itself: the assumption that if these wise experts think some sort of treatment or procedure is good for you, it is your duty to submit to it, and even that they are entitled—by virtue of their scientific understanding and promise of benefit—to force it on you."[18]

Cotton himself was a true believer in his nonsense, and he performed large scale prophylactic tooth extractions on both of his sons, both of whom went on to commit suicide in their middle age.[19]

Lobotomies: The Brilliant Treatment to Quiet the Deranged and Agitated that Ended Up "Cutting Off the Nose to Spite the Face"

The only Nobel Prize that was ever awarded that is related to psychiatry was the Nobel Prize for Physiology or Medicine in 1949 to Portuguese neurologist Antonio Egas Moniz, the originator of the lobotomy surgical procedure. The prize was in celebration of "discovery of the therapeutic value of leucotomy in certain psychosis."[20]

It was 1936 when psychiatrist Walter Freeman performed the first prefrontal lobotomy on a housewife in Kansas. Freeman wanted to find a more efficient way than drilling into a person's head like Moniz did, and he created a ten-minute ice pick procedure. Freeman is reported to have gone on to have performed about twenty-five hundred lobotomies. Known as a showman, he once performed twenty-five lobotomies in one day. To shock his audiences, he also liked to insert picks in both eyes simultaneously.[21] Freeman was banned from performing lobotomies in 1967 after he had done a third lobotomy on a longtime patient of his who hemorrhaged and died. Some nations had already outlawed lobotomies as early as the 1950s, including the

Soviet Union (!) which said that lobotomies were "contrary to the principles of humanity."[22]

Roy Porter, emeritus professor in the social history of medicine at Wellcome Institute for the History of Medicine at the University of London, who was considered by the *British Medical Journal* "the greatest medical historian of his generation,"[23] observed that writing the history of the surgery through the eyes of the families of patients brought many testimonials to how much easier it was to live with the now placid patient who had been so unmanageable to the family earlier. At the same time he recognized that the procedure became a byword for medical barbarism and medical trampling of patients' rights.[24]

❖ My own experience as a clinical psychology intern in the 1950s at a totally kosher (accredited) US government Veteran's Administration psychiatric hospital was that not only deteriorated chronic patients were given "well-intentioned" lobotomies in the hopes of "alleviating the[ir] suffering," but that the procedure was done on young adults, some of whom had not been the recipients of serious efforts at less violent therapies previously. In fact, through the years I have been haunted by the memory of one young man in his early twenties, like I was at the time, who was showing a lot of free-flowing anxiety, which of course was never translated into a call of his potential to be healthier, and then this young man dared to have the guts and the wherewithal to escape from the hospital—God bless him!—but was forcibly brought back and then sent for a lobotomy. I felt terrible for him. Quite obviously I was identifying with my age peer. In fact during those years, I myself was suffering intense anxiety attacks, but I had the privilege of psychoanalytic treatment twice a week on a nice leather couch at the university hospital and not a lobotomy! The lobotomy was obviously a punishment for his daring to defy the rules of the all-powerful hospital that in so many ways pretended to itself to be "well-intentioned."

One is similarly reminded of the fate of McMurphy played by Jack Nicholson in the unforgettable film, *One Flew Over the Cuckoo's Nest*, based on a novel by the same name.[25] A BBC review of the "strange and curious history of lobotomy" quotes "one of Britain's most eminent neurosurgeons" saying that the operation was "bad science . . . the fact that they [the patients] were totally ruined as social human beings probably didn't count."[26]

A Boston University Web magazine on Walter Freeman summarized the outcomes of lobotomies in this way: "Lobotomies frequently have nasty side-effects such as: death, epilepsy, loss of motor function, loss of cognitive abilities, blunting of personality and emotion, and incontinence." Nonetheless, fair disclosure requires us to add that the previous sentence is followed immediately by the remark: "It is worth noting, however, that some patients did improve in relation to their pre-operational state." The same entry then goes on to report, without any evaluative remark, that one of John F. Kennedy's siblings, Rosemary, whom the world knew of as "mentally handicapped" in reality had undergone a lobotomy at age twenty-three.[27]

Recently, NPR carried a touching story of a fifty-six-year-old bus driver in California who was on a quest to find the story behind the fact that he underwent a lobotomy as a twelve-year-old. The man is quoted as saying "If you saw me, you would never know I had a lobotomy. The only thing you'd notice is that I am very tall and weigh about 350 pounds. But I have always *felt* different—wondered if something is missing from my soul. I have no memory of the operation, and never had the courage to ask my family about it."[28]

If we go back to the era in which lobotomies thrived as a legitimate treatment to see what scientific assessment of results said at the time, we find a report in the *Canadian Medical Association Journal* in 1967.[29] The author studied 150 patients who had undergone lobotomy between 1948 and 1952. He assessed them first in 1952 and then again in 1962 when he was able to reach 116 of the patients. Serious scientific work. Were the results "good"? Reportedly, 67 percent improved sufficiently to live outside of the hospital, although 26 percent did have periods of relapse, and the most significant complications were that 12 percent suffered epilepsy and 91 percent showed a personality defect. The author's conclusion in this 1967 article was that "if pre-frontal lobotomy is used for selected cases of intractable mental disorder only, it is has probably found its proper place in psychiatric treatment."

My own reaction is "There but for the grace of God, go I." There are a lot of things for which I am grateful in my life—among them not having been sent to Auschwitz and not having been sent for a lobotomy.

The larger point of this and the previous horror story is that these are the things that are done in the names of science and medicine when a basic fallacy is adopted in trying to cure psychological problems through bodily interventions. This fallacy then joins with the fact that institutions of medicine that we all need so deeply, and to which so many times we are more than grateful for saving our lives and giving us health, often entitle themselves to unchecked powers to perform stupid, brutal, procedures on people And then for the longest time the professionals involved lie to themselves and to society about their use of unchecked power and allowance of violence and deny brazenly the harm they are doing. Sadly enough, all of the above are characteristic of fascist-mind thinking. Democratic mind hates lobotomies and the whole configuration of forces that made this era possible.

ARE MENTAL HOSPITALS INHERENTLY TOO TOTALITARIAN, OR CAN THEY CONTRIBUTE TO A DEMOCRATIC MIND?

It also seems right to look at the institution of mental hospitals, if only because these are the settings in which the horrendous physical treatments of many mental problems take place! The subject of mental hospitals is in its own right a huge and fascinating one and of the utmost importance for the many people who definitely need a period of protection and concentrated care. The subject is much bigger than we can examine in this book. But what does behoove us is to take a bird's-eye view of the institution of mental hospitals from the perspective of the question of whether they are inherently totalitarian institutions that suppress human experiencing and individuality, or can they really contribute to the kind of treatment for free and alive minds and people that we are encouraging.

Perhaps surprisingly, my answer is *yes* to both questions, despite the fact that, to the best of my knowledge the prevailing modes of treatment in most mental hospitals aim to suppress symptoms and are not at all loath to so by quieting, drugging, and re-socializing people to conform to their normative and politically correct ways of behavior. On the other hand, I know of hospitals, and I had the privilege of working in such a hospital for several years, where the goal of treatment is to free patients to become more of their natural selves and to fulfill their better potential. Treatment in such good hospitals also often enough includes restraints on destructive behaviors, physical and mental. But these restraints are applied and conveyed in messages of genuine caring for the patients and the other people in their life, and not for the purpose of quieting the troublemaker down or retaliating, consciously or unconsciously, for what a fearful or troublesome pain in the ass the patient has been.

There is a part of me that actually loved working in a good hospital. Because this is a setting where patients can enjoy total care, it is possible to undertake stronger therapy interventions than one does in an office setting, where the patient goes home and has a return appointment a week later. One example for me is the much greater ease of doing what I call "naturalistic family therapy," where the therapist does not pace the session and is not careful about controlling the intensity of interventions, but instead relentlessly describes to a patient and family what communications are taking place between them from minute to minute. It is not long before longtime defenses and hiding places are exposed in new ways![30]

It is very interesting to me that the *fix-symptoms-hospitals* are frequently characterized by a strictly hierarchical professional structure, among other things with what I call make-believe staff meetings, where staff members may not even know that they are not daring to think of ideas that differ from the direction coming from on high. The *genuine* hospitals on the other hand lean more often toward genuine staff collaboration, where staff members at (almost) all levels are more authentic, and the collective atmosphere is one of greater respect for fellow staff members as well as patients.

In the United States today—as well as a number of other countries—many of the big cavernous mental hospitals of yesteryear have been closed. They were for the most part horrors where human beings (including doctors and nurses) and bureaucratic systems have strong control over others (that's what *One Flew Over the Cuckoo's Nest* is about). Even good private psychiatric hospitals where more decent treatment was offered have had to close their doors because of legal rulings that denial of symptom-erasing drugs can be a justification for huge medical litigation.

But are the mentally ill really better off with the closing down of hospitals? There is evidence that a really significant number of these handicapped people are now the occupants of heavily overflowing jails in the United States. A joint study of the Alliance for Human Research Protection and the National Sheriff's Association in 2010 reported, "More than three times more seriously mentally ill persons [are] in jails and prisons than in hospitals. . . . America's jails and prisons have become our new mental hospitals. At least 16 percent of inmates in jails and prisons have a serious mental illness. In 1983 a similar study reported that the percentage was 6.4 percent. . . . These findings are consistent with studies reporting that 40 percent of individuals with serious mental illnesses have been in jail or prison at some time in their lives."[31]

My own summary position is that I have great respect for the much-needed institution of mental hospitals, which in a variety of really tough clinical situations are no less than lifesavers and give people a chance to pull out of dangerous and horrible tailspins. But I dislike deeply the frequently authoritarian-hierarchical way hospitals operate; the bad atmosphere of staffs who are competitive with one another and disrespectful and insensitive in their collaboration and not dedicated to patients; and the flagrant overuse of medical procedures to stop symptoms at whatever costs, and so often without any effort to understand the symptoms as communications.

On the other hand, I love the few hospitals whose atmosphere and organization breathe respect for people—the staff to one another and the staff with patients—and create a genuine house of therapy and healing. Like every societal institution, mental hospitals as organizations and communities are collective extensions of the choices each of us as individuals must make between fascist ways of operating versus more democratic, respectful, and potentiating worlds of interaction between staff and with patients.

Well-known sociologist Erving Goffman coined the term "total institution" for mental hospitals, along with other places that take over and confine a person's life completely. Goffman has included mental hospitals in a list that includes orphanages, monasteries, military organizations, prisons, and concentration camps. In his book *Asylums*, Goffman is eloquent in his description of how mental hospitals socialize patients into being good patients, which means harmless and dull and inconspicuous, and makes the powerful point that this in turn reinforces the chronicity of severe mental illness.[32] Goffman's classic work was done a long time ago in 1955–1956 at Saint Elizabeth's Hospital in Washington, D.C., which housed seven thousand patients and was well known as representative of the full-blown "cuckoo's nest" treatment of the time. His book contributed a great deal to the deinstitutionalization of mental hospitals—which we see has not been entirely a blessing, but certainly was a well-intended move to secure better care for mental patients. But the very serious question to be asked—even over and over again by all of us who have any connection to treating mental disorders—is whether the methods we use, including the many medications psychiatrists prescribe, are or are not educating for and inducing conformity and non-beingness?

DIFFERENT CULTURES OFFER PEOPLE DIFFERENT "SYMPTOM REPERTOIRES"

We conclude this chapter with the observation that a huge variety of symptoms have been reported from different cultures around the world, and this is true also from different eras of Western history. To contemporary Westerners, many of these may appear exotic and perhaps humorous, but the plain and very important point is that mental illnesses are not so much disease entities like the *DSM* catalogs, but varying expressions of patients' misery, protest, and disconnection from the real world and their real work and relationships. Thus there are cultures in Asia where a murderous rage followed by amnesia is a known symptom and it has earned in English the very recognizable name of "amok." Asia has also given us "koro," which is a terrifying certainty of a man that his genitals are retracting into his body. The Middle East has given us "zar," which at least sounds happier in that it evokes a runaway episode of laughing, shouting, and singing. In our day and age, one syndrome that has come from Asia, "sudden unexpected nocturnal death syndrome" (SUNDS), is a dead-serious condition and is exquisitely psychosomatic.

A medical historian at the University of Toronto, Edward Shorter, writes that different cultures organize different groups of symptoms to express mental distress and/or how to go mad: "We might think of the culture as possessing a 'symptom repertoire'—a range of physical symptoms available to the unconscious mind . . . in some epochs, convulsions, the sudden inability to speak or terrible leg pain may loom prominently in the repertoire. In other epochs patients may draw chiefly on such symptoms as abdominal pain, false estimates of body weight and enervating weakness as metaphors for conveying psychic stress."[33]

A reviewer of Ethan Watters's *Crazy Like Us: The Globalization of the American Psyche*, illustrates very clearly how a capitalist juggernaut promotes pills as well as the conceptions that seemingly justify the pills.

> GlaxoSmithKline, the producers of Paxil, introduce[d] new conceptions of sadness and depression to Japan. Previously, Japanese psychiatry and popular thinking only acknowledged a rare and very severe form of depression, which required institutionalization. Medical anthropologists and open-minded psychiatrists were feted in exclusive holiday resorts and received generous honoraria for their willingness to share their insights with CEOs and marketing experts. A smart marketing campaign then presented new images of depression—after all, experience in the Western world had demonstrated that marketing disease leads to much higher sales that marketing specific cures. Ask-your-doctor commercials appeared everywhere, de-stigmatizing depression and encouraging individuals to take charge of their own condition by requesting prescriptions. At the same time (around the year 2000), as we now know, the evidence in favour of Paxil (and many other SSRIs) remained flimsy, incomplete, and inconclusive. Undesirable side-effects (including, possibly, akathisia, violent behaviour and increased risk of suicide) had been deliberately swept under the carpet. Nevertheless, marketing campaigns do not let questionable science stand in the way of good sales figures.[34]

CONCLUSION

To conclude our discussion of a medicalized psychiatry: There are a great many studies that demonstrate a variety of thinking mechanisms that lead us to see and confirm whatever it is that we want to believe in. Daniel Kahneman is a Nobel Prize–winning researcher who has done a great deal of work in this area and has many a sad observation to make about the irrationality of our supposedly rational thinking. Kahneman's original work was done with a colleague, Amos Tversky. In one of their early studies they described how an "*availability heuristic* permits people to approximate frequency on the basis of how easily the target comes to mind but more memorable events are not necessarily more frequent, thus people overestimate the number of deaths in fires but underestimate the number of deaths due to stomach cancer. Similarly, a clinician may easily recall several times in which a certain intervention was associated with a remarkable improvement in a patient's symptoms, but may not recall that on many other occasions the technique was ineffectual and even counter-productive." [35]

Pharmacological treatment of mental conditions can be disastrous. Too many times they wreak havoc on a patient's physical condition because they are the wrong medication and/or because they are overprescribed. The disastrous outcomes can also be true even of medications that do work but at the same time convey to a person that he/she does not have the emotional and spiritual capacity to solve their problem, and that they *must* have the assistance of a physical agent. A heavy reliance on medications often conveys that one cannot expand one's capacity for bearing, containing, surviving, and growing out of tension, hurt, and discomfort. The meds convey a lack of faith or hope that the brilliance of the creative process (through which many a Demosthenes has become a great public speaker) may overcome the dysfunction, especially with the help of a knowledgeable and kind guide (therapist). Often there is also a further message that the person is *always* to need a continuation of such chemical assistance.

The overly medicalized interpretation of mental illness is not only a power play that assigns dominance to the medical profession in the treatment of mental disorders, including the rationale it provides pharmaceutical companies to treat virtually everything with pills, it is also spiritually and philosophically an escape from—I dare say, *soul*. If a condition is purely medical, then there is not much point to understanding deep feelings, and certainly not unconscious feelings. Even the concept of psychosomatic processes becomes superfluous, despite the fact that this concept very much includes serious attention to physiological processes. I think medical psychiatric procedures should be used to assist patients to work psychologically and spiritually at their psychological issues, with counseling or psychotherapy being the major treatment modality in most cases. Centuries ago Hippocrates wrote, "Natural forces within us are the true healers of disease."[36] In our times a talented surgeon, Bernie Siegel, observed: "I am convinced that unconditional love is the most powerful known stimulant of the immune system. If I told patients to raise their blood levels of immune globulins or killer T cells, no one would know how. But if I teach them to love themselves and others fully, the same changes happen automatically. The truth is: love heals."[37]

About Psychological Disturbances:

> *Macbeth:* Canst thou not minister to a mind diseas'd,
> Pluck from the memory a rooted sorrow,
> Raze out the written troubles of the brain,
> And with some sweet oblivious antidote
> Cleanse the stuff'd bosom of that perilous stuff
> Which weighs upon the heart?
> *Doctor:* Therein the patient
> Must minister to himself.

—William Shakespeare, *Macbeth*[38]

NOTES

1. Marcia Angell, "The Epidemic of Mental Illness: Why?," *New York Review of Books*, June 23, July 28, 2011.

2. Irving Kirsch, *The Emperor's New Drugs: Exploding the Antidepressant Myth* (New York: Basic Books, 2009); Daniel Carlat, *Unhinged: The Trouble with Psychiatry: A Doctor's Revelations about a Profession in Crisis* New York: Free Press, 2010).; Robert Whitaker, *Anatomy of an Epidemic: Magic Bullets, Psychiatric Drugs, and the Astonishing Rise of Mental Illness in America* (New York: Crown, 2010).

3. Angell, "The Epidemic of Mental Illness."

4. Ibid.

5. Ethan Watters, "In the Age of Globalization, West Exports Mental Illness Too," *International Herald Tribune*, January 10, 2010 (from the *New York Times Magazine*). Also see Ethan Watters, *Crazy Like Us: The Globalization of the American Psyche* (New York: Simon & Schuster, 2010).

6. Rael D. Strous, "Psychiatry during the Nazi Era: Ethical Lessons for the Modern Professional," *Annals General Psychiatry* 6 (2007): 8.

7. "Eugenics Committee of the United States of America (in the 1930's). Outstanding Leaders in American Intelligentsia Were Avid Supporters of the Eugenics Movement in the 1930's," in Israel W. Charny, ed., *Encyclopedia of Genocide* (Santa Barbara, CA: ABC Clio, 1999), 220. This document was originally retrieved from the archives of Bryn Mawr College.

8. Andrew Scull, *Madhouse: A Tragic Tale of Megalomania and Modern Medicine* (New Haven, CT: Yale University Press, 2005). See a review of the book: Joel Donchin, "Nobody Dared Say That the Doctor of the Soul Is Naked or Crazy," *Haaretz–Sefarim*, November 30, 2005 (Hebrew); and Joel Donchin, "When the Shrink Goes Nuts: The Historical Lessons of This Hair-Raising, True Story about a Psychiatrist Who Wreaked Havoc Have Not Yet Been Learned," *Haaretz English Edition*, December 1, 2005. The same story appears in the two languages, but the different titles convey messages that seemed deserving of being recorded here. Quotations in the text are from the English language article.

9. Robert Darby, "American Psycho: Another Surgical Temptation," (review of Andrew Scull, *Madhouse: A Tragic Tale of Megalomania and Modern Medicine*), H-Histsex, https://networks.h-net.org/node/6056/reviews/7139/darby-scull-madhouse-tragic-tale-megalomania-and-modern-medicine.
10. Donchin, "When The Shrink Goes Nuts."
11. Ibid.
12. Ibid.
13. Ibid.
14. Ibid.
15. Ibid.
16. Darby, "American Psycho."
17. Ibid.
18. Ibid.
19. Ibid.
20. *Wikipedia*, s.v. "Lobotomy," retrieved April 30, 2014, https://en.wikipedia.org/wiki/Lobotomy
21. PBS *American Experience*, http://www.pbs.org/wgbh/americanexperience/features/transcript/lobotomist-transcript/
22. Margarita Tartakovsky, "The Surprising History of the Lobotomy," *World of Psychology* (blog) Psych Central, http://psychcentral.com/blog/archives/2011/03/21/the-surprising-history-of-the-lobotomy/.
23. Bill Bynum, "Roy Porter, the Greatest Medical Historian of his Generation Dies at the Age of 55," *British Medical Journal* (March 9, 2002), http://www.bmj.com/content/suppl/2002/03/09/324.7336.DC1.
24. Roy Porter, *The Greatest Benefit to Mankind: A Medical History of Humanity from Antiquity to the Present* (Waukegan, IL: Fontana Press).
25. Ken Kesey, *One Flew Over the Cuckoo's Nest* (New York: Viking, 1962). Film by United Artists released in 1975.
26. Hugh Levinson, "The Strange and Curious History of Lobotomy," BBC News, November 8, 2011, http://www.bbc.com/news/magazine-15629160.
27. Becca Tarvin, "The Lobotomy: An Old School Mental Health Treatment," *The Quad*, April 16, 2010, http://buquad.com/2010/04/16/lobotomy/.
28. "My Lobotomy: Howard Dully's Journey," NPR (November 16, 2005), http://www.npr.org/2005/11/16/5014080/my-lobotomy-howard-dullys-journey
29. A. Miller, "Lobotomy Patient—a Decade Later: A Follow-up Study of a Research Project Started in 1948," *Canadian Medical Association Journal* 96, no. 15 (April 15, 1967): 1095–1103.
30. Israel W. Charny, "Recovering the Lost Art of Naturalistic Family Therapy: Prospective and Perspective," *Journal of Family Psychotherapy* 25, no. 2 (2014): 99–116.
31. E. Fuller Torrey, Aaron Kennard, Don Eslinger, Richard Lamb, and James Pavle, *More Mentally Ill Persons Are in Jails and Prisons than Hospitals: A Survey of the States* (Arlington, VA: Treatment Advocacy Center, and Alexandria, VA: National Sheriffs Association), pamphlet.
32. Erving Goffman, *Asylums: Essays on the Social Situation of Mental Patients and Other Inmates* (New York: Anchor Books, 1961); See also Helen Lester and

Lindal Gask, “Delivering Medical Care for Patients with Serious Mental Illness or Promoting a Collaborative Model of Recovery?,” *British Journal of Psychiatry* 188, no. 5 (2006): 401–2.

33. Edward Shorter, “The Americanization of Mental Illness,” *New York Times*, January 8, 2010.

34. Hans Pols, Review of Ethan Watters, *Crazy Like Us*, *h-madness* (blog), July 24, 2010, http://historypsychiatry.com/2010/07/24/review-ethan-watters-crazy-like-us-the-globalization-of-the-american-psyche-new-york-free-press-2010/.

35. Amos Tversky and Daniel Kahneman, “Judgment under Uncertainty: Heuristics and Biases,” *Science* 185, no. 4157 (1974): 1127). See also Daniel Kahneman, *Thinking Fast and Slow* (New York: Farrar, Straus and Giroux, 2011).

36. G. E. R. Lloyd, ed. *Hippocratic Writings* (London: Penguin, 1984).

37. Bernie Siegel, *Love, Medicine and Miracles: Lessons Learned about Self-Healing from a Surgeon’s Experience with Exceptional Patients* (New York: Harper Perennial, 1998).

38. William Shakespeare, *The Tragedy of Macbeth*, Act V, Scene 3.

Chapter Five

DSM-Thinking Is Oblivious to the Human Condition

Returning Psychiatry to the Unconscious, Human Relationships, and Value Choices

IF YOU CRITICIZE *DSM*, ARE YOU NEGATIVISTIC, OPPOSITIONAL, OR SHOWING CHUTZPAH?

The history of psychiatric nomenclature and its frequent and major name changes through the years is fascinating in its own right, and illuminates how much psychiatric syndromes reflect the mores and prejudices of a given generation. Thus, drapetomania was a formal diagnosis in the United States before the Civil War for "an ailment that causes slaves to be possessed of a desire for freedom and to want to escape."[1]

The basic reference of today's Psychiatry is the current *DSM* manual.[2] Critiquing the *DSM* used to be so scary. There was an aura surrounding this Bible-like opus that was brought down to the people toiling in mental health from the Sinai of psychiatry that prompted attributing to the critic a crime or sin of heresy, revolution, or at the least plain old *chutzpah.*

The politically correct concept was that *obviously* the *DSM* was correct. It was official, wasn't it? It couldn't possibly have earned the publication and distribution that it did without the agreement of many wise men. Who are you to say that it is wrong or that something is missing in the basic mode of defining more and more medical-like categories of illness?

I remember very well the tension accompanying my raising a few major criticisms of *DSM* in my lectures in the university to a course on psychopathology, where I realized that my young students were simultaneously doing their field work in hospitals, clinics and agencies where the staffs were overwhelmingly bowing and scraping in deference to the Establishment *DSM* system of diagnosis.

The massive power that *DSM* language and ideas gathered is a strong example of how a wrong idea can be adopted by officialdom, and how demands for obedience can quickly imbue the idea with a tyrannical status—with sanctions and punishment for deviance. "Fortunately" the process of *DSM*–thinking has grown more and more absurd and extreme from edition to edition so that by now there are floods of criticisms of many aspects of *DSM* by many people from many fields, including large numbers of psychiatrists, some of whom have been the well-known leaders in the field and its *DSM* thinking.

I believe that contemporary "*DSM* psychiatry" represents a flight and an escape from vital human experiences—including anxiety as a constructive call for our potential personal growth, including the desirability, if not necessity, of spiritual growth and integrity, and the ability to make choices of meaningful goals and wholesome means to reach our goals. The *DSM* escapes almost completely understanding the role of the unconscious, minimizes the significance of human relationships, and overrides and denies a basic *psychological* conception of human behavior.

IGNORING DOING HARM TO ONESELF OR TO OTHERS, AND IGNORING RELATIONSHIPS TO OTHERS AND TO THE WORLD AS KEY SOURCES OF MENTAL DISORDERS

Promoted by the American Psychiatric Association, the *DSM* is the basis of a formal system of diagnosis in a vast psychiatric health empire, including a multimillion-dollar insurance reimbursement industry. With so much prestige and actual power added to its auras of medical and scientific knowledge and certainty, many practitioners have refrained, even fearfully, from criticisms of the *DSM*. Nonetheless, there has also been a considerable dissatisfaction of many mental health practitioners for many years, especially but not only by nonmedical practitioners of psychotherapy, and now increasingly also by major psychiatric figures.

For example, one psychiatrist who is interested in a more scientific basis for psychiatric diagnosis where psychiatrists would demonstrate much higher rates of agreement with the diagnoses of one another than is true today concluded that *DSM* diagnosis is *descriptive* and in effect has the psychiatrist calling the patient whatever the patient complains of symptomatically. In contrast, medical diagnosis is normally anchored far more in concepts of the basic damage caused by that illness and is based so much more on scientific observations of the processes that underlie the symptomatic complaints of the patients. This psychiatrist argues that this more basic kind of diagnosis is what psychiatry needs to cultivate for the future.[3]

There have been many criticisms of the *DSM* that the diagnoses lack empirical foundations; there is an arbitrariness of many definitions; there is also a lack of perspective about how many symptoms are widespread in the everyday lives of so many ostensibly normal people and therefore are better understood as existential efforts at coping with the human condition than as illnesses; and especially, certainly for many family-oriented therapists, the *DSM* fails to relate to major *relationship* aspects of mental health disturbances and how major relationship problems are in their own right mental health issues as well as major causes of many psychiatric conditions and dysfunctions.

Family therapy has contributed a great deal of knowledge of the impact of lost love and of hurt and anger in basic human relationships and their basic roles in a score of psychopathological conditions. For example, a very high frequency of losses of a key loved one or a relationship is found prior to the onset of many cases of depression, suicide, a number of known psychosomatic conditions, and even major killers, such as heart disease and cancer, that are too little recognized also as including psychosomatic processes in many cases. *DSM* is also all but oblivious to a person's relationships to events in his era and world, like earthquakes, hurricanes, poverty, social disorganization, political upheaval, migration, epidemics, and holocausts.

A major statement of an alternative approach to *DSM*-type diagnosis through "relational diagnosis," or the diagnosis of disturbances in interpersonal relationships, appeared in 1996 under the leadership of Florence Kaslow. *The Handbook of Relational Diagnosis and Other Dysfunctional Family Problems* culminated a noteworthy process of a good number of years during which Kaslow, a distinguished psychologist who was the founding president of the International Family Therapy Association, pioneered bringing together a broad-ranging coalition of mental health organizations to create a possible supplemental diagnostic point of view focusing on people's experiences in relationships.[4] In a rare show of cooperation between often competing professional guilds, Kaslow successfully led an admirable and impressive coalition of organizations that included the Division of Family Psychology of the American Psychological Association, American Association for Marriage and Family Therapy, American Orthopsychiatric Association, American Psychoanalytic Association, International Psychoanalytic Association, Group for the Advancement of Psychiatry of the American Psychiatric Association, and the National Association of Social Workers. Unfortunately, the process that was initiated did not culminate in a comprehensive diagnostic menu that describes relationship disorders.

My sense of the *DSM* is that it is too much in love with its supposed medicalizing and thereby represents a flight away from seeing the human being as a multilevel organism whose mind is under the considerable control of personal psychodynamic issues. These psychodynamics include:

- *unconscious* dynamics in our lives of basic loves and hatreds
- a variety of *unconscious structural mechanism*, such as our being drawn to go too far to excesses, and to our drive or need to bring matters to completion, that also contribute to going to extremes
- an *instinct for self-defense* that characteristically leads to perceiving oneself as the injured, aggrieved party in conflicts, and then "justifies" hatred and retaliation in respect of one's conviction that one is operating in self-defense
- *powerful responses to basic interpersonal relationships* such as hurt, rejection, betrayal, exploitation, trauma, and so on.

My most important criticism of the *DSM* is that psychiatric and psychological disturbances should always be seen both in terms of the extent of one's personal disabilities and how much one is doing harm and disturbing good living in oneself, as well as the extent to which one is doing harm to others—either or both.

Implementation of the above concept would mean that, at long last, one cannot be defined as psychiatrically normal while engaging in such heinous behaviors as child abuse; spouse abuse; insulting, dominating and brutalizing other people such as one's workers; or terrorism and genocidal mass murder of civilian populations. Common sense has always told us that, however widespread, these are sick and disturbed behaviors, certainly not normal actions or the kinds of behaviors that the mental health disciplines want to *recommend* to people as "normal," but our mental health professions have never had the guts to confront such behaviors by defining them formally and authoritatively as "sick." Psychology and psychiatry need to disavow such behaviors and declare them thoroughly not acceptable in the repertoires of sane and wholesome people. At the same time, note that although these are disturbances of mental health, the mental health disciplines still must turn over people who injure and destroy others to legal punishment, because these behaviors are, first and foremost, criminal insofar as they involve doing serious harm to other living creatures.

Perhaps the single most vocal critic and downright opponent to *DSM-5* has been Allen Frances, a psychiatrist who—believe it or not—was the key director of the *DSM-IV* project. Frances has been pouring out article after article such as "The Inmates Seem to Have Taken Over the Asylum" [5] and "Where Have All the Normals Gone?"[6] and has appeared on TED's weekend news as well as on his own blog with "The *DSM-5* Follies as Told in Its Own

Words."[7] At the same time Frances has *not* turned against the whole *DSM* establishment and in fact continues to defend the *DSM-IV* that he edited.

From my point of view, what he is saying is that *DSM-5* has gone way too far in adding a bunch of ridiculous diagnoses that in turn serve to justify more medications, but for all of his wisdom and eloquence, Frances has not renounced entirely the underlying faulty theory base of all *DSM*s to date. For example, he still keeps everyday problems of relationships outside *DSM*. I agree with him that *DSM-5* is a "wholesale imperial medicalization of normality," and because I know it is important to take clear note of a patient's symptoms, I even agree with him when he says, "I am a great defender of psychiatric diagnosis and treatment"—but only when it is done well and within its proper sphere.

My thinking is that *DSM* is off in its basics from its outset and that the medicalizing is getting worse and worse in the successive editions. Throughout, the *DSM* schema also fails to project a picture of a human being who cannot only get himself into the hot water of mental problems but who can do that to other human beings in his life, and that *both* the psychiatric conditions that center on the self and those that are defined by hurting others are deeply related to a person's intimate relationships—especially family, and in turn are also expressions of society-wide trends, for example, going crazy through becoming violent in the United States which is such a mad culture of violence.

Carol Tavris is a sociologist and an accomplished popular science writer. In an article in the *Wall Street Journal* entitled "How Psychiatry Went Crazy,"[8] she unfolds quite responsibly the history of *DSM* editions and in particular reviews two recent books, Allen Francis's *Saving Normal*,[9] and Gary Greenberg's *The Book of Woe*.[10] Tavris is normally a solid factual writer and yet on this topic one senses her mounting anger. She writes:

> The goal of "precision medicine" in mental health is a mirage. The *DSM* committees already tried their damnedest to support their diagnoses with neuroscience or biomarkers, but no lab tests yet exist for depression, schizophrenia, bipolar or obsessive-compulsive disorder, or, for that matter, any other mental disorders. Efforts to find explanations in genes, neurotransmitters, "chemical imbalances" or brain circuits have, Dr. [Allen] Frances writes, "turned out to be naïve and illusory."[11]

Overall, the *DSM* is so busy defining whether human life experiences constitute diagnosable medical conditions or not that it fails to portray real people in their everyday life experiences in a way that fits good old common sense understanding of the differences between healthy and sane responses to the life cycle and human condition versus nutty, disturbed, and ethically rotten reactions.

DSM's diagnostic errors go in two directions. On the one hand, emotional upsets are welcomed as more business for psychiatry and over-diagnosed. As we read from several wise thinkers, some conditions of being upset and even symptomatically anxious can be very healthy statements of creative turmoil in the course of creative work or perfectly appropriate responses to personal crisis, and should not be diagnosed as illness or over-treated. Granted, the *DSM* does try to avoid to some extent this kind of error and leave room for natural and transient upset but not enough, and its basic error of an absoluteness of a polarity between psychiatric illness and health also leads many psychiatric practitioners into "crazy" exaggerated diagnoses. This pattern was shown irrevocably by the brilliant research of David Rosenhan.[12] In his classic work "on being sane in insane places," Rosenhan sent false patients to mental hospitals to present a description of a single isolated disturbed experience. Granted, Rosenhan's subjects described a hallucinatory experience, but only one fleeting experience, and otherwise they behaved perfectly normally, as indeed they were. Nonetheless, every one of them was soon hospitalized, and for no less than several weeks; and when discharged, were crowned, and potentially forever stigmatized with no less severe diagnoses than psychosis—in most cases "chronic paranoid schizophrenia."

The other side of errors in *DSM* psychiatry is that it ostensibly accepts many of the worst, ugliest, and meanest sides of human nature as *normal.* Of course, probably one understandable reason is that because so many of us human beings engage in evil behaviors, diagnosing so many human beings as disturbed from a medical point of view could create a problematic situation that we would be left with too few normals. Thus, being a nasty person and lording it over others in personal or work relationships is wrongly omitted from contemporary psychiatry as a very real and commonplace disturbance. There are many power freaks everywhere, and in so many cases they are the "successful" people of their times. Personally, I believe that the truth should prevail, and if at any given time a majority of people are infected with a plague, the correct diagnosis nonetheless should be made that the majority are ill. If at any given time a majority of human beings are crazy enough to do harm to others when a professor or a religion or a government tells them to do so, we need to say this horrible truth.

Later in this chapter we will be looking again at the very fine old work by famous psychiatrist, Karl Menninger and two psychologist colleagues in the famed Menninger clinic, Martin Mayman and Paul Pruyser, who clearly put their emphasis on a basic dynamic process in the development of all emotional disorganization and psychiatric symptomatology. They say that the rotten human propensity to hurt other people up to and including actual destruction of the lives of millions of people is hard at work symbolically in the everyday psychology of all of us individuals, and manifests in the psychiatric symptoms that we all display to some extent. They explain that every symptom expresses both a wish to hurt someone and accomplishes that hurt to some degree if only in a symbolic way. Sometimes this is completely obvious to everyone, as in an act of a criminal nature. But some aggressive element is always there even if it is completely and utterly divorced from any conscious aggressive intent and even if it is concealed from view.[13]

Painfully, I ask how many contemporary mental health therapists have the slightest idea of this concept. So much of contemporary treatment focuses exclusively on making people feel better. Thus in contemporary psychiatry and even in much of contemporary psychotherapy, we see the current "star roles" of "positive psychology" or CBT-cognitive behavioral therapy. And even in most family therapy, the dynamics of inner anger and inner desires to hurt others are largely forgotten and neglected in our times. Were Menninger, Mayman, and Pruyser wrong and behind the times? Or have we in our current world of mental health joined an *Age of Quiet-It-Down, Fix-It-Now, and Smile-Smile-Smile*?

To earn psychological clearance, function well—it doesn't much matter what you are doing. The *DSM* diagnoses are oriented most of all to a person's capacity to function effectively and very little to the value meanings of a person's functioning. If a Nazi guard starts shaking and trembling because of pangs of conscience, according to *DSM* psychiatry, he is in a disturbed state (personally, if I were the guard's doctor, I would like to congratulate him on his conscience and then try to help him pull together the strength to join in underground activities against the evil Nazi machine). But if the Nazi guard feels just fine, eats well, and sleeps well and is untroubled by the fates of his victims, he is a *DSM* specimen of psychiatric health. Ugh. The *DSM* says as much: Be like your society tells you to be, no matter how stupid, cruel, totalitarian, your current culture is!

The *DSM* lacks a guiding value conception. Medicine in general has much more of such a value conception in its devotion to protecting and extending life. Instead of holding up competent functioning as its prime value, psychiatry needs a larger perspective of defining *pro-life behaviors* as normal and desirable, and *anti-life behaviors* as sick and undesirable. In other words, being psychiatrically disturbed is not to suffer a breakdown into upset or incompetence if one is called on to give Milgram-electric shocks or to mow people down at Babi Yar (being upset at doing such things deserves to be honored). It is a disturbance of proper mental health when one *does* administer the Milgram-shocks or machine gun the Jews at Babi Yar.

My point of view is that the key or basic standard of mental health is not blind "good adjustment" to your surroundings, but a principled forceful stand on behalf of protecting and fulfilling life, first your own life, and then, too, the lives of others. With this formulation we can say unambiguously that it's wrong for you to flagellate yourself, even if your church or Jonestown leader tells you to do so, and it's wrong to harm and kill unarmed innocent others even if you are commanded to do so.

THE MEDICALIZING OF MIND AS A PHARMACEUTICAL "SHOWROOM," AND HOW *DSM* HAS BECOME A BIG FINANCIAL OPERATION TO SELL MORE AND MORE DRUGS

There have also been criticisms of the *DSM*, and more broadly of the contemporary psychiatric establishment, that knowingly or unknowingly (*consciously or unconsciously*!), the *DSM* is seeking to formulate psychiatric conditions and modes of services so that it can sell more of its wares and services to the public to address these conditions. As reported in one newspaper exposé, the profession of psychiatry is accused by any number of critics of promulgating "new diseases or syndromes to sell drugs." According to one assistant professor of immunology in a French hospital, this practice "was already common in psychiatry and appears to be spreading" to other medical specialties.[14] The specific example under discussion in the above newspaper article was that of "sexual dysfunctions" in women as a syndrome of lack of desire and arousal, a state or condition that certainly *does* exist in a number of women—and I add a number of men too. The newspaper report proposes correctly that the point is not only how many women suffer this state, but that the medical profession is "attempting to "medicalize" the lack of libido that some women may have because of tiredness, stress, or aversion to their partner, where in fact the root cause of their condition are to be found in the mind or elsewhere." (My comment is that it is good to see recognition of aversion to one's partner, but treatment for that is not through pills!) *DSM* and selling medicines go hand in hand. In many ways *DSM* is a capitalist game, meaning a tool for extending the power of a priestly profession (psychiatry), an incredible and even obscene money maker for psychiatry's flagship organization, and a justification and kind of cover-up promoter selling medicines!

If you have a condition that is listed in the *DSM*, then the pharmaceutical firms can sell you a medicine for that condition. There are many criticisms of psychiatric medications. We have already reviewed the extent of the effectiveness of psychiatric medications. Here we will refer briefly to some other major difficulties.

- There are any number of psychiatric conditions where serious critics contend that the rate of prescriptions has gone wild. Thus, a recent critical review by Alan Schwarz in the *New York Times* reported that the number of children on meds like Adderall and Concerta has exploded to 3.5 million (from 600,000 in 1990!) The author notes that even the pharmaceutical executive who introduced Adderall in 1995 "strongly opposes marketing the stimulants to the general public" because of the dangers. The executive calls them "nuclear bombs" warranted only under extreme circumstances."[15]

- There are tough side effects to many medications including, variously, irreversible tremors ("tardive dyskinesia"), weight gain, interference with concentration such as for driving, inhibiting children's growth (height) and more. Thus the seemingly more innocent Ritalin-like stimulants that can improve learning ability have been implicated as retarding growth and in some cases causing tremors, while the anti-psychotic drugs have notorious side effects. Shouldn't these side effects constitute serious considerations before prescribing?
- The *meaning* of medications for patients often includes a reinforcement of their experience and belief that they are and will be unable to contribute meaningfully to their own improvement.
- It has been suggested that the "pill-popping culture" fostered by psychiatry predisposes any number of people to possible habits of finding other "happy pills" on the drug scene.
- Too many pills are used to heal symptoms without accompanying counseling that addresses the human heart of the problem: Antidepressants without exploring what is pushing a person down; sex potency enhancers that are divorced from respect, genuine caring, and loving of one's partner, also along with these "positive emotions," a healthy use of power and seduction; anxiety relievers that are set to work on their own without reference to what is terrorizing the patient and/or enraging them, or what wish or talent is it that the patient is afraid they may not be able to fulfill.
- "Psychiatry/*DSM*/Medications Inc." [my word construction—there is no such company in existence] are a mammoth business of intertwining interests and payoffs, including the fact that there have been many revolting revelations of how pharmaceutical companies evade, deny, and conceal the dangerous side effects of their drugs.
- Finally we repeat from the discussion in the previous chapter: A good number of studies have demonstrated about several psychiatric conditions, including bipolar disorders, depression, anxiety, and more, that combined psychotherapy and medication are significantly superior to medication alone; and other studies have shown that long-term improvement is best achieved by psychotherapy and not medications.

The Unreliability of *DSM* Labels, and Teaching People How to Be Crazy

Another large issue was described in a far-ranging and fascinating review of the changes in American psychiatry over the years by veteran psychiatric leader Donald Bloch. He concluded that many times psychiatry tells the public how to behave poorly and what are to be the prescribed ways of being disturbed that will fit the psychiatric services that the Establishment wants to promote.

"'Mental illness' and effective treatment have all too often been defined—without this being explicit—in whatever language extends the hegemony of one of the guilds in the field. Over time, a curious reversal takes place: from 'I provide what you need' to 'You need what I provide.'"[16]

Another serious critique of *DSM* concerns the process of major changes in the nomenclature from one edition to the next. In a number of cases these changes in language imply a major change in the conceptualization of mental illnesses, which is not articulated honestly and has not been derived from definitive scientific studies whose results justify the change in language. Thus I have commented on the dropping of *neurosis* from the approved lexicon and will be discussing it further, and I will also tell the fuller story I know on the elimination of *paranoia* from the list of paranoid disorders. There have been many other changes in different areas of psychiatric diagnosis. For example, in respect of the designations of types of depression, is there really no such condition as *involutional melancholia* or a depression of meaninglessness and loss of purpose connected with old age? Or in respect to changes in the subcategories of schizophrenia (including some which have been given very odd-sounding word constructions), where has the aimless, wandering *simple schizophrenic* of yesteryear gone; and was Soviet psychiatry so wrong in postulating a similar category of *vegetative schizophrenia* for people who act aimlessly and turn themselves into dependent exploiters of their families and/or their community, and thereby are crazily unable to conduct their lives independently?

DSM implies that the changes it introduces each time are an expression of and in response to new empirical knowledge, so that a heavy pall of seeming dereliction of responsibility to science seems to be cast on the practitioners who do not jump to adopt the official changes. In fact, little and often no evidence at all is presented to back up, explain and justify many of the changes. Further, the language changes in *DSM* often issue from committees of people who engage in complex mixes of learned discussion and politics, where the latter often enough overwhelms the former. For example, the decision that was made years ago to regard homosexuality as an entirely benign alternative sexual orientation—which among other things pays no attention whatsoever to psychological constancy and the wholesomeness of the attachment between lovers—was taken at a given committee meeting of the American Psychiatric Association that was attended by a lobby of gay representatives who had planned and maneuvered in advance to attend in force in order to win the vote, and this is what they did. And ever since, it is dogma that few will dare to raise even for further discussion.

NMH Head "Divorces" *DSM* but Not the Biology of Mental Illness

Psychologist Jonathan Shedler is well known for masterful analytic reviews of researches about psychotherapy and psychopathology, which have been published in leading journals in the field such as the *American Psychologist.* He is perhaps best known for his article "The Effectiveness of Psychodynamic Psychotherapy" "that was a breakthrough statement that established psychodynamic psychotherapy as an evidence-based effective treatment.[17]

In 2013 Shedler posted on his Facebook page a major statement that no less than the head of the National Institute of Mental Health (NIMH) has asserted, in Shedler's words, that "the *DSM* is useless for understanding mental health problems and that its fundamental purpose—that mental health conditions can be classified meaningfully on the basis of overt symptoms—is flat out wrong."[18]

Shedler says about NIMH director, Thomas Insel that "since he is a medical doctor, he offers a medical rather than psychological example." He quotes him: "Imagine treating all chest pain as a single syndrome without the advantage of EKG, imaging, and plasma enzymes. In the diagnosis of mental disorders when all we had was subjective complaints [cf. chest pain], a diagnostic system limited to clinical presentation could confer reliability and consistency but not validity."[19]

According to Shedler, "NIMH will no longer fund research based on *DSM* diagnosis." He calls this "a seismic shift." He is deeply critical of the many years of "*DSM* research." He says: "The self-appointed guardians of science decide what does and does not count as an 'Empirically Supported Therapy.'" He uses the same platform also to critique the historic bypassing of psychodynamic therapies by many of the stalwart scientists of *DSM* thinking. "No matter that most people go to therapy for reasons that don't fit neatly into *DSM* categories. Proponents of 'Empirically Supported Therapies' manage to dismiss voluminous research on the benefits of psychodynamic therapies."[20]

But in truth the news to which Shedler refers is not at all altogether good. The same director of NIMH accompanies his wisdom about the unreality, lack of validity, and lack of explanatory power of *DSM* categories with still another embarrassing and frightening escape from the *human* nature of psychological disorders. "Mental disorders are biological disorders," he announces with certainty.[21]

The director of NIMH goes on to describe the launching of an important project entitled the Research Domain Criteria (RDoC) in which, happily, several levels of information will be assembled alongside one another including genetics, brain imaging, and cognitive science, all obviously important, and at least the latter refers to *some* of the experiential processes in the human being we are talking about—the what and how a person is thinking and framing experiences.[22] But still not a word appears about the other complementary side of the coin of *thinking*, namely *feelings*.

Mental disorders of course have physiological correlates, and in some cases direct physiological causes, and in many cases they are psychosomatic expressions of the dynamic processes that are taking place in the human being, which means that physiological processes are playing a significant role alongside and with the psychological, but for the most part, essentially mental disorders are *not* physiological—they are *human* responses to life and its challenges and blows.

How bizarre and frightening it is to see how much mental health professionals can escape from the soul of man. The mechanistic symptom-controlling therapies we are bound to get from such escapism will not help people very much to cultivate the courage and wisdom for living out the mysteries of their life passage. Thus in a major review of the concept of well-being in a special issue of the *American Psychologist* on "happiness, excellence, and optimal human functioning," Ryan and Deci identify "three innate psychological needs—competence, autonomy, and relatedness—which when satisfied yield enhanced self-motivation and mental health and when thwarted lead to diminished motivation and well-being."[23] Where are these concepts in the *DSM*? What in the world is psychiatric ill health if not disturbances in competence, autonomy, and relatedness? But *DSM* wants biological-like syndromes and not the human mind, soul, or machinery for experiencing and relating to other people. And that is too wrong for words.

The Deletion of Psychological Mind from the *DSM*

In the course of the unfolding changes in successive editions of the *DSM*, many mental health professionals have felt that the overall thrust and metamessage has been not only to medicalize psychiatric disorders more and more, but also to attempt to medicalize many basic psychological processes and existential aspects of the human condition.

In general, as we see in repeated discussions of different conditions throughout this book, there has obviously developed in contemporary psychiatry a massive flight from psychotherapy to medical-pharmaceutical nostrums for *everything*: from depression—no more broken hearts, losses of hope, and unbearable unconscious rage at one's enemies; to panic attacks—no more fearfulness of not being as competent and self-actualizing as one hopes and prays to be, no more anxiety about being seen as inadequate or undesirable by others or nervous anger about feeling unsure of oneself; to autism—long since defined as completely unrelated to qualities of parental care as some brilliant therapists have stated, but they are not even allowed to be mentioned in many circles.[24]

Many practitioners feel that what the *DSM* is telling us is that the era of psychodynamic understanding that much of our human behavior is mediated by our inner mind and orchestrated along with powerful *unconscious* drives is over. If one wants to be professionally successful in this era of a medicalized psychiatry, one needs to get on the bandwagon of a brave new world of physiological dynamics, where the promise is that soon, soon, miracles of medical cures of psychiatric conditions will parallel the magnificent life-saving achievements the medical profession is achieving in overcoming cancers and heart diseases.

No erection? Repeated premature ejaculation? Ignore how the man feels toward women, or his image of himself (again, see Karl Abraham's brilliant work in 1917,[25] which I take to this day as my best guide for successful treatment of premature ejaculation). Instead, at best prescribe the excellent exercises of Masters and Johnson,[26] but without looking at inner meanings, and also medicate with Viagra and the later medications for erectile dysfunction, both indeed wonderful advances that *may* well do the trick, but if not, tough luck—it has been declared that there is no longer a linkage between one's unconscious and use of one's penis. In her outstanding work, *The New Sex Therapy,* psychiatrist Helen Kaplan[27] made exactly the point that one cannot and should not treat sex difficulties without first attending to feelings and relationships.

Hatred and murderous schemes in the royal family? Take Prozac and/or call the police, but don't bother with the interpersonal and spiritual bedrocks of relationships in the royal family or what Boszormenyi-Nagy and Spark wisely called the "invisible ledgers" in every family.[28] Apropos, the fact that there are some reports of increased or at least a notable number of homicides by people on Prozac should be ignored, and if possible the data should be suppressed.[29] Long live the *DSM*—whatever edition we're up to and whatever the new names it promotes.

The overall or metamessage of *DSM* psychiatry is that most, if not almost all, mental problems are diseases like migraine, asthma, influenza, heart disease, and cancer that befall people—and are to a large extent based on their genetic predispositions. There is very little personal control of one's mental health. According to this conception, personal choices of one's ways of thinking, feeling, and living are not very determining of one's mental health.

The unconscious is dead and gone. Sometimes I think the day is coming when the new medical psychiatry will declare they have found the gene nodule responsible for genocide. After all, it can't be a psychological or moral choice. Nothing is.

NEUROSIS—A WORD AND A CONCEPTION OF THE UNCONSCIOUS THAT HAVE BEEN EXPELLED FROM CONTEMPORARY PSYCHIATRY

The exiling of the unconscious is expressed vividly in *DSM*'s handling of the classic topic of *neurosis*, a subject that was at the core of the emergence of the grand exploration of mind in twentieth-century psychiatry—and I would add led to the transformation of the field of psychiatry into an intriguing and forward-looking profession giving new hopes that our human minds and behavior would someday be better understood and channeled.

The neuroses were dropped in *DSM-III*. "The omission of the *DSM III* diagnostic class of Neuroses has been a matter of great concern to many clinicians, and requires an explanation," said the *DSM-III*.[30] The strained explanation then given included a differentiation between *neurotic disorder*, which is taken to refer to *descriptions* of neurotic states and *neurotic process*, which "should be used when the clinician wishes to indicate the concept of a specific etiological process involving the following sequence: unconscious conflicts between opposing wishes or between wishes and prohibitions, which causes unconscious perception of anticipated danger or dysphoria, which leads to rise of defense mechanisms that result in either symptoms, personality disturbance, or both."[31] *Huh?* The explanation continues that "although many psychodynamically-oriented clinicians" believe that the above unconscious process plays a central role in *neurotic disorders*, there are also other explanations such as "social learning, cognitive, behavioral and biological models"—very true, but hardly an explanation for outlawing "neurosis."[32] The conclusion was that there will be some continued use in the *DSM* of the concept of *neurotic disorder*—but heaven forbid not of neurosis, with its implications of a core of *unconscious* dynamics. Go to sleep, Sigmund.

Scientifically it *is* quite true that there *are* multiple pathways to the buildup of a neurotic disorder, and that unconscious conflicts are only one of these pathways and not necessarily the unique and inevitable cause of all neurotic reactions. In this sense, the revision by the American Psychiatric Association was a step forward in science of openness to new concepts such as negative behavioral conditioning, wrong cognitive maps, and to a more complex interactive patterning of multilevel causes. For example, in any given patient an undue physiological reactivity to fear may interact synergistically with a learned psychological style of undue helplessness when one is under attack or faced with a challenge. But the stronger thrust of the linguistic change by the American Psychiatric Association of removing the classic honored word *neurosis* from its lexicon is to send a message that the very concepts of an *unconscious* and *unconscious processes* were hereby removed from the halls of the new psychiatric "science," which is to be rechanneled more and more to mechanistic and physiological processes. Psychiatry has thus moved from the wonders of psychological mind to an almost uni-dimensional identification with otherwise welcome new-age medical advances in mapping brain physiology, the genetics of illnesses, and dazzling (though also dangerously injurious) pharmaceutical developments for control of human behavior through the physiological mechanisms. *But the meta-message is: Forget psychology.* And also: *Be sure to buy our medication.*

But human beings, our brains very much included, are more than only brilliant physiological creatures. There are profound emotional and ideational contents inside of every one of us human beings, and to many of us it is scientifically clear that emotions and ideas produce physiological expressions of themselves, and not only that physiological patterns in turn trigger emotions and ideas—which they do. If I am afraid of my mother, or my boss, or a neighbor who is from a different racial/ethnic group, my fear and rage will variously trigger physiological responses of a racing heart, sweat, and endocrinological rage reactions. All of human experience is simultaneously *psychosomatic*—psychological experiences triggering and initiating physiological reactions. All physiological processes are simultaneously *somatopsychic*—body experiences triggering and initiating psychological reactions. We human beings are marvelous complex integrations of mind and body. That is one of the great brilliances of the human condition. *DSM* psychiatry has tilted severely only toward the somatopsychic—the influences of physiology on mind and behavior, and is in flight from the no less awesome beauty of the power of the former—the influence of mind both on the body and of course on behavior.

Deposing and excommunicating, as it were, the time-honored word *neurosis* also conveys an attack on and disavowal of a whole century of the wonderful foundational works of psychoanalytic psychiatric and psychological pioneers. These pioneers left us a great legacy of understanding man as a *psychological* creature—existentially fearful of aloneness and coping with ultimate death; frightened of not being able to fulfill one's potential; fearful and guilt-ridden at not protecting various others such as one's parents; needing and desperate to be loved and to love; frequently tempted to withdraw from life to protect one's bruised ego; needing to be anchored in a stable and trustworthy set of object relations; given to powerful angers, hatred, and worse; and overall, desperate to find and give meaning to one's existence. This is the basic "stuff" from which psychological explanation of mental and relationship problems is best understood, and much of it takes place unknowingly in the unconscious mind.[33]

Again I will acknowledge respectfully and joyfully that it is a celebration of scientific progress that psychiatry has been *adding* additional levels of understanding, such as a person's history of social learning of traits like undue fearfulness or aggression; awareness of the behavioral conditioning a person has endured, for example, traumatic experiences that cut in deeply to a person's "memory chip" whose recording or memory of the trauma is later easily re-evoked in situations that remind one of one's original trauma; understanding the cognitive structures that promote errors in living, for example, a need to never fail or show vulnerability; or understanding physical and psychological processes that greatly affect overall development and behavior, for example, an attention deficit disorder or a hearing loss that expose a child to intense feelings of incompetence and inadequacy. Nonetheless, any and all human experiential processes, even many experiences that derive from purely physiological processes, need to be understood as being mediated through and linked up with the essential psychological nature of man.

Premenstrual Syndrome (PMS), for example, may very well be triggered by hormonal processes, as may be the case for some postpartum reactions; and yet the way in which a premenstrual woman feels about herself and her femaleness was shown many years ago to be a decisive factor in her ability to process the uncomfortable changes in her physiology.[34] And the ways in which a young woman does or does not trust herself to be nurturing and not to be destructive to her new baby is central in treating and processing the postpartum experience.[35] Is psychiatry a branch of medicine and science that can afford to dispense with all old studies and findings? Were the early explorers and discoverers of the unconscious all old medicine men and witches of a prescientific era? I don't think so.

The arbitrary dismissal of *neurosis* from the professional club was a message that the unconscious and all its devotees have been banished by the new bearers of power in psychiatry—more medical, biological, supposedly scientific. Concomitantly, certainly more business-like people have stepped in with many new pills and serums to dispense, and infinitely more managed packages of care designed to make many more people comfortable and freer of worries, but not necessarily more wise, loving, or better people.

In sum, *DSM* psychiatry declares the unconscious "dead" or nonexistent; and dismisses insultingly the accumulated knowledge and psychoanalytic methodology for arriving at more knowledge of unconscious processes. *DSM* thinking's meta-message is that what is politically correct in psychiatric circles is medicalizing and more medicalizing.

PARANOIA—A CATEGORY THAT MIGHT HAVE HELPED DEVELOP A PSYCHIATRY FOR THE HITLERS AND BIN LADENS THAT HAS BEEN MADE TO DISAPPEAR—*POOF!*

Paranoia is a category that was traditional in psychiatry through *DSM III*, but was dropped quite unceremoniously in *DSM III-R*, a transitional revision published in 1987.[36] There was only a bare statement in the appendix that gave no explanation for the change, and by the time *DSM-IV* rolled around, it simply didn't exist anymore. (Note the difference from the sister word, "paranoid.")

At first glance, this category is very appealing because it was defined in the group of psychoses, or far more severe states than personality disorders, yet it did not refer to the decompensation and everyday nuttiness of paranoid schizophrenics, and one might have hoped it offered a definition that would describe the disorders of at least some of the worst tyrants and destroyers in human history—people who for a long time (too long) are "successful" in their madness and rottenness.

This is how paranoia was described in *DSM III*:

> The essential feature of paranoia is the insidious development of a paranoid disorder with a permanent and unshakable delusional system accompanied by preservation of clear and orderly thinking. Frequently, the individual considers himself/herself endowed with unique or superior abilities.[37]

I had not tracked this change in *DSM III-R*, which I had allowed myself to treat at the time perhaps mistakenly as a transitional book that I did not have to study and was awaiting the appearance of the next full revision. By the time the *DSM-IV* appeared in 1994, the diagnosis was simply missing. I then wrote the American Psychiatric Association on December 14, 1994, to ask to be referred to an explanation of the changes in the classification of paranoid disorders, and I noted that "because of my particular research concerns on various aspects of human destructiveness and evil, I would be grateful for an early reply." A not-early reply was received close to eight months later, dated August 4, 1995, which simply referred me to *DSM III-R*, pages 409–30, and indicated that there "the changes to Paranoia which you describe in your letter are explained." But in fact, on page 420 of *DSM III-R* there is no more than a note that the previous diagnosis of "Paranoia," which has been dropped, is replaced by "Delusional (paranoid) disorder: Specify type: erotomanic, grandiose, jealous, persecutory, somatic, unspecified." The same category of "Delusional (paranoid) disorder" is also made into the main category for the overall group of "Paranoid Disorders," and it is noted that the category has been broadened from either persecutory delusions or delusions of jealousy to other delusional themes as well and refers to the listing of types above, and that in order to qualify for a diagnosis the duration of delusions has been defined as lasting at least one month, which should have correctly canceled out all the diagnoses of the fake illnesses in the Rosenhan study, of course, but in everyday psychiatric reality even one delusion was gleefully embraced.[38]

But why was paranoia dropped? There is no explanation at all. It is enough to make one suspicious!

So, are the Hitlers, Stalins, Maos, and Bin Ladens and all of their ilk accounted for in psychiatry? Damn them! They are in fact superior master killers on grand scales. But are they described sufficiently by "delusional (paranoid) disorder?" In a way, *yes*: delusional (paranoid) disorder—persecutory, grandiose, and unspecified types—does have something to do with them, I think. But something huge also is missing. Beyond the familiarity of a classic term, the concept of *paranoia* seems to convey far better a broad panoramic madness that has a better fit to these monsters. There was a greater power in this no-longer-available category in its definitional emphasis on highly systematic delusional thinking, also, importantly, in the fact that the overall functioning of the paranoiac does *not* necessarily appear disturbed. And, as stated, the paranoiac person may regard himself as superior—to which I add bitterly that indeed the paranoiac characteristically does excel in his devotion to his own superiority and to killing life! The characterization of an effective and even brilliant-seeming madman who is living out a delusional scheme has been lost. The paranoid disordered people who are left for the most part need to act and look more obviously crazy in order to qualify for a diagnosis, Therefore, capable and crafty leaders of nations and terrorist groups are not likely to qualify, even if they are committed to mass murdering.

Admittedly, a major problem with the category of paranoia was that it was virtually never used in clinical practice. Generally, people who are "caught" or brought to see therapists to get diagnosed have failed to build absolute power and have shown some breakdown in their functioning, and it is their failures that lead to their being entered as clients into the mental health system. There have been few professional voices in the history of mental health that have had the courage to identify early on political leaders who were to be, or even already were, dangerous mass killers as paranoiacs.

In democracies, moreover, there have been legitimate concerns with the possible abuse of power by psychiatry in some efforts to offer psychopathological diagnoses of bona fide political leaders. And in less democratic countries, a mental health professional who would identify a leader or emerging political leader as disturbed, even by virtue of a genocidal ideology, would be risking imprisonment or death. A further problem for ethical mental health clinicians is that in our daily work we respect the fact that we offer our diagnoses to and for people who have asked for our services, or in community health contexts that properly authorize us to conduct our work with people who need to be evaluated for their own welfare even though they are unable to ask for psychological or psychiatric help, such as the involuntarily hospitalized mentally ill, criminals serving out prison sentences, or clients of the social welfare system. When clinicians on their own volunteer a diagnosis of a prime minister or president, there is a serious violation of the norm of non-imposition of mental health services without authorization.

Nonetheless, there has to be a way of creating a clear definition that says that planning to kill many people, and taking steps to do so, are—as common sense tells us—nuts, crazy, disturbed, and out of control, as well as in violation of the core of what needs to be a universal categorical imperative against murder. At the least, official definitions of the medical specialty of psychiatry and of psychology should take a clear stand that mass murdering is unhealthy, crazy, and unacceptable: "*The Surgeon General advises that mass killing is bad for your life and for the lives of your many victims!*"

Someday society will need to have a reasonable science-based mechanism for identifying people whose thinking is systematically organized toward mass destruction as very disturbed psychologically and also ethically as criminal. The need for such a diagnosis is all the greater when the paranoiac person is very much succeeding in consolidating political power. The endless Hitlers, Stalins, Maos, Pol Pots, Saddam Husseins, bin Ladens, and Abu Bakr al-Baghdadis of our world *are* crazy people who are responsible for leading campaigns of destruction against society's very capability for enabling people to live normal everyday lives.

I have a fantasy that someday, when the mental health field will have reached a greater maturity and scientifically proven objectivity, all national leaders will have to undergo an annual checkup by an international mental health board in order to retain their "license" to be a national leader—similar to how pilots of aircraft have to pass a periodic examination. In these examinations of national leaders we would look very much for signs of a malignant paranoia, as well as the signs of any lesser disturbance of excessive power strivings (a condition discussed below in this chapter). In a sense, these are disturbances that are common occupational hazards of people who gain power, and many leaders bring a potential for these disturbances or the actual beginnings of such conditions to the job from the start.

I think that the concept of paranoia was probably a very correct one. Granted, it would need to be used carefully and only after an extreme process of systematic persecutory thinking has consolidated, but it is quite real, and it is very different from the delusional disorders that are accompanied by *breakdowns* of functioning that make a person an obvious psychiatric case. The gravest danger with paranoiacs is their very capacity to function very well in the service of their purpose to destroy lives.

It is also an important clinical observation that any number of these monsters become increasingly "mad" and that their destructiveness often expands toward increasingly limitless plans of killing. Power indeed corrupts, and absolute power indeed corrupts absolutely.[39]

Bloodlust and killing are addictive and can trigger an increasingly insatiable thirst. The only "trick" that could save *millions* of human lives is for humankind to have the knowledge and guts to identify the monster killers in the making at early enough stages and within the framework of an effective legal-political system so that they can be stopped. Clearly this is a job for psychiatry and psychology, along with law and political science, and our professions are still far, far away from doing the job.

Intriguingly, along with the official silence of *DSM* and the absence of a coherent philosophical view in mental health about such matters as ethnic and racial prejudice, slavery, torture, terrorism, persecution, and genocide, one nonetheless finds many a mental health writer bemoaning one or more of these phenomena. In the wake of major historical cataclysms in particular, there are waves of excellent senior mental health thinkers who put themselves to the wheel of trying to understand human destructiveness. Thus World War II Nazism brought us distinguished psychiatrists such as Silvano Arieti[40] and Viktor Frankl,[41] and distinguished psychologists such as Erich Fromm[42] and Rollo May.[43] The wild destruction of the World War II nuclear era brought the work of psychiatrist Robert Jay Lifton;[44] Vietnam's hell brought us more of Lifton as well as social psychologists Herbert Kelman and Lee Carpenter,[45] and the relentless repetition of genocides has led to the work of a number of psychologists including this author,[46] Steven Baum,[47] James Waller,[48] and Ervin Staub.[49] But no matter how well known and well received are some of the above, the basic field and the basic texts of mental health have not really incorporated the truths of evil, cruelty, power gluttony, stupid conformity to norms of destruction, and lust for murder into a basic conception of the nature of the human species.[50] The latent desire in psychiatry to explain and account for these overwhelming human behaviors leads both to nonsense—such as one book that presents the thesis that Napoleon, Stalin, and Hitler all suffered manic-depressive psychoses, hence the mass killings they executed[51]—and to a not small number of seminal works on how our human mind goes off the deep end away from any humanity. But overall, there is largely a roaring silence—denial—that homo sapiens are killing shits.

IS THERE A "LEAKING" OF THE UNCONSCIOUS INTO THE *DSM* THROUGH THE DIAGNOSIS OF FACTITIOUS DISORDERS?

Nonetheless, amazingly, the good old unconscious did make it into the *DSM*. Here we link up once again, however briefly, with our earlier discussion of so-called factitious disorders. As we saw, *DSM* defines factitious disorders as seemingly genuine psychiatric disturbances that look like known physical or mental disturbances because the patient unknowingly (*unconsciously*!) wishes to appear that way, even though the patient isn't *really* disturbed. It is very much emphasized in the *DSM* that these disorders are *not* consciously willed, and that there is no intentional or willful effort to appear ill in order to gain material benefits from the disturbed condition. But, of course, in commonsense language the fact that people choose to appear ill is in its essence a mental disturbance. The real disturbance in a factitious disorder is an unknowing wish to present oneself as disturbed. If this is not willful *conscious* behavior, then it is certainly behavior deriving from *unconscious* processes.

So for all its aspersions toward a more secure place in biological-medical sciences, the *DSM* has admitted the existence of an unconscious that is powerful enough to create pictures even of complex serious psychiatric disturbances. Blessed be the unconscious after all; for it has left its mark even on the *DSM* Establishment, which couldn't help itself and unknowingly (yes, unconsciously) let on that psychiatric disturbances can be sought, chosen, and favored by one's unconscious mind and aren't necessarily or only illnesses that are "visited" on a person.

Of course the *DSM* "thinks" it only happens a little of the time. In fact, in the course of my clinical work, as I read reports from psychiatrists and psychologists about patients who come to see me, I hardly ever see an actual recording of a diagnosis of factitious disorders; and although I don't have systematic data, my hunch is that such diagnoses—not the condition itself—are quite rare in the psychiatric-diagnosing world. But my own belief is that the unconscious process of a *choice* to suffer and continue suffering emotional symptoms happens a good deal of the time—that at least at some level *most* psychiatric disorders are unconsciously invited, elected, and celebrated by the patient, and that therein lies an essence of many a psychiatric disturbance. In general, I think that throughout life most of our human experiences are mediated through, coordinated with, and monitored by our unconscious "black boxes." Personally, it makes the theater of life infinitely more fascinating to me.

Are Excessive Strivings for Power Covered in *DSM* Diagnosis?

The most superficial look at human life confirms that power, very much including excessive striving for power, makes a good deal of our world go round. Yet this subject is not accounted for in a meaningful way in contemporary *DSM* diagnosis. I have authored in the psychiatric literature a proposal to establish a new diagnosis of a personality disorder of excessive power strivings. This proposal was originally published in an established and somewhat influential psychiatric journal following a round of critical reviews of the article by several psychiatrists on the editorial board, but nonetheless it seems to have had little impact to date on the known thinking of the psychiatric establishment.[52] How much of the proposed diagnosis of excessive power strivings is in fact already included in *DSM* diagnoses of personality disorders? Elements of a personality disorder of excessive power strivings will be recognized in several existing diagnoses, especially narcissistic, antisocial, and paranoid personality disorders, paranoia and its renamed heirs, and perhaps also borderline disorders. One reviewer of my proposal to diagnose excessive power strivings said that "one could label the tyrants at issue as at least mixed personality disorder with antisocial, narcissistic and paranoid features" so that "another diagnosis isn't necessary." One answer to this criticism is that it turns off altogether the spotlight on *power*—bossiness and tyranny—and hides the really human feature in a mumbo jumbo of our professional pseudo-disease categories that makes us forget how people are feeling and behaving.

In all of the above categories of personality disorders—as is basically the focus of *DSM* diagnosis—the emphasis over and over again is on the suffering, incompetence, and dysfunction of a person, and not at all about seeking power over other people. In the *DSM*, the general diagnostic criteria for a personality disorder specify that "the enduring pattern leads to clinically significant distress or impairment in social, occupational, or other important areas of functioning."[53] The description therefore does not seem to relate to countless everyday instances of those who are out, "successfully" and ominously, to "corner the market" of success in order to concentrate an arrogant and possibly deadly power over others.[54] People who are "on top" and eminently "successful" in their superiority do not earn a psychiatric diagnosis.

The criteria for antisocial personality disorder emphasize patients getting into trouble with society by reason of their deceitfulness, impulsivity, irritability, aggressiveness, reckless disregard for the safety of self or others, and irresponsibility, rather than because of the essence of their harmful intentions and actions toward others.

The definition of paranoid personality disorder picks up on situations where one's power strivings flood over into hostile wariness, suspiciousness, and accusativeness of others who are experienced and seen projectively as seeking to use their power to block, overcome, and destroy one's own power, where these concerns are obsessive and flood the mind with conspiratorial and revengeful fantasies, preoccupations, and schemes. A paranoid who is an ebullient, outwardly confident personality full of pseudo-leadership charms and populace-pleasing charisma would not earn the diagnosis (see the discussion of paranoia above).

The overall emphasis in the definition of borderline personality disorder is on personal weakness in the offending person and not on what they do to others. But almost every therapist who has struggled with borderlines will tell you that they (borderlines) do plenty of discomforting, disappointing, and troubling of others. In the diagnosis of a borderline personality disorder there are exploitation and abuse of others; a pattern of unstable and intense interpersonal relationships (e.g., marked shifts of attitude from idealization to devaluation, manipulation of others for one's own ends); and inappropriate, intense anger or lack of control of anger. One might speculate that in some cases power seeking is a kind of antidote to inner borderline experiences of not being sure of oneself, and that the search for power is to compensate for or to protect against this torment. It is intriguing that in Hitler's psychological history one discovers that throughout his grandiosity and destructiveness, there were many statements of a morbid fearfulness of being exposed and "seen" in his essence. A physician to Hitler described how Hitler never allowed him to examine him naked, how Hitler was constantly abusing his body, and how his psychosexual development remained very incomplete. Indeed, when the fortunes of war went badly for him, Hitler reverted to more acute symptoms of emotional instability, as if this were the hidden truth waiting all along behind his megalomania.[55] But as I stated earlier the trick we are after is to identify these dangerous bastards earlier, *before* these monsters wreak an unforgivable hell on Earth, and the focus on efforts to control power over others will give us such information much earlier.

In none of the diagnostic categories mentioned is there an emphasis on the perversion of power in everyday contexts of life in one's family or at work or in the course of rising in organizational, communal, or political leadership—the period of time before the excessive power is consolidated when it is important to spot a nascent dictatorial personality.

In a kind of overall "add-on" to the *DSM*,[56] there is a section on "Abuse and Neglect."[57] For a moment one's hopes soar. There is attention to abuse after all, including diagnoses of "Child Physical Abuse," "Child Sexual Abuse," "Child Neglect," and "Adult Maltreatment and Neglect Problems," which includes a range of physical or sexual violence to a partner or group, neglect, or psychological abuse—also to and by spouses and partners. *Bravo!* Our real world of so much real abuse is not being overlooked by clinical mental health after all. In fact in *DSM-5* there has been real progress in acknowledging these are real problems that come to the attention of mental health clinicians.[58] Yet, still, in *DSM-5* as in the previous edition, *DSM* introduces the entire chapter with a firm statement that "the conditions and problems listed in this chapter are not mental disorders."[59] Heaven help! Why are these conditions listed? "Their inclusion in *DSM-5* is meant to draw attention to the scope of additional issues that may be encountered in routine clinical practice." [60] In other words, the listing is for the benefit and welfare of us clinicians more than it is about the people we treat. Mental illness and beating, raping, exploiting, and neglecting other people abusively remain two separate worlds of human experience and meaning. Sometimes they overlap, but they are not to be integrally related to one another. In any case, the abuse of other people in its own right does not constitute psychiatric disturbances. The *DSM continues to say what it did in 1994*: "These problems are included because they are frequently a focus of clinical attention among individuals seen by health professionals."[61] *Whatever that means.* Abuse of others isn't really the province of psychiatry and mental health. It is only a subject of psychiatry because people come to psychiatrists to complain of these problems, and you have to pay attention to the public—the customer is always right. But in no way are these behaviors ipso facto expressions of deep disturbances of mind. No matter that these are problems that literally plague us human beings, they are not really psychiatric problems.

Racist Personality Disorder

It is relevant to note that the need for a new psychiatric diagnosis that addresses aggressive acting out, delusions of grandeur, and prejudices specifically against racial or ethnic groups of people also has been brought up in the psychiatric literature. A psychiatrist, Willie Hamlin, proposed, in my opinion wisely, a diagnosis of a *racist personality disorder*, which is specifically concerned with people who denigrate, dehumanize, or persecute racial minorities,[62] but evidently his proposal too had little impact on the profession.

The indicators of the racist personality disorder that Hamlin proposed included: disordered personal and social interactions; inappropriate acting out of projected and displaced feelings; irrational and at times hostile behavior; delusions of grandeur; stereotypic actions and reactions, especially in dealing with individuals of certain skin color or sociocultural backgrounds; use of overgeneralizations as poor substitutes for appropriate and rational judgments about members of different sociocultural groups, race, religions; little ability to view human beings in other than "all good" or "all bad" categories ("splitting"); and proneness to aggressive and/or assaultive behavior, particularly when under the influence of alcohol or drugs. Hamlin's proposal is a statement that the overall subject of taking hostile power over other people basically has not been dealt with in psychopathology, notwithstanding the fact that for many of us the real-life phenomena of prejudice, discrimination, and persecution of others are *a quintessence of human madness*.

Psychopathology as Rooted in Everyday Human Experience

Discomfort and dysfunction are important aspects of the human condition. Nothing in the above criticisms of the *DSM* is intended to imply that there is no such thing as psychopathology, nor that the descriptions of common conditions that are included in the *DSM* are not grounded largely in legitimate observations and descriptions of dysfunctional behaviors. The main point of many of the criticisms rendered is that the *DSM* tends to disconnect symptoms from their being rooted in human experience, including the individual's unconscious experiences of ways of constructing their life—such as what we are calling a fascist or democratic mind style. There is little recognition of the impact of basic relationship experiences with people—such as hurt, abandonment, and anger at intimates—nor of the basic spiritual and value choices that people make such as whether to be victims or perpetrators.[63]

Interestingly, although family therapy represents a major advance of recognizing the profound significance of relationships and that psychopathology often is rooted in or triggered by problems in one's basic intimacy relationships and not only in the individual's mind, many family therapists also have denied and ignored aspects of inner experience and unconscious emotions and thoughts. Writing in the *Australian and New Zealand Journal of Family Therapy,* Paul Gibney observed:

> It seems that as family therapy has moved more and more away from "inner" pathology, i.e., pathology located in the individual, to "outer" pathology, i.e., pathology located in the systemic interaction, a curious thing seems to have happened. . . . Eventually, a notion of "pathology" seems to have been lost altogether in the family therapy literature. Upon reflection, tragically, a number of associated concepts also "left the building" at the same time—"illness," "sadness," "madness," "melancholia," and "tragedy" rarely seem to rate a mention in the family therapy literature. . . . Family therapy, while originally having some clear ideas as to what constituted "pathology," has failed to provide a rigorous conceptualization of "pathology." So schools of therapy have emphasized the "outer" more and more, e.g., the "family game," linguistic activity, "cultural discourse." The whole notion of individual pathology and a conceptualization of pathology seem to have disappeared from family therapy literature.[64]

Gibney concluded:

1. Pathology needs to be given further consideration in family therapy discourse. Pathology can be seen as a "knowing of sadness" and as a "knowing of suffering," and as a "knowing of dis-ease." The aim here is to honor people's suffering, their lived experience, to "sit with it" and to allow ourselves to be as uncomfortable as we need to be to give genuine witness to their stories. This knowing of their

sadness (and our own) is in service of valuing their experience, as opposed to the often obscene rush in which they are invited to distance themselves from their experiences.

2. With that knowing of suffering, "feelings" and "emotions" are once again central to the therapeutic enterprise. The therapist is moved by the therapeutic process: he or she feels and intuits. "Seeing" and "questioning" surrender their privileged positions, to become just other activities in the therapeutic domain, as opposed to the main techniques.
3. Pathology can be given a privileged role, as a messenger of the necessary.[65]

IS IT MORE MENTALLY HEALTHY TO EXPERIENCE EMOTIONAL PROBLEMS AND WORK AT COPING AND SOLVING THEM THAN TO BE A "NORMAL" WITH NO PROBLEMS?

For all of us, mental health necessarily includes living respectfully and energetically with a great many significant faults, limitations, and errors that all of us make, and taking responsibility for them and working to correct them. Mental health is not achieving a symptom-free or problem-free existence. In fact the appearance of such sublime states of perfection in itself almost always is a sign of an existing or looming problem. Thus, in medical conditions, too, people who have "never been sick a day in their lives" are described by some physicians as worse risks for coping with illness because they don't know "how" to be ill and recover. With respect to psychological health, "perfect marriages" characteristically are recipes for humdrumness, sexlessness, infidelity, and breakdown; and perfect kids often do not star as adults. A report from the Center for Disease Control says, "Stress helps children develop the skills they need to cope with and adapt to new and potentially threatening situations throughout life."[66]

Note, clearly there is no doubt whatsoever that children who are abused physically or mentally are at very high risk for many problems and disabilities, including health problems, but the literature also recognizes potential contributions of adverse experiences to the development of greater resiliency—for some children. In my practice over the years I have seen a notable number of such adults and they and their stories take my breath away in admiration, even though in many cases their very resilience has proved to be at the expense of desirable tenderness and readiness to connect intimately.

We have already met one of America's great psychiatrists and psychoanalysts, Karl Menninger, one of the leaders of the famed Menninger Clinic for many years in Topeka, Kansas.[67] Menninger was one of the first to acknowledge that *some mental difficulties are the lot of every person*. Together with his colleagues, Martin Mayman and Paul Pruyser, in their brilliant and humane book they say wisely about psychological abnormality and health. "It is now accepted that most people have some degree of mental illness at some time, and many of them have a degree of mental illness most of the time." They further argue intriguingly: "This really should not surprise anyone, for do not most of us have some physical illness some of the time, and some of us much of the time?"[68] With regard to the nature of man, the Menninger team observed:

> Life is more than permutations in the DNA molecule as the Fifth Symphony is more than vibrating air. And mental illness is more than an aggregate of errors in body physics and chemistry. It is a universal human experience which has a salvage function in maintaining the vital balance.[69]

The overall conclusion that the Menninger team reached was *the desirability of working hard at making oneself a positive, loving and productive person*. In other words, genuinely desiring and trying to be a constructive related person is more the essence of mental health than how many concrete symptoms of mental disturbance are or are not present. It is not so much the presence or absence of *DSM*-like symptoms that defines real mental health and illness. Love of people, work, and of life itself are the real point of it all and the basis for possible cure of many psychiatric conditions.

Similarly, veteran pioneering psychologist Albert Ellis observed after many years of his work that there is a virtual "impossibility of achieving good mental health" so long as one tracks concretely the lapses, errors and drops in any person's functioning.[70] Shedler, Mayman, and Manis[71] point out forcibly that the *absence* of symptoms of anxiety and upset are often indicators of a more serious absence of healthy processing of life and its existential and realistic dilemmas than the presence of symptoms that are to be managed and worked through constructively.

In my own clinical experience, I have seen, paradoxically, very psychiatrically sick people in whom I have experienced with pleasure and excitement a fight for recovery and life that generally boded well for their recovery and future. And I have seen seemingly symptomless people whose spirit for life was so lacking that one had to expect the worst was yet to come, as it often did.

Good mental health includes processing our manifestations of poor mental health well more than it means maintaining a pose of no problems whatsoever. Healthy people are upset, make mistakes, and encounter ugly sides of their spirits and personalities. They work at overcoming, correcting, taking responsibility for, and transcending the undesirable but nonetheless very human parts of themselves. Healthy people apologize to themselves and others and strive to be better persons, whereas the psychiatrically unhealthy people dig themselves in deeper and deeper into anti-life thinking and behaviors and do not work at correcting them.

Very much like our language for a democratic mind, the Menninger team concludes that the goal of psychiatric treatment is not simply "reinstatement of the status quo ante ('recovery' in the popular sense), but . . . the development of new potentialities and transcendence of previous levels of vital balance to a state of being 'weller than well.'"[72] This is a psychiatric orientation that offers hope and purpose, Menninger, Mayman and Pruyser are the kind of therapists I want to have when I need help—and not a classifying *DSM*ologist.

DSM-5 KNOWS THERE ARE MANY OTHER FORMS OF EMOTIONAL AND MENTAL PROBLEMS, BUT IT HAS OUTFOXED ITSELF

Just as the subject of "Abuse and Neglect" is pushed into the section on "Other Conditions," the same "comedy" is also played out in respect to many other conditions, especially where interpersonal relationships are clearly involved.

Is it really comedy? It is so sad and intellectually offensive, but it is also hard not to laugh as the American Psychiatric Association's *DSM* experts face huge problems of their own creation. My sense is that since they are on a "holy crusade" to make as much of mental-psychological problems sound like good-old biological-medical problems, they don't know what in the world to do with a whole series of quite serious and important types of human behaviors that even they simply can't force into biological-sounding concepts. So if their initial axiom-opener is that all mental problems are biological, when they hit mental disorders that they can't fit in, they have nowhere to go but to put them in an "other" category while continuing to state that these disorders are not mental disorders.

You have to be totally "schizo-out-of-it" not to know that so many of the "other" conditions draw endless numbers of people to psychiatrists and other mental health facilities. The upshot that I call so funny and yet sad and also offensively corrupt is that we now have a situation where huge numbers of people go to psychiatrists (and other mental health clinicians) for these conditions and psychiatrists certainly accept them and earn a good living from them, but in their official books they say loudly that they are not treating psychiatric conditions! That is why the *DSM* has to refer to these conditions as "Other Conditions That May Be a Focus of Clinical Attention." Isn't it a bad joke and a gross ethical violation for a professional to treat conditions that are not within the domain of his training and expertise?

We saw that Menninger, Mayman, and Pruyser are very unimpressed by the various discrete psychiatric conditions that are spoken of as if they represent genuinely different syndromes, just as in biological conditions like smallpox and lung cancer. No, they say. "Relative normality or mental healthiness [ranges from] one end of the scale to a zone of abnormality, or maladjustment or mental ill health at the other end of the scale."[73] What is called for in psychiatric diagnosis is an understanding of the overall ways in which a person organizes his or her "external and internal affairs" (meaning lifestyle and use of mind).[74]

As we saw earlier, they also put their finger on the human propensity to be angry, hostile, and willing to harm others, a basic dynamic process that gets out of control in the development of all emotional disorganization and psychiatric symptomatology, and critical issues for all of us throughout our lives, just as we all display psychiatric symptoms to some extent throughout our lives.[75]

What else is missing from the *DSM* subject matter? We now have a situation that in addition to subjects of outright clinical disturbance that really are not covered, such as suicidality and neurosis and paranoia, *DSM* is also weak in describing a great many very common other everyday human problems, which it defines as the "other" conditions. These include:

- Relational Problems
- Problems Related to Family Upbringing
    - Parent-Child Relational Problem
    - Sibling Relational Problem
    - Upbringing Away from Parents
    - Child Affected by Parental Relationship Distress
- Other Problems Related to Primary Support Group
    - Relationship Distress with Spouse or Intimate Partner
    - Disruption of Family by Separation or Divorce
    - High Expressed Emotion Level within Family
    - Uncomplicated Bereavement
- Abuse and Neglect
- Child Maltreatment and Neglect Problems
    - Child Physical Abuse
    - Child Sexual Abuse
    - Child Neglect
    - Child Psychological Abuse
- Adult Maltreatment and Neglect Problems
    - Spouse or Partner Violence, Physical
    - Spouse or Partner Violence, Sexual

- Spouse or Partner Neglect
- Spouse or Partner Abuse, Psychological
- Adult Abuse by Nonspouse or Nonpartner

- Educational and Occupational Problems
    - Academic or Educational Problem
    - Problem Related to Current Military Deployment
    - Other Problem Related to Employment
- Housing and Economic Problems
    - Housing
        - Homelessness
            - Inadequate Housing
            - Discord with Neighbor, Lodger or Landlord
            - Problem Related to Living in a Residential Environment
        - Economic Problems
        - Lack of Adequate Food or Safe Drinking Water
        - Extreme Poverty
        - Low Income
        - Insufficient Social Insurance or Welfare Support
            - Unspecified Housing or Economic Problem
- Other Problems Related to the Social Environment
    - Phase of Life Problem
    - Problem Related to Living Alone
    - Acculturation Difficulty
    - Social Exclusion or Rejection
    - Target of (Perceived) Adverse Discrimination or Persecution
    - Unspecified Problem Related to Social Environment
- Problems Related to Crime or Interaction with the Legal System
    - Victim of Crime
    - Conviction in Civil or Criminal Proceedings without Imprisonment
    - Imprisonment or Other Incarceration
    - Problems Related to Release from Prison
    - Problems Related to Other Legal Circumstances
- Other Health Service Encounters for Counseling and Medical Advice
    - Sex Counseling
    - Other Counseling or Consultation
- Problems Related to Other Psycho-Social Personal and Environmental Circumstances
    - Religious or Spiritual Problem
- Other Circumstances of Personal History
    - Problem Related to Lifestyle
    - Adult Antisocial Behavior

- Child or Adolescent Antisocial Behavior
- Problems Related to Access to Medical or Other Health Care
  - Nonadherence to Medical Treatment
  - Overweight or Obesity
  - Malingering
  - Wandering Associated with a Mental Disorder
  - Borderline Intellectual Functioning

"Hail, hail, the gang's all here!" At last we have a list of many of the problems that are recognizable and real in our human lives. So did the *DSM-5* manage after all to pull the chestnuts out of the fire?

Well, *yes*, the list speaks well for itself; but *no* nonetheless, for remember these are *not* psychiatric disorders, conditions, or problems; they are "Conditions That May Be a Focus of Clinical Attention." The list is squeezed literally into the last pages of the *DSM-5 Desk Reference* almost as a kind of afterthought—or in classical psychodynamic language as an *undoing* of the terrible neglect of these vital real-life topics up to now in the *DSM* edifice of recognized psychiatric conditions, illnesses, problems, or dysfunctions.

In an afterthought that would be almost comical were it not so sad, the *DSM* adds that the physician "may" want to include in the medical record of a patient such "useful information on circumstances that may affect the patient's care."

Oh well, such are the "circumstances of life (referring to the *DSM* statement that these problems are "circumstances that may affect the patient's care.")

CONCLUSION

Would it be really so difficult to put together a simple-to-understand classification of human dysfunctions problems or mental conditions? Such a list should include—

1. A scale for the degree of dysfunction one is suffering and the harm that one is doing to oneself—one's sense of comfort and freedom from mental distress, capacity to cope with life and its distresses and challenges, and plain old well-being, happiness and satisfaction.
2. A scale for the degree of harm that a person is doing to others, including in one way or another ruining another person's life, making a person feel rotten, lousy, dumb, incompetent, unlovable, or other things such as the trauma imposed on others by walking out of a close family relationship in a way and at a time that the others experience as being abandoned, and

also the extent of one's readiness to take responsibility and correct harm being done to others.

Of course, this way of thinking calls for a basic change in *DSM*-thinking. Like many others, Carl Jung observed the tortuous path on which new ideas are set by the prevailing Establishment of the time:

> In studying the history of the human mind one is impressed again by the fact that the growth of the mind is the widening of the range of consciousness, and that each step forward has been a most painful and laborious achievement. One could almost say that nothing is more hateful to man than to give up even a particle of his unconsciousness. Ask those who have tried to introduce a new idea![76]

A psychiatric classification system that is more true to real life and every-day human experience could make a lot of people—professionals and laymen alike—a lot more comfortable than current *DSM* mumbo jumbo.

> Reveal the unconscious tendencies which lie behind actions and reactions and which influence development and determine the relations of life itself. . . . The state of introversion finds there below in the shadows of the unconscious the substitute for the upper world which it has abandoned.
>
> —Carl Jung[77]

NOTES

1. Joe Sharkey, *Bedlam: Greed, Profiteering and Fraud in a Mental System Gone Crazy* (New York: St. Martin's Press, 1994), 1.
2. American Psychiatric Association *Diagnostic and Statistical Manual of Mental Disorders: DSM-5*, fifth edition revised (Washington, DC: American Psychiatric Association. See chapter 2, note 3 for our sequence of citations for *DSM-5, DSM-IV*, and *DSM-III*.
3. Avi Peled, "Virtual Reality and Psychiatry" (paper presented at Conference on Psychotherapy and Virtual Reality, Tel Hashomer Hospital, Tel Aviv, Israel, August 2003).
4. Florence W. Kaslow, ed., *Handbook of Relational Diagnosis and Other Family Dysfunctions* (New York: Wiley, 1996).
5. Allen Frances, "The Inmates Seem to Have Taken Over the Asylum," *Huffington Post*, July 12, 2013.
6. Allen Frances, Where Have All the Normals Gone?," *Huffington Post*, May 2013.
7. Allen Frances, The *DSM-5* Follies, as Told in Its Own Words," *Huffington Post*, February 9, 2012

8. Carol Tavris, "How Psychiatry Went Crazy: The 'Bible' of Psychiatric Diagnosis Shapes—and Deforms—Both Treatment and Policy," *Wall Street Journal*, May 17, 2013.

9. Allen Frances, *Saving Normal: An Insider's Revolt Against Out-of-Control Psychiatric Diagnosis: DSM-5, Big Pharma, and the Medicalization of Ordinary Life*. New York: William Morrow, 2013). See also the author's proposal for a better diagnostic system in Frances Allen, *Essentials of Psychiatric Diagnosis* (New York: Guilford Press, 2013).

10. Gary Greenberg, *The Book of Woe: The DSM and the Unmaking of Psychiatry* (New York: Bluer Rider Press/Penguin Group, 2013).

11. Tavris, Carol "How Psychiatry Went Crazy."

12. David Rosenhan, "On Being Sane in Insane Places," *Science* 179, no. 4070 (1973): 250–58.

13. Karl Menninger, Markus Mayman, and Paul Pruyser, *The Vital Balance: The Life Process in Mental Health and Illness* (New York: Viking Press, 1963). 170.

14. "Drug Companies Are Accused of Creating Dysfunctions to Lift Sales," *International Herald Tribune*, January 4–5, 2003, 1 An earlier *New York Times Weekly Review* feature story summed up the issue similarly: "Many new disorders develop powerful lobbies in the therapeutic and political worlds, critics say, because of the *DSM*'s far-reaching influence in health-care spending . . . . There is a clear motive for defining new mental disorders and marketing psychiatric medications for adults." Joe Sharkey, "You're Not Bad, You're Sick. It's in the Book," *New York Times Weekly Review* (September 28, 1997), 1, 4.

15. Alan Schwarz, "The Selling of Attention Deficit Disorder," *New York Times*, December 14, 2013.

16. Donald A. Bloch, "Cautionary Tales" (reviews of Emily Fox Gordon, *Mockingbird Years: A Life in and Out of Therapy* [New York: Basic Books, 2000], and T. M. Luhrmann, *Of Two Minds: The Growing Disorder in American Psychiatry* [New York: Alfred A. Knopf, 2000], *Readings: A Journal of Reviews and Commentary in Mental Health*, 15, no. 3 (2000): 6.

17. Jonathan Shedler, "The Effectiveness of Psychodynamic Psychotherapy," *American Psychologist* 65, no. 2: 98–109.

18. Jonathan Shedler, "Is NIMH Brilliant, Stupid, or Both?," *Psychology Today* (October 2013), http://www.psychologytoday.com/blog/psychologically-minded/201310/is-nimh-brilliant-stupid-or-both.

19. Ibid.

20. Ibid.

21. Ibid.

22. NIMH Research Domain Criteria (RDoC), http://www.nimh.nih.gov/research-priorities/rdoc/nimh-research-domain-criteria-rdoc.shtml.

23. Richard M. Ryan and Edward L. Deci, "Self-Determination Theory and the Facilitation of Intrinsic Motivation, Social Development, and Well-Being," *American Psychologist* (Special Issue on Happiness, Excellence, and Optimal Human Functioning) 55, no. 1 (2000): 68–78.

24. Bruno Bettelheim, *The Empty Fortress: Infantile Autism and the Birth of the Self* (New York: Free Press, 1967); Frances Tustin, *Autism and Childhood Psychosis*

(London: Hogarth, 1973). Both Bettelheim and Tustin reached therapeutic triumphs in any number of cases, so that by any scientific standard one at least has to pay attention to their work, but as we have seen they are an anathema and generally not allowed to be mentioned.

25. Karl Abraham, "Ejaculatio Praecox," in *Selected Papers of Karl Abraham* (New York: Basic Books, 1957 [1917]).

26. William H. Masters and Virginia C. Johnson, *Human Sexual Inadequacy* (Boston: Little, Brown, 1970).

27. Helen S. Kaplan, *The New Sex Therapy: Active Treatment of Sexual Dysfunctions* (New York: Brunner/Mazel, 1974).

28. Ivan Boszormenyi-Nagy and Geraldine Spark, *Invisible Loyalties: Reciprocity in Intergenerational Family Therapy* (New York: Brunner/Mazel, 1984)

29. Leah R. Garnett, "Prozac Revisited: As Drug Gets Remade, Concerns about Suicides Surface," *Boston Globe*, May 7, 2000. Ironically, a Letter to the Editor of *Haaretz Magazine* (English edition) two years later on March 1, 2002, by a Dr. Hannah Schwartz complained about the newspaper printing an advertisement for Seroxat, a new version of Prozac. The writer argued: "A more responsible approach would have informed the readers that only recently, on June 6, 2001, a U.S. court in Wyoming ruled that it is liable to cause a person to murder someone or commit suicide." The writer continues that the jury in the above case decided the drug manufacturer should pay the plaintiff (the widower of the murdered daughter) compensation of $6.4 million! The writer also noted that complaints have also been made against the manufacturer of Seroxat over its failure to disclose information about the risks of addiction and the side effects that occur when one stops using the drug. "This is a controversial medication that requires psychiatric supervision and is not a safe and 'trendy' wonder drug, as the article suggests."

30. American Psychiatric Association, Introduction, in *Diagnostic and Statistical Manual of Mental Disorders, DSM-III* (Washington, DC: Psychiatric Association, 1980), 9–10.

31. Ibid., 9.

32. Ibid., 10.

33. See Seymour Epstein, "Integration of the Cognitive and the Psychodynamic Unconscious," *American Psychologist* 49, no. 8 (1994): 709–24. This article in the prestigious "home journal" of the American Psychological Association concludes that even nonclinical psychologists recognize "the existence of two parallel, interacting modes of information processing: a rational system and an emotionally driven experiential system," or *cognitive* and *psychodynamic unconscious* systems. If you don't believe it, says Epstein, look at the conflicts that abound between the heart and head, or the appeal of superstitious thinking. "It is evident . . . that non-rational thinking is highly prevalent and that even when people know their thinking is irrational, they often find it more compelling than their rational reasoning" (712). See also Mick Power and Chris R. Brewin, From Freud to Cognitive Science: A Contemporary Account of the Unconscious," *British Journal Clinical Psychology* 30, no. 4 (1991): 289–310.

34. Arthur Jersild of Teachers College, Columbia University divided a group of young women who suffered PMS symptoms into two experimental groups, one

of which experienced noteworthy reduction of PMS discomforts after working on greater acceptance of themselves, and their bodies as women. See Arthur T. Jersild, *In Search of Self* (New York: Columbia University Press, 1952).

35. Joseph Rheingold, a psychiatrist at Harvard University, described at great length the unconscious fears of many women who suffered severe postpartum symptoms, including psychotic reactions, of their transmitting to their new babies harmful doses of anger, hatred, and rejection which they themselves had suffered unknowingly from their mother. According to Rheingold, it is these fears that are at the heart of the postpartum reactions. Over the years, I have successfully applied this paradigm in treatment of postpartum reactions several times. See Joseph C. Rheingold, *The Fear of Being a Woman: A Theory of Maternal Destructiveness* (New York: Grune & Stratton, 1964); and Joseph C. Rheingold, *The Mother, Anxiety and Death: The Catastrophic Death Complex* (New York: Little, Brown, 1967).

36. The transitional volume was: American Psychiatric Association *Diagnostic and Statistical Manual of Mental Disorders: DSM-III-R*, third edition revised. Washington, DC: American Psychiatric Association.

37. American Psychiatric Association, *DSM-III*, 197.

38. Rosenhan, "On Being Sane in Insane Places."

39. This is the classic statement of Lord Acton, a nineteenth-century British parliamentarian. See R. J. Rummel, *Power Kills: Democracy as a Method of Nonviolence* (New Brunswick, NJ: Transaction Publishers, 1997).

40. Silvano Arieti, *Will to Be Human* (New York: Delacorte, 1975).

41. Viktor Frankl, *Man's Search for Meaning* (Boston: Beacon Press, 2006).

42. As noted, Erich Fromm's books include: *Escape from Freedom*, 1941; *Man for Himself*, 1947; *The Sane Society*, 1955; *The Heart of Man: Its Genius for Good and Evil*, 1964; and *The Anatomy of Human Destructiveness*, 1973. I'm adding to this list: *On Being Human* (London: Bloosmbury, 1997). Many of Fromm's books are being continuously republished. All these books were very meaningful for me, and I probably drew from his works and wrote more papers in college and graduate school on Fromm than any other source. My personal favorite is: *The Heart of Man: Its Potential for Good and Evil.* I love the title and appreciate his confrontation of this basic choice for all of us humans.

43. Rollo May, *Power and Innocence: A Search for the Sources of Violence* (New York: Norton, 1972). Rollo May died in 1994. A year later his last book that he was reported proofreading two days before his death appeared: Kirk Schneider and Rollo May, *The Psychology of Existence* New York: McGraw-Hill, 1995). The publisher recently announced it is reissuing this seminal text.

Schneider appears in a 2013 multiauthor volume: Arthur C. Bohart, Barbara S. Held, Edward Mendelowitz, and Kirk Schneider, eds., *Humanity's Dark Side: Evil, Destructive Experience, and Psychotherapy* (Washington, DC: American Psychological Association, 2013). A review of the book by Paul Efthim in the *New England Psychologist* (April 2014) gives the following information (abstracted from http://www.nepsy.com/articles/book-reviews/humanitys-dark-side-evil-destructive-experience-and-psychotherapy): *Humanity's Dark Side* grew out of the famous debate between Rollo May and Carl Rogers regarding evil, destructive behavior, and the question of whether therapists need to confront the dark side with their patients in order to be effective. The May-Rogers debate was about conflicting views of human nature. May criticized Rogers for minimizing humans' potential for acting in negative and destructive ways. One of May's key concerns was that the Rogerian approach was so focused on warmth and empathy that it discouraged patients from accessing and experiencing anger and other destructive emotions and behaviors.

44. Robert Jay Lifton, a psychiatrist, has been a brilliant and prolific voice of reason probing man's destructive behavior and the critical "underground issue" of man's search for immortality (the latter is referenced separately in this book). Among his works: Robert Jay Lifton, *Death in Life: Survivors of Hiroshima* (New York: Random House, 1968); Robert Jay Lifton, *Home from the War: Vietnam Veterans—Neither Victims nor Executioners* (New York: Simon & Schuster, 1973); Robert Jay Lifton and Eric Markusen, *The Genocidal Mentality: Nazi Holocaust and Nuclear Threat* (New York: Basic Books, 1990); Robert Jay Lifton, *The Nazi Doctors: Medical Killing and the Psychology of Genocide* (New York: Basic Books, 2000).

45. Herbert C. Kelman, and V. Lee Hamilton, *Crimes of Obedience: Towards a Social Psychology of Authority and Responsibility* New Haven, CT: Yale University Press, 1989).

46. Israel W. Charny, *How Can We Commit the Unthinkable? Genocide, The Human Cancer* (in collaboration with Chanan Rapaport, foreword by Elie Wiesel) (Boulder, CO: Westview Press, 1982). Paperback with title change: *Genocide, the Human Cancer: How Can We Commit the Unthinkable?* (New York: Hearst Professional Books, 1983); Israel W. Charny, ed., *Genocide: A Critical Bibliographic Review* (London: Mansell, 1988); Israel W. Charny, ed., *Encyclopedia of Genocide* (2 vols.) Santa Barbara, CA: ABC-Clio, 1999 Publishers); Israel W. Charny, *Fascism and Democracy in the Human Mind: A Bridge between Mind and Society* (Lincoln: University of Nebraska Press, 2006).

47. Steven K. Baum, *The Psychology of Genocide: Perpetrators, Bystanders, and Rescuers* (New York: Cambridge University Press, 2011). See also his excellent work on anti-Semitism: Steven K. Baum, *Antisemitism Explained.* Foreword by Shimon Samuels (Lanham, MD: University Press of America, 2008). Steven Baum is the editor of the *Journal for the Study of Antisemitism.*

48. James Waller, *Becoming Evil: How Ordinary People Commit Genocide and Mass Killing* (New York: Oxford University Press, 2002).

49. Ervin Staub, *The Roots of Evil: The Origins of Genocide and Other Group Violence* (New York: Cambridge University Press, 1989; Ervin Staub, *Overcoming Evil: Genocide, Violent Conflict, and Terrorism* (New York: Oxford University Press, 2011).

50. I can start with the Holy Bible to show murder and mass murder as rooted in the human psyche and history. Our very gods (of many faiths) have their moments of instructing the faithful to commit mass murder. If you want, pick up a history of just about any people and you will find dark chapters of evil actions everywhere.

51. D. Jablow Hershman and Julian Lieb, *A Brotherhood of Tyrants: Manic Depression and Absolute Power* (Amherst, NY: Prometheus Books).

52. Israel W. Charny, A Personality Disorder of Excessive Power Strivings, *Israel Journal of Psychiatry* 34, no. 1 (1997): 3–17.

53. American Psychiatric Association, *DSM–IV*, 633.

54. A disgusting as well as a gripping portrayal of everyday exploitation of power over "suckers" in the stock market, and the deadly corruption of the lives of the power brokers can be seen in the Academy Award winning film, *The Wolf of Wall Street.* The story was obviously inspired by the horror of Bernard Madoff's swindle of all times.

55. Dennis L. Breo, "Hitler's Final Days Recalled by Physician," *American Medical News* (October 11, 1985), 1, 56–71. The physician's name was Ernst Gunther Schenk, then eighty-one years old, who was described as the only surviving physician who was in the bunker with Hitler hours before Hitler committed suicide. In addition to his eyewitness account, Schenk reported that he studied the medical records on Hitler kept by Hitler's personal physician, Theodor Morell. The *AMA News* reports that Schenk was to publish a book in German by Bavarian Connection Publishers in Munich, *Patient A—Adolf Hitler and His Private Physician, Professor Theodor Gilbert Morell*, which I have not succeeded in locating. However, an Internet search did reveal a book with a different title by Dr. Morrell. It appears both in a German edition and in an English translation—*but* with a maddening twist: the editor of both editions is the infamous British historian David Irving, who in later years was identified by a British court in no uncertain terms as an out-and-out anti-Semite who lionized Hitler and engaged in blatant denials of the Holocaust. One can hardly recommend any books by this man, but we can take note of the information they may provide about Hitler from his doctor: Theodor Gilbert, Morell, *Die geheimen tagebücher des Dr. Morell: Leibarzt Adolf Hitlers /* [herausgegeben von] David Irving. (München: Goldmann, 1983); Theodor Gilbert Morell, *Adolf Hitler, Medical Diaries: The Private Diaries of Dr. Theo Morell*, edited by David Irving (London: Sidgwik & Jackson, 1983).

56. American Psychiatric Association, "Other Conditions That May Be a Focus of Clinical Attention," *Desk Reference to the Diagnostic Criteria from DSM-5* (Washington, DC: American Psychiatric Association, 2013.

57. American Psychiatric Association, *DSM-5 Desk Reference*, 358–59.

58. Ibid. Two sections that follow the above are "Child Maltreatment and Neglect Problems," 359–62, and "Adult Maltreatment and Neglect Problems," 363–67.

59. Ibid.

60. Ibid.

61. American Psychiatric Association, *DSM-IV*, 682.

62. Willie T. Hamlin, "Racism Is a Personality Disorder" (unpublished pamphlet, 20 pp), personal communication, retrieved August 14, 2014, http://the3cs.com/racist_personality_disorder.pdf. Willie T. Hamlin, MD was the director of the Institute for Child and Family Psychiatry, in Silver Spring, Maryland.

63. Albert Camus, *Neither Victims nor Executioners* (Eugene, OR: Wipf and Stock, 2008 [1946]). The overriding value that Albert Camus proposed is that as much as possible we direct ourselves neither to be victims nor victimizers.

64. Paul Gibney, "Family Therapy: Inner, Outer and the Issue of Pathology," *Australian and New Zealand Journal Family Therapy* 17, no. 4 (1996): 173–90.

65. Ibid., 186.

66. J. S. Middlebrooks and N. C. Audage *The Effects of Childhood Stress on Health across the Lifespan* (Atlanta, GA: Centers for Disease Control and Prevention, National Center for Injury Prevention and Control, 2008). See also Jessica Laheyjan, "Why Parents Need to Let Their Children Fail," *Atlantic* (January 29, 2013); Eliana Dockterman, "'Cool' Kids More Likely to Have Problems Later in Life," *Time* (June 11, 2014); Patricia Logan-Greene, Sara Green, Paula S. Nurius, and Dario Longhi, "Distinct Contributions of Adverse Childhood Experiences and Resilience Resources: A Cohort Analysis of Adult Physical and Mental Health," *Social Work Health Care* 53, no. 8 (2013): 776–97.

67. Karl Menninger, Markus Mayman, and Paul Pruyser, *The Vital Balance: The Life Process in Mental Health and Illness* (New York: Viking Press, 1963).

68. Ibid., 401.

69. Ibid., 417.

70. Albert Ellis, "The Impossibility of Achieving Consistently Good Mental Health," *American Psychologist* 42 (1987): 364–75. See Ellis's original basic work: Albert Ellis and Robert A. Harper, *A Guide to Rational Living* (Englewood Cliffs, NJ: Prentice Hall, 1961); Albert Ellis and Robert A. Harper, *A Guide to Successful Marriage* (North Hollywood, CA: Wilshire, 1961); Albert Ellis and Robert A. Harper, *Creative Marriage* (Secaucus, NJ: Lyle Stuart, 1961). See also Albert Ellis, and Debbie Joffe Ellis, *Rational Emotive Behavior Therapy*, third edition (Washington, DC: American Psychological Association, 2011).

71. J. Shedler, M. Mayman, and M. Manis, "The Illusion of Mental Health," *American Psychologist* 48, no. 11 (1993): 1117–31.

72. Menninger, Mayman, and Pruyser, *The Vital Balance*, 401. This same conclusion has been reached by many other thinkers over the years. The shorthand my generation was taught of Freud's conclusion in this respect was that to be emotionally healthy one needed to be able *to work and love well* (though, granted, in those days the concept of love had no few overtones of a greater emphasis on good sexual performance and less on caring and treasuring the person). Thus too, we saw that in a much more recent publication of a *Special Issue of the American Psychologist on Happiness, Excellence, and Optimal Human Functioning,* Ryan and Deci concluded that there are "three innate psychological needs—competence, autonomy, and relatedness" which characterize mental health. See Richard M. Ryan and Edward L. Deci, "Self-Determination Theory," 68.

73. Menninger, Mayman, and Pruyser, *The Vital Balance*, 150.

74. Ibid., 162.

75. Ibid., 170.

76. C. G. Jung, H. G. Baynes, and C. F. Baynes, *Contributions to Analytical Psychology* (London: Routledge & Kegan Paul, 1928).

77. C. G. Jung, *Psychology of the Unconscious: A Study of the Transformations and Symbolisms of the Libido: A Contribution to the History of the Evolution of Thought* (New York: Moffat, Yard, 1916).

Chapter Six

The Wisdom and Tools of Multiple Schools of Psychotherapy

Treatment of psychiatric conditions can focus on at least three different levels: relief of symptoms, correction of inner errors in one's way of life, or a combination of both. In addition, the focus of treatment can be on either or both the individual or relationships—most often on marriage or parenting, at times with the extended family, or other relationships such as at work.

Psychotherapy can be directed to several different goals for an individual or for a relationship:

- Level 1: Relief of symptoms and correction of harmful behavior
- Level 2: Healing and correction of the inner emotional, cognitive, and/or spiritual lacunae and errors of judgment that are generating the symptoms
- Level 3: A combination of the above, which means a degree of relief of symptoms and correction of behavior to relieve major distress to put a stop to major damages of one's own life and/or to the lives of others; and meaningful healing and correction of the inner ways of feeling, thinking, and making ethical decisions from which the distress and damage are being created

Practicing and prescribing a single mode of treatment for all people and conditions is comparable to a physician's use of any single medication or therapeutic procedure for *all* medical conditions. Philosophically, this single-minded approach—which is still very widespread in mental health—qualifies for what we are calling fascist-mind thinking: blind loyalty and obedience to a stipulated ideology of treatment that is ultimate and not to be questioned. It is clearly an approach that in its essential structure is mentally unhealthy and offers lousy treatment for many patients even though it is the right treatment for some patients.

DIFFERENT THERAPY STROKES FOR DIFFERENT FOLKS

People go to therapy when they get too upset to handle life, are scared that something is really wrong with them mentally or emotionally, experience a breakdown in their ability to function, or are terrified or already deeply hurt about losing a love relationship. These are obviously justifiable reasons for going to get help from a psychological health practitioner. Psychotherapy, quite similarly to medicine, is certainly intended to give a degree of relief of severe emotional pain, repair malfunctioning, and assist in generating energy and hope to renew more effective functioning.

But also very much like good medicine, psychotherapy is a classroom for learning *how* to correct the faults and errors that create our conditions of pain and dysfunction, and *how* to go about everyday normal life much more healthfully and satisfyingly, including as much as possible preventing the onset of disturbances that are waiting to "come at us" because we are doing things unwisely. I am always excited when a physician or dentist *teaches* me how to take better care of myself. Thus—

- What a boon it was when, after endless cavities, a dentist taught me how to floss my teeth.
- With aging I learned the sad truth that the skin I live in was losing its natural lubrication and getting so dry that it actually tingled with hurt; and what a relief it was to be taught by my doctor to put on a nourishing cream while I was still wet after showering.
- "We can fix that up with surgery," says many an orthopedist to many a severely aching back; while Alexander Technique and Feldenkreis teachers and osteopaths say, "Here is the way you do these stretching exercises." I love these exercises—plus have overcome at least two "incurable" spinal problems through such exercises—first, thanks to the healing-teaching hands of good teacher-therapists (especially Alexander Technique and [British] Osteopathy), as well as Feldenkreis, and then continuing on my own.

For so many years the most accepted mode of psychoanalytic-psychodynamic therapy was a well-meaning invitation and expectation for patients to bring up from within the critical information as well as tools for understanding and recovering from their symptoms. There are many brilliant and genuinely helpful aspects to this kind of therapy, but such therapy has proven appropriate and helpful (even very helpful) only to a very small minority of patients. A majority of people simply cannot produce, or bear experiencing, the free associations and dreams from which understanding is to be developed; and a majority of people cannot generate from within their own selves really helpful ideas and especially the will power to change their ways of life. And only a minority of patients can bear the intensity of a full encounter with their "transference reactions" to their therapist so that negative feelings toward the therapist ("negative transference"), which can be a very helpful basis for learning about oneself, too often brings on premature termination of the treatment.

For years, many a genuinely well-meaning therapist continued to provide a blank screen onto which the patient was to project their innermost self, and many a treatment situation became one where there was nobody in the room who knew what to do to move ahead. Moreover, most psychoanalysts themselves had little knowledge and few to no ideas about relatively simple corrective procedures that could help people break bad cycles of pain and dysfunction. Thus I never heard of a purely psychoanalytic therapist who would coach a man how to:

- Recover from premature ejaculation by entering the vaginal garden and sit there quietly enjoying the beautiful world before galloping his horse forward
- "Relish failing" if that was going to be the case when giving a fearful public address
- Speak firmly but carefully and respectfully to a child or to a spouse about feeling insulted and pushed around—after first practicing how to do so in the therapy sessions.

Along came alternative therapies that contributed many of the missing wisdoms of counseling the patient through *active* procedures:

- Humanistic therapy shamelessly introduced new levels of appreciative acceptance and cultivation of pleasures of the senses, including a more naked sexuality. (At the first meeting of the newly formed American Association of Humanistic Psychology, I found some members actually came to a session naked—those were revolutionary times in psychology with all the excesses of revolutions).
- The behavioral therapists gave us working ideas how to desensitize even bitterly locked-in symptoms, such as desensitization of phobia—for example, a woman who had not left home including to go to work for over a year—or how not to reinforce wild behavior and how to reinforce the good behaviors of a child.
- Family therapists (also known as systemic therapists) came along and introduced the "Elementary, My Dear Watson" procedures of having people

in relationships actually tell one another truthfully what they were feeling, hating, wanting, and so on, and taught people *how* to speak even of terrible matters in ways that gave a real chance for correction and growth for all concerned.

- Existential therapists reintroduced forgotten natural wisdoms of knowing who you really are, how you really are living your life, and what is really happening all around you, for better and worse, in your era of history. So that much of therapy then includes accepting—even with thanks—whole batches of limitations, burdens, bad breaks, and so on that inevitably turn up in the existential fates of all of us along with reaching hopefully for fuller and more joyful uses of our natural faculties, talents, and potential creativity.

How do we feel about a physician who has one standard treatment—say the wonderfully useful medication of aspirin that does so much good for any number of situations—which he gives *every* patient, from a sore throat to cancer to ulcers to kidney stones to headaches, ad infinitum. That is what is happening when *one and only one* of the psychotherapies is presented by mental health practitioners to *every* patient who comes across their doorstep. Endless books can be written about the arrogance, stupidity, zealotry, and cruel insistence of therapists on the one specific wonderful technique of therapy with which they identify—and characteristically such therapists' insistence that any other form of therapy is beneath contempt. It is amazing how a large group of very intelligent, and for the most part quite decent caring people, can live out such a fascist way of insisting on a single ideological truth.

In truth, just about every technique of therapy does offer us impressive helping techniques, but each patient in their life situations and relationships requires a *selection* of techniques to fit their needs. Psychotherapy is a collection of many ways of treating people who need help to rearrange their ideas, feelings, behaviors, and ways of living. Every patient deserves a selection of the techniques that are most likely to be helpful.

Moreover, many patients, if not most, need and deserve *combinations* of several techniques in a wise sequence. The notion that to combine techniques is a violation of god-given precepts has made so much of psychotherapy far less effective than it can be, far more a variation on wishful faith healing and a frightening representation of fascist thinking in the course of what should be an ennobling democratic experience of freeing people to a good life.

Integrative Psychotherapy

Psychotherapy that is integrative designs a selection and cocktail of techniques for each person or relationship (in marriages, families, or other relationships). This is a welcome new development in the field, though it is not exactly new and in fact has been around for at least twenty years. For a long time, the concept of integrative therapy was an esoteric liberal idea that did not have that much clout in the politics of psychotherapy alongside the more mainstream "political parties" of major schools and approaches. Is the concept of integrative psychotherapy now gaining a stronger place? I think in the intellectual literature of the profession maybe yes, but I doubt that it has become a way of thinking that is encouraged with any enthusiasm in most departments, clinics or institutes.[1]

Philosophically, integrative psychotherapy is built on a democratic concept of a pluralism of methods of helping. At the core of all therapies is the relationship between therapist and patient.[2] The needed and appropriate techniques to be used are to be chosen from many options and, thank heaven, there are a lot of tools in the toolbox.

There are different times when what is called for is lots of:

- Deep sympathy
- Quiet acceptance
- Interpretation of self-defeating patterns
- Explanation and acceptance of the inadvertency of mistakes and errors coming out of one's original personal history
- Teaching new and more effective ways of going about specific functions and/or broader aspects of life
- Criticism for hurting and harmful behaviors—to one's self and/or to others
- Anger at insulting or assaultive behaviors by the patient to people in their lives
- Teaching how to love
- Therapist feeling and conveying love for the patient
- Therapist feeling and conveying combinations of love and anger for the patient (à la Donald Winnicott, who taught that this combination in turn instructed the patients how both to love and hate people in their lives[3]).
- More and more techniques

The chart that follows gives some picture of how there are many varied approaches and techniques that a therapist can apply to the very same existential focus or problems in living. We see here six different modes of therapy: Expressive-Narrative, Psychoanalytic-Psychodynamic, Cognitive, Behavioral, Family-Systemic, and Existential. There are others as well. Moreover, in each mode of therapy therapists have available to them considerable further variations in methods. The art and science of psychotherapy call on therapists to make the most responsible selections of techniques and integration of techniques for a given patient or family group.

WORKSHEET: BASIC PROCESSES IN DIFFERENT METHODS OF PSYCHOTHERAPY

		at the core of all therapy: THE HELPING RELATIONSHIP				
THERAPY PROCESS & GOAL / *EXISTENTIAL EXPERIENCES*	*Expressive—Release of Emotional Concerns, Personal Narrative*	*Psychoanalytic, Psychodynamic—Insight and Transference Work*	*Cognitive—Correction of Mind Paradigms*	*Behavioral—Correction of Behavior Patterns*	*Family, Systemic—Treating Hurts and Anger, and Upgrading Relationships*	*Existential—Accepting Life Realities, and Learning Best Use of Natural Equipment*
Desire & Ambition						
Anxiety						
Loss						
Incompetence						
Fulfillment						
Anger, Hate						
Violence						
Longing, Love, Loyalty						
Limitation, Decline, Death						

The requirement that therapists select different and multiple techniques of helping is a more democratic way of thinking about therapy compared to a fascist imposition of a single technique that is defined absolutely as always the one and only correct way.

The integration of different modes of emotional experience—sympathy, active counseling, warmth, affection, anger, and more—also represents a democratic kind of assembly of different sides of human experiencing.

RECONSIDERING THE PRESENT "FIX-IT-NOW" ERA IN PSYCHOTHERAPY

Is psychotherapy more about helping people with symptoms, helping with their style of living, helping with their personal relationships, or all of the above? All of the above.

There is no question that people very often come to psychotherapists precisely because they are ailing and suffering—although it is also true that many people come to therapy when they have begun to feel better and are ready to grow in a deeper way in their personality and character and/or in relationships. In any case, obviously the first job of a helping professional is to offer relief of distress.

However, to my regret, our modern age of do-it-now, instant-fix and instant-experiences has led an increasing number of therapists into stopping just there. Fix the pain and the patient has been served. This is also what many of the blessed damned insurance companies will pay for and not much more. And obviously the pour-medicine-down-their-throat psychiatry of our age is designed essentially to clear up symptoms. The fact that in *some* cases relieving palpable suffering indeed frees finer aspects and strengths of people's personalities to renew themselves without further professional help is not unimportant, but I think that in a majority of cases the symptoms bespeak very real complications and errors in people's management of their mind—their thoughts and feelings, style of life, and personal relationships—and that most of us will benefit from a good teacher-therapist to help us.

One must also add that in some cases relieving symptoms can do a serious disservice to a patient. The reason is that the person may now be freer to do some very wrong things to him- or herself or to others that wouldn't have been possible when the person was feeling so lousy and down and out. Thus, a depressed person who responds well to antidepressant medication can then go and commit suicide (see elsewhere our discussions of the tragic scandal of tens of thousands of such cases!). Even in family relationships, reducing a divisive alienation and encouraging old warmth to re-flower before really dealing with the deep-down hurt and anger can literally speed up further breakdown, including divorce.

There is the obverse problem in classical psychoanalysis, where a suffering person appears to be pleading for help, and according to the good books of psychoanalysis the therapist promptly leads the patient through basic techniques of meeting up with his or her deepest inner self to an intensification and worsening of the breaking down symptoms that brought the patient to treatment to begin with. Only the strong of heart and mind patients who can generate from inside of themselves a sense of relief that they are now seeing a trustworthy helping person will benefit. The many whose life experiences have left them more battered, empty, and untrusting cannot attach hope and promise to their relationship with the therapist, especially if the analyst is using classical technique and doing nothing much more than being present and asking for free associations and dreams. What this means is that those relatively few people who are privileged underneath it all to enjoy a basically strong and fertile personality can undergo the full perilous journey of psychoanalysis. Instead of getting stuck on removing symptoms, psychoanalytic therapy can get stuck on going deep, deep into the treatment of bedrock problems in the patient's personality It is a technique that can be wonderful and has been helpful (often very helpful) in many cases but only to a very small number of patients.

Overall, I believe there are two parts to psychotherapy. The one part of therapy that is generally to be emphasized in the initial and early stage of treatment pertains to symptom control, removal, and reduction—help in living with troubling symptoms. The second part, of therapy should bring about a significant educational or counseling experience for learning how to improve the management of one's mind, style of life, and personal relationships. Personally, I feel responsible for the first aspect of therapy of reducing suffering—people get into such distress and agony and really need help; but I find myself more genuinely excited and enlivened by the second part of therapy for improving one's life style.

The counseling experience also can be seen as involving two major processes, the first one stopping or correcting very wrong—meaning destructive—ways of functioning (and it will be recalled that in this book such "wrong" always refers *both* to destruction done to oneself *and* destruction done to other people); the second one learning or generating from one's creative wisdom new styles and guidelines for coping with life and fulfilling and joying oneself. The therapist needs to exercise good judgment about how much to counsel actively, suggest, or direct the patient to better ways of living, and how much to rely on and even require the patient to generate new ideas and resolutions for his or her own living. The difference is between a therapist-teacher and a therapist who supports the patient's "Eureka experiences"; both are constructive modes, and a wise mixture of the two can add to the quality of the therapy.

Here are some examples of the two parts of therapy:

- A not-so-young male patient requests help for chronic premature ejaculation. The shortest path to possible help is through the brilliant sexual behavior exercises first created by Masters and Johnson which do help many a man.[4] (Such exercises were sorely lacking for many years while psychoanalysts delved deeper into underlying emotional issues.) But in many cases what is needed even before teaching the patient the above exercises is a review of the ways the man feels about himself, and to his inner image of his mother, as well as his feelings towards his partner when he is making love to her. It makes common sense, doesn't it? As mentioned before Karl Abraham identified three main causes of "ejaculato praecox": undue self-involvement, anger at and hatred of the woman, and selfishness.[5] My own experience working with these dynamics has been that they can enable successful therapy. There are cases where couples received very fine treatment with sexual behavior tasks and for a time reported much success and pleasure, but it was not long before the scene shifted to grim outcomes because the core issues had not been addressed, and it became clear that treatment needed to be directed at the core problems of each of them and in their relationship.[6]

- A couple comes to therapy because they are battling, insulting, or in other ways showing great disrespect for one another. Teaching the couple how to listen better to one another, show respect for one another's feelings and work together toward mutually agreed resolutions even when there is continuing disagreement is fine.[7] But what about the underlying feelings toward one another? And what about the need of one or the other to express disrespect, hateful anger, screaming demands? How much of these behaviors are rooted in the specific relationship, and how much do they bespeak dark currents of troubled emotions and poor ethical standards in one or both partners which should be addressed *before* or at least *alongside* teaching the couple to communicate through guided exercises?

- A woman paralyzed by engulfing depression comes to a therapist seeking help. The first order of business is to relieve and lighten her symptoms. In this difficult case there may be at least a period of time that one wants to enable the patient the benefit of antidepressant medication. But what does it mean to treat the symptoms of depression without finding out in what ways and why the patient is giving up on her life, how much she is unconsciously seeking to hurt herself over and above the very real hurts and problems that life has dealt her? Most important, many of us therapists believe, is the question whether the depressed person is *very* angry at someone and does not know and does not process and release that anger? As has already been noted, there are too many cases where "successful" treatment of depressive symptoms alone has led to tragedy. Moreover there are studies that show good results, and in some cases a distinct long-term advantage, for therapies that seek understanding of feelings and meanings over therapies that are more plainly symptom cures.[8]

THE DIFFERENCE BETWEEN DIAGNOSTIC LISTS OF SYMPTOMS AND INTERPRETATION OF LIFE MEANINGS

One major conclusion about the mess of contemporary psychiatric diagnosis is that there has been a serious lack of differentiation between describing symptoms and interpreting them. This makes all the difference in the world when one goes into therapy. Naturally a psychologist or psychiatrist needs to describe how a person is functioning, including the ways in which the person is responding to stresses and transitions in life. But there is much more to *understanding* symptoms, putting them in contexts of their meanings for the person, and seeing them in a perspective that differentiates between breakdowns of personality versus breakdowns under stress that can be creative and possibly launch a better reorganization and new emotional growth.

Moreover, it is high time to face the truthful facts that *all* us human beings experience and react to stress. Many of our reactions are bona fide full-blown symptoms of discomfort, lack of confidence, and upset, but these do *not* qualify us as psychologically or psychiatrically disturbed or pathological. Do you or have you suffered any of the following?

- Feeling nervous and not your real self in a social situation?
- Being scared of a new job?
- Nervous about finding a new meaningful relationship?
- Hurt and angry in a relationship?
- "Breaking down" when you have had a breakup of a relationship with a lover or spouse?
- Deep mourning over the loss of a dear person in your life?
- Upset at not being accepted to the college or position you wanted so much?
- Humiliation—even being "broken"—by losing your job?

- Bewilderment at the rejection of your major project?
- Distress by a break-in to your home?
- Distress over the news of barbaric mass murder of members of your faith or whatever affiliation?
- Anger and feeling beyond hope at the rise of out-and-out fascist laws, persecutory taxation, or police actions in your supposedly democratic country?
- Worried sick about the possibility of being seriously physically sick?

If yes, you are *human*—and not a *DSM* item. In many cases it is an excellent idea to go for psychological help to overcome these difficulties and in general to advance one's emotional growth. Furthermore, it is only natural that when a person presents any of these difficulties of living that the mental health professional will give the difficulty a meaningful name, but this needs to be done carefully without sliding into giving the name of a bona fide psychiatric condition with all of its heavier implications. Being anxious does not mean necessarily an overall anxiety neurosis; being depressed does not necessarily mean a person is suffering the clinical entity of depression. And even when a "larger" diagnosis is justified, the clinician needs a language that recognizes when a person is struggling with a basically healthy crisis versus conditions where a person has broken down and surrendered their vitality.

I think that personally I may have suffered all of the conditions listed above, and yet, I feel I have been living a miraculous and wonderful life. If you don't experience a fair number of the above, check if you are alive (as in the geriatric joke that if you wake up in the morning without any pains in your body, you may be dead). If you want to be wise, go for help to get more connected to your inner experiencing and emotions.

LIFE MEANINGS THAT CAN BE MISSED WHEN TREATMENT AIMS ONLY AT SYMPTOMS

The philosophy we are advancing is that the desired goals of psychological and psychiatric treatment are a combination of helping people to relieve their anguish, or other crazy-making symptoms, and helping people to identify and correct major errors in their ways of experiencing and organizing their lives, especially the deeply personal meanings that are being played out in their primary relationships.

Treating psychiatric symptoms alone, or treating a person with the explicit aim of immediate relief of troubling symptoms may teach people how to—

- put energy into relief of discomfort more than into more basic problem-solving

- believe they are weak, vulnerable, disturbed, defective, and not the stuff of growing people and leaders in life
- be dependent on experts outside of them for solutions to life's problems
- be too dependent—perhaps to the point of becoming addicted—on chemical substances to banish discomfort and fear
- escape from authentic experiencing of truths about themselves and their way of life and their human relationships

Here is a case example of integrative treatment and its long-term outcome:

❖ She was a frightened, nervous worrywart girl. She pulled her hair compulsively (to a point of earning the scary-sounding formal diagnosis of trichotillomania), and experienced unnerving vaginal pain quite quickly after penetration in intercourse (thereby earning another terrifying name of dyspareunia). She was scared stiff about being able to find and hold a relationship with a man.

In long-term intensive individual psychotherapy, plus some family therapy, attention was given to reducing the aura of her parents superworried disaster-imminent way of life. She improved tremendously. She reduced her hair pulling by about 80 percent and overcame her vaginal pain also by about 80 percent, but most of all she fought successfully to correct her way of approaching life with too much fright. Altogether, she earned the jackpot and completed her education in a meaningful profession, fell in love and married a decent man, and had several healthy beloved children.

Some ten years later she came knocking at the therapist's door once again and asked for help first of all to reduce the remaining two 20 percents—her hair pulling, and if not vaginal pain then her feeling indifferent to lovemaking ("I can't care about intercourse so much; it's for him," which she herself knew was not the greatest way to go.) But most all she asked to increase her capacity for humor, joy, and happiness, and quite wisely, she asked to be more able to transmit this way of living to the children she loves.

She wrote me after a session: "I agree that the best way for me to have a good influence on my children is simply for me to find and create joy in myself and to fill the house with it as much as possible. I really know that I grew up in a home in which there was absolutely no legitimacy to genuine happiness. There was much more room for misery, suffering, and worry than for empathy. But I am happy that today I am in a different place, and I believe that the home in which my children are now growing up looks and feels different and this will only get better!"

If you look up her symptoms in contemporary books on psychopathology and treatment, you will find lots of absolutely meaningless recommendations for medications that often don't work, and not a word about joy and working to cultivate joy instead of "pulling one's hair out."

THE DRAMA AND BLESSING OF GENUINE PSYCHOTHERAPY

There *are* psychotherapeutic techniques for reducing symptoms, and they should be used when a patient is suffering painfully or is tied up in knots and unable to make any progress in what was intended to be depth psychotherapy devoted to redesigning the patient's way of life and relationships.

Therapists can and should give a full ear and a full heart to the unloading of stories of trauma and deep hurt. Therapists can and should give needed advice for distress, such as helping people caught in a spiral of insomnia, teaching parents how to respond to a child who has gotten into a cycle of uncontrollable tantrums, helping couples when one spouse is abusive, helping people stem discomforting anxiety attacks, and more. The silent, poker-faced, seemingly all-knowing therapist is useless in the above and many other situations where people really need immediate guidance and help.

But it makes very logical common sense that if therapists can, they should try to help a people with the *sources* of their discomforts. The sources inevitably involve the ways in which people are running their lives—including "running their minds," feelings, and values—and the truths of their relationships with others (very much including their spouse and children), the atmosphere and meaningfulness of their work, and also their relationships with extended family and community. Therapy that addresses any of these so obviously central arenas of a person's life experience is bound to have a "kick" that is stronger than what chemical substances can deliver. By analogy, sure you can get happy on a good beer or scotch, but you can damn well get happier in a more soul-filling way if you succeed in loving yourself and others.

And now there enters on our stage of human experience a further hidden yet also so obvious source of the way each one of us feels and behaves. Every one of us was once a small tyke. We needed so much in the way of physical and emotional nourishment. We needed parental protection, reassurance, guidance, and teaching. And it does not require a Wikileak for us to know that a huge number of us didn't get what we needed! Instead, many of us were subjected to a parent (or two) who was:

- infantile
- weak

- innocently naive
- selfish
- possessive
- nasty
- harmful and abusive—sexually, physically violent, or emotionally

Oh dear psychiatrists and managers of pharmaceutical companies, you too were once children weren't you? And is it remotely possible that you too were influenced by anything like the above? And do you think any of these above formative atmospheres of early life could have created any of your own mental health problems or the psychiatric conditions of your patients?

Depending on your biology and the specifics of your experiences with your parents, you grow up happy or sad, confident or nervous, driven by obligation or motivated by commitments to good things: evangelical-coercive-tyrannical or respectful-enabling-empowering of others. Doesn't it sound reasonable that if a person enjoys a therapy experience in which that person can (a) replay the major experiences of his or her childhood, and (b) connect to major ways of functioning that an in-depth psychotherapy can give, this person will have a wonderful second chance to make his or her life much better?

"For the fun of it" we now add a considered question as to what the therapist and the school of therapy to which he or she belongs intend for us? Is my therapy going to be a mode of being that is dependent on someone else pretty much for the rest of my life? There is at least one South American country where therapy is for no less than *all through life*. I have seen intelligent capable people from this country who have been seriously damaged by this form of "over-medication." The goal of almost all therapy should be to arrive at the *end* of therapy with the patient ready to go out capably with their "certificate" to their independent life.

Intriguingly, the process of good therapy basically parallels the growing up of a healthy child. It includes some degree of good healthy anger and fighting with one's therapist, an increasing freedom to see the therapist objectively, including the therapist's weaknesses and limitations, and if all really goes well, a lovely sense of friendship and potentially a warm lifelong inner connection. (In the immediate years following my psychoanalysis, I had many an internal "conversation" with my former therapist, especially when I showered, and fifty-plus years later a deep gratitude and love continue in my heart.)

All of which leads to a further obvious truth that just as there are lots of lousy parents, there are lots of lousy therapists. In both cases, it is true that many of them are innocent of conscious malicious intent. It is obviously going to be hard to impossible to get anything good out of one's second chance if one's therapist does therapy according to the books, but without heart, and

- is possessive (your success in therapy is my success; you must succeed in therapy *for me*),
- is dictatorial, ritualistic (*you must come so many times a week*),
- restricts experiencing and free speech (*remember we never talk about* [forbidden topics according to the school of therapy]),
- is insufficiently trained for the kind of therapy being conducted,
- is dominated by personal weaknesses and errors in life choices
- is not working at making progress in personal growth,
- is mainly out to make a buck and doesn't give a damn in a real way.

Successful psychotherapy—

- frees people to be alive, enjoy and use their real talents, work both at accepting and correcting their quite real defects and weaknesses, and live with a sense of meaning and commitment to life for themselves and other human beings
- helps people to be able to love *and* hate, be independent *and* dependent, strong *and* vulnerable, self-confident *and* unsure or humble, ethical yet also capable of pulling a not-so-bad fast one, and more of the brilliant pallet of natural human experiences.[9]
- restores and opens the heart to any number of people who have been left out in the cold; so that although every one of us is and ultimately will be alone as hell on the bottom line of it all, we become less abandoned and less alone in our lives.

Are you still hungry for some pills?

Of course there are downsides to psychotherapy. Aside from the bad luck of lousy therapists, lots and lots of treatment, especially for certain conditions, doesn't work or doesn't work as well as we would hope. That's true of just about everything in medicine and all of life, isn't it? But overall, for many (though not all) psychiatric conditions and relationship disorders, there is a great deal of success in psychotherapy. A good number of researches show this, and show that the long-term gains of a deeper psychotherapy last more significantly than simple removal of symptoms, such as treatment of depression by medication. Besides, if psychotherapy can really help us to clean up and improve the ways in which we are going about our lives every day and night, to fulfill more of who we really can be and want to be, and to be more decent lovers and friends, we've gained a lot more than getting rid of the headaches.

THE MIRACULOUS CURES BY INNOVATORS OF A NEW THERAPY

Here is an offer you can't turn down: I can almost guarantee you remarkably great success with a new method of psychotherapy if you will be so kind as to create it.

Actually, I may have messed up some portion of the miracle by being the one who is suggesting to you that you be an inventor, because I have intruded to some extent into your own natural excitement and your understandable self-satisfaction that you yourself—or you and your colleagues—are inspired to have as the creative innovator(s). Such excitement and pride then play major roles in the further choreography, where we see the innovator strongly dedicated to the patients who are receiving their new treatment. These patients certainly benefit greatly from the dedicated involvement and interest in their welfare. (It's enough to make many other patients crazy with jealousy, given their doctors' indifference or mechanical styles—in our day and age rarely lifting their heads from their computer screens.)

Great news! We have just created a new method of treatment for the dread illness of schizophrenia! You wouldn't believe it, but what we do is administer electric shocks to the patient—don't worry, we are constantly watching out for them that they don't get hurt. They go into grand mal convulsions, sleep it off, and after a number of sessions show marked improvement in their psychiatric condition. Why? Because we have definitely corrupted the electric pattern of their illness. Who are we? We are two Italian psychiatrists named Cerletti and Bini and the year is 1938. We are not at all con artists. We are so excited over how we can help these pathetic people. We are getting over 80 percent cures of schizophrenics. Our treatment is going to be enormously popular all over the world.[10]

Fifteen years after the innovation of electroconvulsive therapy (ECT), I was being trained in a series of accredited psychiatric hospitals in the United States (two Veterans Administration hospitals and a New York State hospital). In one of these, the authority presiding over staff conferences in which patients were assigned a course of treatment such as ECT or lobotomy was no less than the Big Boss chairman of the excellent psychoanalytically oriented department of psychiatry at my university hospital (for a time he was the psychiatrist responsible for the psychiatry section of the definitive *Merck Manual*). Several mornings a week I saw patients assemble passively and dutifully—to me it seemed like many of them were very downcast—to take their places in a conveyor belt–like sequence that headed into the operating room where ECT was administered. Personally, I could not help but be reminded of other people lining up for other rotten procedures similarly administered by authorized personnel—let the reader guess what I'm talking about—and I was aghast and furious. But I was a student in training without a voice, and to speak up also would have endangered my being kept in the program. I did have some compensation as well the funny experience that my own psychoanalytic treatment lying on a couch twice a week was in an office at the university hospital just a few doors down the hall from the office of that same guru chair of the department, and in my free association I frequently expressed my democratic freedom of free speech just a short distance from his office to curse the daylights out of the fascist who was prescribing the shocks and lobotomies.

I am not the only one who has had severe reservations about ECT, with or without grand mal seizures (a later version of ECT does not produce seizures). An article in *Medical History* that accompanied an exhibit of the first ECT machine at the Museo di Storia della Medicina della Sapienza at the University of Rome in 2011 notes suggestively that "ECT was developed within the context of Fascist Italy" and goes so far as to conclude that "the Bini-Cerletti apparatus was at one and the same time a blessing, a hope, a lie, and a profitable commercial product."[11]

But I really don't doubt that Cerletti and Bini were telling the truth. I have an image of them greeting each patient with *genuine* interest, touching them sympathetically, and following with pleasure the course of their recovery. Note how every single one of *these* procedures, doubtless in itself, is very real therapy! It became more and more obvious to me, and over the years has become an established scientific truth that *caring about patients getting better is a super-powerful treatment technique* even in tough and even in some untreatable conditions—physical and mental.

Do you want to see the same phenomenon at work in a more lovable area of mental health that has to do with the ability to make sexual love?

Please proceed to our laboratory for treatment of your failure to enjoy an orgasm—ladies, or for your coming too quickly—gentlemen. Our therapists will be Dr. William Masters, gynecologist, and the lady who was his co-therapist and researcher, Virginia Johnson (who I was sure for years was a psychologist until I watched the delicious TV series *Masters of Sex* and learned that she never completed her formal undergraduate education).[12]

You are now going to enjoy a basically very constructive treatment that in effect provides you with sexual behavior exercises for retraining you to go through the natural cycle of sexual experience more fully and effectively. The exercises begin with a lot of wholesome touching of one another, and then there will be more advanced exercises that will culminate in a wonderful climactic orgasm, Ladies, or in a respectably paced ejaculation, Gentlemen.

Note, both of you, that the exercises will be taught with a special emphasis on deepening the pleasure of *your* sensory experience.

Were these great researchers-authors ever excited about their work! Man, did they ever get super results. In their breakthrough book, Masters and Johnson reported, in entirely properly dry scientific language, successful results of 90 percent and more!

I remember reading and studying their book very soon after it was published, both as a horny guy and also as the instructor of the first or second course in Israel on treatment of sexual problems (my colleague at another university whom I did not know at the time and I have never been able to figure out which of us came first—note the playful double entendre). I realized that after years and years when psychotherapists had not a word of advice to give patients about these dysfunctions, and where patients had to wait months and years until their deeper work on their personality problems might bear fruit in better sexual functioning, these were instructional techniques and training exercises that could be immediately helpful. But then my heart sank when I ran into the 90-plus percent figures Masters and Johnson gave for their success, because I knew that there ain't no significant human foible or problem that is amenable to such hugely successful corrections.

Sure enough, the years went by and, as we saw, a psychiatrist, Helen Kaplan, pushed ahead and taught us how the Masters and Johnson techniques must be preceded and combined with work both on the relationship between the sexual partners as well as the deeper psychology of the partner who is symptomatic.[13] Later empirical research, such as by Levay and Kagle,[14] showed that roughly one-third of patients who received Masters and Johnson's treatment retained their improvement over time, and that the other two-thirds needed to be referred for a more comprehensive treatment of the relationship and personalities along with the behavior tasks, and now about half succeeded in the broader therapy and about half did not.

Again I have no reason to doubt that Masters and Johnson were reporting their results sincerely and honestly. Just go look at the TV series and you will see how, with all their personal limitations which we also learn about, both of the two innovators are absolutely devoted to the new-fangled improvements in lovemaking that they are pioneering. And devotion is in its own right therapy—very good therapy.

THE "GUARANTEED" SUCCESS OF ANY SYSTEMATIC SCHOOL OF PSYCHOTHERAPY

I can also almost guarantee you remarkably great success if you follow in a kosher way the rules and prescriptions of *any* systematic school of psychotherapy.

The mind game goes something like this: Since you are practicing a recognized method of therapy, with its history of excitement and hope at the time of its innovation, and since there were so many reports of successful treatment with this method—which in the case of most forms of psychotherapy really is a perfectly helpful technique for some patients, it is going to work some of the time.

As for the rest of the times, no worry: researcher after researcher has shown that the human mind is not only capable but virtually duty-sworn to attribute the outcome it expects to see to an event; and if in fact the outcome seriously betrays the expectation, the mind knows glibly how to explain away the failure so that it doesn't change anything of the belief in the positive outcome.

There are a great many studies that demonstrate a variety of thinking mechanisms that lead us to see and confirm whatever it is that we want to believe in. Daniel Kahnemann is a Nobel Prize–winning researcher who has done a great deal of work in this area—and has many a sad observation to make about the irrationality of our supposedly rational thinking. Kahneman's original work was done with a colleague, Amos Tversky. In one of their earlier studies they described how an "availability heuristic permits people to approximate the frequency on the basis of how easily the target comes to mind but more memorable events are not necessarily more frequent." Tversky and Kahneman observed that "a clinician may easily recall several times in which a certain intervention was associated with a remarkable improvement in a patient's symptoms, but may not recall that on many other occasions the technique was ineffectual and even counter-productive."[15] There are an endless number of medical and surgical procedures that have been seriously destructive but reigned for a long period as the respected treatment of choice (are any such around in our time, pray tell?).

For a therapist there is a beguiling sense of certainty and correctness in following the prescribed checklist of any given procedure that has been laid out by well-known "experts" and leaders in the profession who, of course, are presumed to know what they are talking about. Paradoxically, the prospects for some real healing of the patient really do improve when a therapist follows a systematic sequence also, because the therapist's self-assurance and confident expectation of success are known to affect the outcome.

Basically, however, there are endless problems associated with the regular prescription of a single treatment technique. First of all, it is a blind prescription of the same medicine for just about all ailments, and it is clear that life doesn't work that way.

Any number of family physicians are known to take the course of least resistance and prescribe antibiotics generously say for flu, or say even for the first disturbing symptoms of what will prove to be cancer. I have known personally several cases where a delay of several months of administering antibiotics and watching symptoms allowed cancers to become inoperable.

Now consider a psychotherapy equivalent of a therapist who uses the basic technique of listening to people graciously and sympathetically, no matter what is the clinical reality. At the same time no attempts are made to:

- understand the key dynamic that is creating the present disturbance;
- identify the basic error, fault, or abuse that characterized the formation of the patient's personality in the earliest years of life, or to see a possible interaction between the present key dynamic and the original damage;
- advise, counsel, teach, and encourage the patient to fight back against the people and conditions of life that are contributing to their problematic situation and suffering.

It is as if the instructions to the therapist go like this: *So just plain listen, therapist, with a properly holy face, and make it look like you're helping when you are not necessarily doing much good.* I never forget the quite distinguished psychoanalyst who told me that he had begun treating couples because business was down for requests for individual psychoanalysis, and when I asked him whether he had done any training or learned about the special issues that come up in doing marital therapy he admitted honestly that he hadn't, but he said, "All I have to do is listen and then say a few wise words at the end of the session."

Another major limitation of prescription of any single technique is that often these prescriptions do not provide a context or vehicle for utilizing critical psychodynamic knowledge that has been developed of different psychological conditions. For example, Many psychosomatic illnesses are rooted—originate and are maintained—in major relationship or experiential dynamics that are the driving forces of the physiological processes that create the illness. Thus, in the treatment of asthmatic conditions, for all the biology of allergy and infection, there is also often a deep-seated fear-system of abandonment, either the patient being left alone—say, child fearing being abandoned by his mother—and/or the patient's fear of imposing aloneness on another, generally the same person who they fear will be the one to leave. The fear triggers a rage that—with poetic permission—contributes to a raging cough, which the patient fears will get entirely out of their control and even cause (as it does periodically) death—very much the embodiment of the aloneness that has been feared. Along with medical treatment, a method of therapy that works actively with the rage and fears of abandonment is likely to help the patient meaningfully.[16]

Whatever the hormonal issues, women who suffer a serious post-partum depression—including those who develop actual psychotic symptoms—often are struggling especially with deep fears of being rejecting mothers to their newborn, just as they themselves suffered unconsciously from their own mothers. These women are among the many who never make contact with the inner truth that they themselves were not fully and genuinely welcomed-loved by their own mothers. Their family lives were often intact and entirely proper, and it is as if neither daughter or mother knew that there were some pretty lousy feelings in Denmark. Now the new mother is appropriately terrified that she will do the same mean trick on her baby and she wants to be stopped. Only a method of therapy that works actively to pinpoint the mother's fears of rejecting her baby (and in the process also helps the mother to manage constructively the realization about her own mother's rejecting feelings towards her) is likely to help the patient meaningfully and rapidly.[17]

- He is a capable—even very capable man—with a good business and good services to offer, but he is nonetheless headed downhill toward bankruptcy. Whatever be the very real economic and business realities, he is unconsciously shooting himself in the foot. It is as if his unconscious destiny is to fail. It may be a promise to whoever is inside him—himself, a sibling, or parent(s)—that he must not succeed and is obligated to fail. In many cases such men have either very, very little to say about their fathers, many of whom positioned themselves on the sidelines in their early lives, or they have a bitter critique and a story of having severed their emotional loyalty tie to a too-tough father years before. In other words, these are men without father heroes or models to guide them in winning at their work, especially when stressed and faced with difficulties. Only a method of therapy that works actively to kill off any inner message that he is to fail, and pinpoints the disappointment, longing, and rage at his father with encouragement to "create" a new and better father in himself is likely to help the patient meaningfully.

- She is sliding into her thirties without having a partner, let alone being married, but worst of all she knows inside of her that she is not likely to find one. Over and above the statistical realities and the laws of chance or even the situational realities of where she lives and works, she knows inside of herself, but doesn't want to know that she knows, that she chases them away from her. She is hardly likely to get out of her vicious circle unless she learns and does something about the fact that she is a porcupine or skunk, as it were, who chases the men away from her. Women who are defeating themselves in this way are hardly likely to win a partner without getting help to clear from their hearts the pain and loss of hope that hit them at an early age when they suffered any of the lousy events of being left by a disappearing father or mother, felt deeply unwanted, were seen as rottenly unattractive, or whatever of the many unfair tragedies that befall millions. Only a method of therapy that works actively to release the pain and aloneness in the woman's own development, and to pinpoint the style of dismissal of men who might want to love her is likely to help meaningfully.

The schools of psychotherapy that are largely dependent on the ancient belief that if patients speak from their heart sufficiently they will find the way to get well obviously will fail to help in any number of the above examples. But many later and therefore seemingly more modern and advanced methods of psychotherapy, including those that utilize much more active techniques and interaction with the patient, in many cases also do not have a machinery for releasing and counseling the patient directly about the core dynamics that are driving the system of disturbance. In many cases even when they give patients meaningful exercises to do, they do not provide for "prescriptions" and exercises that address accurately the real specific inner dynamic that is at the heart of the problem, and thereby more effectively point patients toward repairing themselves more fully and more quickly. Psychotherapists need to differentiate between people and situations where releasing one's feelings will do the trick to enable good living, and people and situations where more probing and challenging are needed to break up an unhealthy pattern, and people and situations where thoughtful rehearsals and exercises are needed to enable learning and a mastery of new habits.

There are many different therapy techniques for doing probing and challenging. Thus, Deborah Cabaniss and her colleagues ask, "What makes a formulation psychodynamic? There are many different kinds of case formulations. There are cognitive behavioral therapy (CBT) formulations, psychopharmacologic formulations, and family systems formulations—just to name a few. Each type of formulation is based on a different idea about what causes the kinds of problems that bring people to mental health treatment. . . . A psychodynamic formulation is an hypothesis about the way a person's unconscious thoughts and feelings may be causing the difficulties that have led him/her to treatment."[18]

On the other hand, there are also so many situations in life where problematic, distressing, even worrisome emotional reactions are entirely normal—and in fact—called for. Normal people experience many symptoms. Almost all of us are subject to periodic occurrences of symptoms—nervousness and fright, misery, sweating in anxiety, having trouble sleeping, phobic fear of a situation, feelings of not belonging, suspicions especially of a loved one, shame that one feels to the bottom of one's being, and many more such human reactions to stress. "We all got them"—in fact we need them as periodic responses of our humanness to our fragility and the dangers that haunt the fates of our lives, *and* at the same time as wholesome triggers and challenges to cope and grow.

In the 1950s, the great psychological-psychiatric Midtown Manhattan study was undertaken.[19] Instead of collecting responses from whatever percentage of subjects who would answer a questionnaire, researchers went from door to door to ask everyone questions such as "Do you experience such and such symptoms?" One overwhelming result was that a huge percentage of people reported some bona fide symptoms of mental illness and maladjustment.

More recently an official professional statement by the U.S. National Institute of Mental Health (NIMH) described 30 percent of people in America as *suffering mental disturbance* but without fully understanding the difference between symptoms that may well deserve attention and treatment and more serious disturbances. Fortunately, the NIMH statement at least goes on to qualify its message of doom to say that the really seriously mentally ill register a 6 percent incidence, but it offers no explanation of the earlier alarming figures because it is so stuck theoretically on medicalized thinking rather than understanding our human condition.[20]

Personally, all my life I have had to cope with major visual-perceptual symptoms, but happily I have certainly seen (word purposely chosen) a great deal of very satisfying living. I suffer from an absence of depth perception since birth. There have been more than enough activities that were tough on me, especially in childhood—drawing (forget it), cutting (I could only cut a jagged trail and got very nervous), and more, so *I even had to drop out of kindergarten*. But that year at home I learned to read and was making my way delightedly through a full-blown children's encyclopedia when I entered first grade a year later, and then within a few weeks I was skipped to third grade still and forever heavily handicapped in hand-eye activities but overall quite able to "make a good living" intellectually.

THE KEY TO PSYCHOLOGICAL AND PSYCHIATRIC DIAGNOSIS IS RESPECT FOR LIFE

Once again I return to the two criteria that I consider genuinely correct for a mental health diagnosis. Both are intended to go beyond intellectual abstractions and to be largely recognizable in our real daily lives as humans. I think they make plain common sense, and I hope they transcend cultural differences and qualify as "categorical imperatives" for the mental health to which we want our species to strive.

1. Along with the limitations and conditions a person is "given" in life, how well and self-respectfully is a person "working" with their potential for living? How energetically and wisely does a person protect and bless their life? *Self-abuse, and then denials of abuse of oneself, are psychopathological.*
2. How well does a person respond to the needs of other human beings for respect, encouragement, and protection of their opportunity to protect and fulfill themselves? *Insults, exploitation, abuse, and violence against others are psychopathological.*

There are several good psychological tests and inventories that report information to clinicians with a degree of differentiation between symptoms of stress and existential struggles in processing life, such as the differences between periods of "growing up" and psychological problems that have taken more permanent root in a person. But these instruments too, valuable as they are, largely do not provide a simple clean theoretical framework for appreciating normality with its tensions versus psychopathology with its more rooted destructiveness. Perhaps even more importantly, they also do not make the theoretical leap we propose of seeing mental health both as what we do to ourselves and what we do to others. Like medical lab tests, they bring back to the clinician important information, but often don't give a coherently intelligent overall scan of a person's functioning and a perspective on whether and how much they are trying to live and help others to live versus how much they are putting sticks in the wheels of their lives or other peoples' lives.

To my knowledge there have been two major efforts in recent years of admirable teams of scholars to create improved frameworks for psychological diagnosis, one embodied in a *Handbook of Relational Diagnosis*,[21] and the other in a *Psychodynamic Diagnostic Manual (PDM)*.[22] The work in relational diagnosis adds the missing critical dimension of the state of intimate relationships in a patient's life. The *PDM* adds a welcome probe of the dynamic meanings of a person's symptoms. We reported on the *Handbook* earlier and noted that it was created in a remarkable collaborative effort of many professional associations, but regrettably did not produce a workable diagnostic system. The *PDM*, in turn, was created by a task force of thirty-six outstanding professionals plus four more noteworthy consultants. Again, such collaboration raises hopes for breakthrough conceptions of mental health, but in my opinion regrettably here too the result has been two very rich volumes of information and understanding of psychopathology but not yet an effective workable tool for diagnosis that will free us from the mess we are in with *DSM*-like symptom checklists and convoluted definitions.

The *PDM* also advances us in that it recognizes greater normality of some symptoms and in general emphasizes that:

- Mental health comprises more than simply the absence of symptoms. It involves a person's overall mental functioning, including relationships; emotional depth, range, and regulation; coping capacities; and self-observing abilities.[23]
- Medicine has moved beyond simply describing symptoms. . . . The classification of mental health disorders may have gone to authority mandated in focusing on describing symptoms.[24]

Moreover, *PDM* also adds, though inconsistently, a concept that healthy personality involves forming moral judgments. Redemption! At last! And such indeed are the remarks of many a reader-reviewer of this book that we see in the Internet entries about *PDM*.

But, say I, not quite. Regrettably, redemption isn't here yet for the following reasons: First of all, there are plain old considerations of the usability of a book. This is an 857-page whopper, and there is nothing about the production that makes this book into a comfortably usable product. The pages on which it is printed are perfectly nice (in the usual sense of printing) but are not on tough thin paper (like the brilliant *Merck Manual* has been for years.) Second, the edition for poorer folk that I am holding has a soft cover that does not hold the book sufficiently; if you allow the natural stresses to play in lifting the book, you have to be religiously careful not to have the cover tear off. In plain English, it's a pain in the neck.

But then there is for me another even bizarre problem: Part Three of the book, which is entitled, "Conceptual and Research Foundations for a Psychodynamically Based Classification System for Mental Health Disorders," runs from page 329 to page 837 just before the index. Not that it is a crime to produce long books, but there should be a logical relationship between the parts of a single book, and in this case it is as if there are two separate worlds. The first section includes the classification of mental health disorders, and the second is a collection of important and sometimes even fascinating scientific papers and reviews of issues in mental health diagnosis, but these are not the kind that one thumbs to use in a classification system. They constitute a good old-fashioned sit-down reading book. One has to tote around a heavy and annoyingly precarious monster and doesn't at all feel free to use it in a look-up mode for diagnosing a clinical case, nor do I even feel comfortable doing my beloved sit-down reading of the scholarly chapters because the book even sits physically too heavily on my lap.

OK, OK, but does this manual finally bring us a new and wiser Torah of diagnosis of mental disorders than the symptom-hoarding DSM that you have been complaining about for so long?

Well, yes, well maybe, but no. The main reason for the no, in my judgment, is that the authors have bent over backwards way too far to complement and compliment the *DSM*, or in plain language not to make enemies and alienate people in the establishment to which so many of them are connected. For me, the result is that the serious efforts at new levels of interpretation and classification of mental disorders are fed into and absorbed by the traditional *DSM* nosology. As a practitioner and a person trying to understand mental disorders more fully, I am often left bewildered and disappointed by a feeling that I have been told that I can't *really* exercise my mind freely to understand a mental problem without using the religiously mandated language that psychiatric authorities have laid down for my political correctness. Several reviewers call the presentation of *PDM* as complementary to *DSM* a wise move. One reviewer writes: "This is a bold and accomplished attempt by the psychoanalytic collaborative to produce a diagnostic manual that respects the phenomenological astuteness of the *DSM-IV-TR*, whilst assertively departing from it and offering a personality centered nosology for categorizing psychological difficulties."[25] But another writes, "The *DSM* is unfortunately too entrenched to be dislodged."[26]

Altogether, I am left with some wonderful new diagnostic ideas, not to speak of the hundreds of pages of fine research papers, but in a context where I continue to feel that I don't really have handily available simple make-sense and easy-to-look-up commonsense diagnostic labels, and that I continue to be imprisoned by demands that I stay loyal to the catechism rendered by my superiors.

From my point of view, improved diagnostic criteria such as diagnosis of relationships and attention to psychodynamics are very fine and usable insofar as a diagnostician can get to focus on the criteria given, but in both the above books the results are complex lists that are hard to use. The proposal I am now making is, first of all, to use only two main criteria for all cases so that we gain the advantages of parsimony, inclusiveness, and a sharper focus on key meanings. Above all we place the focus on the meaningfulness of a person's life and capacity for good living more than on symptoms of upset. The stipulation of two interrelated axiomatic definitions of mental health—how we treat ourselves and others—give us a simplified handy basis for psychological and psychiatric diagnosis, and more true-to-life pictures of people.

The proposal I am making of focusing simultaneously on how a person is treating him or herself and how a person is treating other human beings, if adopted, is a major step forward in our basic theory of psychopathology. Mental health is no longer simply feeling good in whatever one is doing in one's life, but is defined by doing the *right* things as a human being, constructing, protecting, and advancing life—one's own life and the lives of others, and not being destructive of life—one's own life and the lives of others. I think this is an expression of a universal ethic. The single defining criterion of mental health is being good to life. After establishing this basic platform it is fine—indeed advisable—to go on to many more criteria such as these previous studies give, but these additional criteria must flow consistently from the basic axioms.

The key to psychological and psychiatric diagnosis and treatment is respect for life. The facts are that all sorts of destruction of life are also built-in natural parts of our human equipment, but the challenge is to put these destructive instincts into minor positions, to sublimate them and channel their power for life, and not to destroy life.

HOW TO SPOIL GOOD THERAPY TECHNIQUES BY EXAGGERATION

Continuing our basic theoretical structure about democratic minds vs. fascist-type thinking, we have also applied the concepts to the thinking and behaviors of therapists and say that psychotherapists' certainties that any single treatment approach fits all people and conditions are, disconcerting as it sounds, also a type of fascist thinking. Why such strong words as "fascist" or "totalitarian"? Because it is the application of an authority-mandated, politically correct way of treating people, instead of a scientifically oriented health practice looking to match the best possible available techniques of therapy to the needs, talents, and limitations of a given patient or family.

As we have said, too often therapists operate in the name of a given professional establishment that imposes with certainty what is often almost like a religiously ordained school of therapy. And heaven help any therapist in the social-professional network of that school of thought or technique if said therapist sinfully deviates from the prescribed ways. Thus, some years ago it was "criminal" for an individual therapist to dare to see another member of the patient's family such as a husband or wife; in much of puritan and litigious America today, a therapist who *dares* to touch the body or even the hand of a patient in friendship and warmth may face charges and a law suit for sexual harassment; and I think that the most emotionally sinful of all actions in the contemporary culture of psychotherapy in the United States for a therapist is to express a clear-cut moral opinion about the behavior of the patient.

For serious students of intellectual history and for psychotherapists who are genuinely interested in helping their patients, a virtual comedy-tragedy takes place in our mental health profession when patients do *not* respond constructively and happily to the specified one and only technique. These patients are soon defined as "highly resistant," because of their resistance and in many cases are labeled the more "seriously emotionally disturbed," which means beyond the reach of the one true method of therapy that of course only does wonders and saves everybody else who is not so perverse.

Years ago I was invited to write a review article about "the new psychotherapies . . . progress or fads?"[27] This was at a time when the field of psychotherapy was just emerging from the certainties of a very few techniques of treatment (mainly psychoanalysis and Rogerian client-centered therapy—which of course vied competitively with one another) and other new techniques were being developed. Basically I respected and celebrated all the new developments, and this is the way I feel forty years later. I recognize that there are very wonderful and valuable aspects of therapy in virtually every school or method that has developed over the years. But is there any one of these many methods that has not been set up officiously and quasi-religiously, if not by their founders then by over-devoted loyal adherent practitioners who go on to demand complete and slavish ritualistic loyalty to mandated procedures and a political kind of loyalty to the technique?

Thus with respect to several major modes of psychotherapy:

Psychoanalysis—this is the brilliant "mother-technique" of penetration into the unconscious mind, but see the many forms of utter nonsense of ritual proscriptions that accompany psychoanalysis through the years: there shall be no small talk or friendship with your patient; give only a selfish minimum of verbal response within the sessions; refuse to listen to let alone speak about issues that deviate from the mining of the unconscious, such as about marital problems, tensions at work, concerns with contemporary social-historical issues in the world, and much more. Thus, it is well known that over a long period of time psychoanalysts *refused* to listen to Holocaust survivors' accounts of the concentration camps and killing camps. "You have a job here to which you must dedicate yourself completely of free associating and talking about life events in your childhood family."[28]

Shamai Davidson, an Irish-Israeli psychiatrist and psychoanalyst who was devoted to treatment of Holocaust survivors summed up his experiences in the field in this way:

> In psychiatry too, the avoidance of the subject of the Holocaust was overwhelming—and I do not believe it has stopped occurring. Through the 1970's,

> psychiatric cases were presented, and reports of psychoanalysis were presented in professional mental health meetings and *not a single remark* was made in respect of the fact that the patient was a survivor, or that the patient's parents were victims of the Holocaust. The extent of denial and dissociation even in mental health services in Israel was not believable.[29]

Psychiatrist Robert Krell, a genial man who is himself a child survivor, wrote a scathing indictment of the "perversion of psychiatry" and how patients' "denial of the events of the persecutions" were "supported by the therapists' own need to deny."[30]

My own experience over the years is that I have heard from one patient after another in the United States, England, Australia, and even in Israel how their psychoanalyst ruled authoritatively that their psychoanalysis was no place to unburden about their Holocaust experience.

> ❖ One American lady psychoanalyst who was herself also a concentration camp survivor who was visiting Israel contacted me to exclaim, "In my own analysis, I was told that speaking about the time I was in a camp was resistance to the therapy. It has simply remained bottled up in me. I can't thank you enough for giving me permission and encouraging me to talk about what happened to me."[31]

I don't think it is an exaggeration to say that the absolute rules created by some psychoanalysts also constitute the kind of censorship characteristic of fascist thinking. Note how this happens in the course of a procedure that is supposedly dedicated to greater freedom of the mind (which it is when practiced well)!

Client-centered or Rogerian therapy—During the heyday of Rogerian therapy there was a whole stock of jokes by graduate students about how the therapist is to reflect *anything* whatsoever that came out of the client's mouth. In this satirical vein, in the unfolding rottenness of our contemporary world, you might have something like, "So, what you want to do is to kill as many people as possible when you blow yourself up as a suicide bomber. I understand you don't really want to waste your life on just a small number of victims." Even according to the politically correct conception of therapy today it would seem to be an absolute violation of the sacred for the therapist to say, "For God's sake, what you're thinking of doing is totally wrong," and for many years the same code would have looked askance at reporting the miserable would-be killer to police or a security agency.

Behavior therapy—Behavior therapy has often given us wonderfully effective techniques that have saved many a wandering and failing psychodynamic therapy where patients were getting much worse because the therapist didn't have the slightest notion about how to tell them and help them to behave in healthier ways in their real lives. So many reinforcement techniques (positive and negative) have proven very wise and helpful. And how helpful it is for therapists and people to know how to count improvement in terms of relative changes in the numbers of incidents (e.g., a reduction in rebellious outbursts of a child) rather than to seek absolute change and perfect behavior. But like all the other therapists inclined to totalitarian thinking, many behavior therapists also turned to open mocking and rejecting everything—like insight, dream analysis, or warm relationships—other than the wares that they were selling.

❖ I was once faced with a situation where I was unable to help a middle-aged couple where the husband had stopped having erections. A colleague behavior therapist virtually promised me that he would save the day. I referred the couple to him and he proceeded wisely to teach the wife and husband to celebrate the man's waking-up-from-sleep erection, and in fact helped them to make good use of it for the first time in some years! He called me to tell me the news himself bursting with pride. But lo and behold—I later learned from my colleague that the man's unconscious caught on that it was being defeated, and he never had another waking-up erection after that. *Mind proved mightier than penis-body.*

Existential therapy—This is my own beloved major mode and philosophical container for thinking about therapy, so of course I will have "only" good things to say (joke). How beautiful is coming to terms with and accepting with a combination of submission and even gratitude the different realities of our lives, including a bunch of those realities that if we could have been in charge of nature and fate, we definitely would not have welcomed. Ah, how beautiful is going with nature and reality and the miraculous invitations of life. But a blind totalistic devotion to existential reverence and integrity have also meant that some halo-anointed therapists don't have the tools to stand up to harder realities, such as people who beat their spouse or kids, thieves and criminals, evil schemers, or even overly good souls who are declaratively "happy" while being passive, unproductive, and dependent on others and need much more than self-acceptance to get them up to take a more real part in life. Being what you "really are" can be the big mistake of a person who is going in a wrong direction.

JUST WHO IS IT THAT OWNS THE THERAPY AND ITS SUCCESS OR FAILURE?

Here are two illustrations of common everyday scenes, the first in the world of surgery, the second in the world of psychotherapy.

- "Damn, he died on me," mutters the surgeon angrily ripping off his surgical mask moments after the poor patient has left the world.
- "I have succeeded in healing such and such number of patients who were [name of psychiatric condition or relationship disorder]," says the psychotherapist who feels his reputation rides on every case (outcome).

It is clear to me that the odds for recovery and emotional health vary objectively for the various conditions we are called on to treat, and also vary objectively with the differing psychological, demographic, sociological, and other characteristics of the patient, as well as the unknown fortune of how a specific patient and a specific therapist do or do not fit one another. But I have always been impressed with the fact that, especially in the deeper therapies where there is a crisis of real choice to be faced by the patient whether or not to break through to grow, and especially in relation to the more complex psychological-psychiatric and relationship disorders, that there is a brilliant and I think spiritual unknown as to which of our patients is and is not going to win—at *their* therapy and life. I am fascinated by the process that we therapists are privileged to observe, accompany, and to some extent treat and influence. But I am convinced that the ultimate real choice-decision and steps taken to bring on health are the privileged choices of the patient in the drama of his/her life. I really mean it that I never know in advance who will win. I can guess. I can cheer in my heart or even out loud for those whom I become especially prayerful and/or hopeful for. But I never really know. It is their miracle. It is their triumph. And it is their loss and tragedy if they don't make it.

I am responsible—very responsible—for the quality of the job I do with them on their behalf, and of course I give myself grades for my professional performance. Moreover, I am open to and at times explicitly seek the judgments of my professional colleagues as to whether I did as good and as correct a job as possible in delivering the techniques of psychotherapy that are available to me and to our profession as a whole at our given stage of knowledge. These judgments of me, by myself or by others, are legitimate and very much needed, because I have a definite responsibility to use the best knowledge available to attempt to help patients. But the outcome of therapy is "owned" by the patients, and there should *not* be judgments of the therapist as a direct result of the outcome. When patients mobilize a marvelous push and consummation of ridding themselves of wrong ways of living and replacing these ways with a resonant commitment and wise efforts to healthier living, it is their win and to their credit. On the other hand, if patients make the effort and don't succeed, or if, as clearly happens, perfectly nice looking intelligent and sometimes even not-so-sick patients don't generate a real drive or follow-through on the real-life steps that are necessary for them to get out of a mental or relationship disability, it is they who don't make it. It is their sad loss, and it is they who pay the price.

In each respective case, the therapist may appropriately celebrate or mourn, but these feelings, too, should be devoted predominantly to the patients rather than to the therapist's ego.

There are actually real treatment implications to these choices with regard to increasing or reducing the odds for the likely success of a therapy. It has long been cautioned that therapists must correct themselves if they find that they want the patient to get well more than the patient wants to get well. Too strong a presence of the therapist's wishes and hopes, or, worse, demands, take away from ownership by the patient of his or her own life and critical choices.

Cases that involve a very serious decision by patients, such as whether or not to commit suicide or whether or not to make a major life change, will show how much a therapist is functioning on behalf of the patient versus his or her own ego or prideful involvement. Thus therapists who because of their concern about how *their* reputation will be affected panic that a suicidal patient may die are also known to panic in their management of the suicidality by:

1. referring patients overly urgently for "psychiatric treatment"—which means putting the case in the hands of a medical doctor and medications so that the therapist will be absolved of responsibility—in the process conveying to the patient the therapist's terror and lack of confidence in patient's ability to negotiate their suicidal feelings, and a considerable expectation of a negative outcome;
2. referring patients for hospitalization in a psychiatric hospital—and in the process again conveying dread and a lack of confidence, which may contribute to the well-known statistics of how many suicidal patients in fact take their lives either in the hospital or immediately after being discharged from the degrading, depressing, uninspiring experience of being protected custodially rather than treated spiritually for the life-determining choice they have to make.

Obviously it all takes us back to the critical aspect of parent-child upbringing as to who is to be the major beneficiary of a child's success and who is to be the major loser in a child's lack of success. Once again, I recall a wonderful lesson I enjoyed being taught early in my career as a therapist by a gifted child psychiatrist who was the director of the children's psychiatric hospital in which I worked. He was an inspiring teacher. He said to me: "If you want a shorthand way for establishing the psychiatric diagnosis of a child and the extent of his disturbance, ask yourself a series of questions, '*For whom?*'

- For whom does the child breathe?
- For whom does the child eat?
- For whom does the child urinate? Defecate?
- For whom does the child smile?
- For whom does the child feel sad? Worried? Happy?
- For whom does the child learn?
- For whom does the child play?
- For whom does the child recover from illness?
- For whom does the child dream of the future?
- And more. . .

My teacher then concluded: Insofar as the answers mount up that the child is functioning, whether well or poorly, *for* someone other than himself, you have a likely measure of the extent of his psychiatric disturbance, and also a meaningful hint as to his prospects in treatment. I found this to be one of the most instructive lessons I ever had in my professional experience.[32]

Alice Miller, a German psychiatrist, wrote a most impressive book titled *The Drama of the Gifted Child* in which she makes the point overwhelmingly clearly that so many of the curses of children's difficulties flow directly from pressures, demands, and intended ownership of children and their experiences by one or both parents.[33] Countless psychotherapies have been devoted—often very successfully but not always—to setting free "slaves" of all ages from such captivity and possessive ownership.

❖ One very adult, thoughtful, and even brilliant patient of mine, a theologian by profession, described the recurring image in his mind of his earnest and dignified (I met her personally) mother opening up her blouse and pushing her breasts at him whenever he would go off too much toward his own independent life, or alternatively when he was weak and chose to regress to self-indulgence. He had come to therapy because he felt so shaky and inadequate and unsure of himself notwithstanding his status as a brilliant theologian.

Have we strayed too far from our larger and central goal of thinking of psychotherapy for building a more democratic mind? Parental possession of a child is in fact a form of subjugation, and dictatorial power over the spirit and freedom of children to grow for themselves. Psychotherapists who stake out too much of a claim on their patients' lives and/or go too far, even in their inner feelings, let alone in their overt behaviors, trying to control the life outcomes of their patients are attempting to boss the lives of others more than to treat–help. This is a professional version of what we prefer to call totalitarian or fascist thinking. Democratic mind frees people to *their* potential, choices, and destinies.

CHOICES TO BE MADE FOR THE GOAL OF THERAPY

It isn't simple. If the therapist goes in with blazing six shooters to clear up *everything* that is troubling a person or a family unit, in a great number of cases the goal will be totally beyond the reach of the patients, and the very effort to treat and cure unresolvable symptoms and issues will guarantee the failure of therapy altogether. In this respect the really important issue is not the therapist's win-lose statistics and pride, but the fact that a failed therapy often sets people back and in many cases contributes to a paralysis for making a new effort to get help from another therapist.

❖ In my first marriage, my wife and I made an effort to get therapy for one of our children. The therapist who had come to us well recommended by a colleague turned out to be an ex-con who had been jailed as a Russian spy and had studied psychotherapy in a distance-learning course while in jail! He really didn't know what he was doing and we had to leave him, but we were demoralized and it took us a few good years before we got our child to another therapist.

The goals of therapy include both "essential" goals and "desirable" or elective goals, not that there is a guarantee that the essential goals will be reached either, but these are the conditions of disturbance that by definition cry out for treatment and correction if at all possible. One of the reasons I liked the good number of years I spent treating patients in psychiatric hospitals was that the severity of the condition that led to the person being hospitalized in effect justified intensive and at times innovative efforts at therapy. But some of these treatments that can be done when there are hospital safeguards including a guaranteed availability of a therapist cannot be done in many cases in outpatient private therapy.[34]

There is a classic Jewish saying, "Don't put an obstacle in front of a blind man." The choice of goals for therapy needs to be both ambitious and circumspect. The choice needs to be both humane and thoughtful.

But there are many times when we treat patients meaningfully for far more than they have asked. Inside *my* head I have had the experience many times of treating people as if for conditions that didn't actually exist, such as potential psychosomatic illnesses, which I had reason to believe loomed ahead in their lives if they did not address certain aspects of their way of being and living. Obviously this is dangerous thinking, if only because it is not grounded scientifically in observations of existing facts, and there is no way of proving that a condition that did not exist was prevented from happening. Still it is all very real. In medicine too, so many treatments and procedures aim at preventing illnesses that there is good reason to believe are on the way. One of the great gifts of science is that it also provides us with a body of information about likely future outcomes of processes that are in motion at an earlier date. Thus, in our field of psychotherapy that we are discussing, I also see indications and warnings of possible breakdown in suicide or madness or criminality and the possibility of preventing some of them from developing through treatment interventions that address the emerging danger. Paradoxically, the failed efforts can prove the point more.

❖ I remember one case of a couple consulting me about the embezzlement of money from the family business by one of their children and my counseling them that they needed to find an attorney who could play a severe judicial-like role and impose on their son a written legal-like document (with plenty of wax on the seal at the end) which would require him to repay the funds (albeit in installments based on his income and resources), and if not that his embezzlement would be reported to the police. The parents did not take my advice. Their son became progressively criminal also in his dealings with people outside the family and in a number of years he ended up in jail.

The assessment of probabilities of dangers lying ahead in a person's life includes a whole variety of psychosomatic illnesses, injury proneness, marital failure, disturbed children, failures in careers, and plenty of good old psychiatric conditions that bespeak an inability to stand up to life's stresses, despair, regrets and shame, overpowering rage, and more.

So here I am on one hand cautioning against setting goals for psychotherapy that patients can't reach, but on the other hand, encouraging setting goals that go even beyond the territory of what are known factual symptoms and issues. Not quite contradictory, but certainly complex and befuddling.

There are plenty of additional considerations as well, such as what are the implications of the outcome of treatment for other members of the patient's family? We also have to think about what contributions therapy can make to the fulfillment of undeveloped or emerging talents in a person, and what price it is worth paying in the way of tension and anxiety to access these talents?[35]

A contrasting side of the same coin can well be whether a therapist should seek changes in a person who is already expressing a serious talent, say such as an artist who is clearly overdoing his artistry (e.g., a "mad" painter or writer), or a devoted scientist who is in the lab "twenty-four hours a day." It may be very clear that therapy will be for the benefit of this person's mental health and/or to the benefit of others in their lives, but therapy that leads to a more sane restructuring of person's life necessarily can also lead to some reduction in productivity. I have had psychology students arguing this question back and forth more than once. Do we want the great art of a crazy guy? Do we care whether the spouse and/or children of a world-class scientist or medical practitioner feel terribly because he is never home with them and they never really enjoy a sense of being together? Personally, even though I love talent, I opt strongly on the side of a more balanced life.

Even in the cases of florid psychiatric conditions there are big-time questions about what should be the goals of therapy. For example, how much should therapy aim for more meaningful interactions with family intimates for a reticent and withdrawn person who can be helped to come out of actual madness so long as the emotional atmosphere and the subsequent demands of life on him are not too challenging? *Real* life on the high wire of fuller marital and family experiences by definition involve a fair amount of natural tensions and conflict, which can be tonics for growth for emotionally healthier people but can break an emotionally weaker person. Each time therapists have a major decision to make in setting the goals of therapy, and there are any number of times where discretion calls for more limited goals. The beautiful metaphors of healing in psychotherapy, which are wonderfully real as far as they go, also have been used to camouflage the great complexities of judgment that therapists are called on to render. Therapists have enormous responsibilities for the judgments they make about what will and won't be attempted. The "answers" to these choices are only partially given by the scientific facts of the ailments of the patient.

Therapist's choices call for profound ethical wisdom, and even a degree of spiritual inspiration for how best to advance as many lives as possible, and the raw truth is that virtually no therapist gets that much training along these lines. *I think* the situation is a little better in medicine, but there too, and in fact in every area of life that I can think of, we all stumble into our various good or bad luck as to the skill and integrity of the professionals who assist us. Do you know anyone who has not had some really bad caper with a teacher, accountant, lawyer, medical doctor, other health care professional, let alone with a shrink? In sum, setting the goals for therapy requires a great deal of clinical knowledge and excellent scientific judgment as well as lots of integrity and inspiration. Good luck to us all![36]

DECIDING WHICH THERAPY IS THE BETTER ONE FOR ANY GIVEN CONDITION AND PERSON

Still and all, it is unnatural not to ask which treatment is preferred for any given condition. The horrible problem is that in too many cases the therapeutic mode that has made it to the head of the current "scientific" hit list with its huge weight of political correctness is really not the best way to go. That's the point also in the amazing development of a widespread use of "alternative therapies" in medicine—in some Western countries there are more patient visits to alternative healers than to conventional physicians. In an impressive number of cases, alternate treatments that were bitterly condemned by organized medicine end up after many years being offered by the medical establishment—today many hospitals and medical centers house departments and programs of alternative treatments.

It is not within our scope in this book to discuss fully the treatment options for each psychiatric condition, but let's look briefly at one example of the research literature about treating depression—the condition most frequently cited as the most common psychiatric disorder of our time. Our purpose is both to learn more about treating this condition, but also to illustrate how there are conditions that are amenable to more than one mode of psychotherapy, and that regardless of the technique what may count the most is the combination of the patient really trying to overcome the problem with the therapist's help and a basically constructive relationship between therapist and patient. The overall good news is that a large number of studies have come to the conclusion that pretty much all psychotherapies are effective.[37]

It is especially important to note that many studies report good results for psychodynamic therapy and/or interpersonal therapy, since in recent years the smart alecks in psychology and psychiatry have shamelessly degraded anything to do with psychoanalysis and its false prophet Sigmund Freud. Thus, a study from São Paulo, Brazil, concluded that interpersonal therapy for depression is superior to placebo, similar to medication, and that its effectiveness did not increase when combined with medication. The authors write that "Overall, IPT [Interpersonal Therapy] was more efficacious than CBT [Cognitive Behavior Therapy]. Current evidence indicates that IPT is an efficacious psychotherapy [for depression] and may be superior to some other manualized psychotherapies."[38] Another study also reported on the significance of attention to the thoughts and feelings of the patient towards the therapist.[39]

How much is therapy for strengthening, maturing, and freeing generativity and creativity? On the surface of things, it hardly seems logical to question whether relief of symptoms and suffering should be put off or delayed by a therapist, nor does it seemingly make sense to question whether the goal of reducing human distress at times should be restrained and kept to a minimum. After all, what red-blooded person is not out to feel good and free of major pain? There are a million sayings about how life is for feeling good and taking as much pleasure as one can while one can, and not wasting life on bad feelings or suffering.

But it turns out that the subject is deserving of much more serious thinking. Very often, people reach new heights of pleasure and meaningfulness and creativity precisely *because* they first had to endure big-time discomforts—anxiety, indecision, fearfulness, and even major failure in their earlier efforts before they could put together a really winning effort. Thus, this can be true in respect of developing an ability to love. This can be true in respect to being able to rise to new heights of leadership. It is also true on a "molecular level" of learning how to feel well and live well with one's body and physical capacities, where it is only after some pretty serious skirmish with illness or disability that a person may really connect to their privilege of health and create a healthy lifestyle. *New York Times* columnist, David Brooks, whom we saw writing about pain as "holiness," has also written eloquently:

> When people remember the past, they don't only talk about happiness. It is often the ordeals that seem most significant. People shoot for happiness but feel formed through suffering. . . . Suffering gives people a more accurate sense of their own limitations, what they can control and cannot control. . . . Even while experiencing the worst and most lacerating consequences, some people double down on vulnerability. They hurl themselves deeper and gratefully into their art, loved ones and commitments. The suffering involved in their tasks becomes a fearful gift . . . and very different than that equal and other gift, happiness, conventionally defined.[40]

PSYCHOTHERAPY BENEFITS GREATLY FROM A DEMOCRATIC PLURALISM

Healthy controversy in a profession is "democratic" and it is also a path toward progress. Rigid beliefs in a given single theory or approach, accompanied by refusals to entertain and use information that comes from other theorists or from different techniques obstructs progress (and constitute fascist thinking). And since we are talking about a clinical field of treatment of human beings, the result is shortchanging and harmful to many patients who don't receive the more promising treatment that is available.

For many years there have been babyish tyrants who have walked large on the land of psychotherapy with a dumb and coercive insistence on one or another school of thought and therapy. At any given point the seminars and especially the workshops such gurus would conduct in themselves were impressive and charming as they would describe, basically authentically, the beneficial outcomes of cases treated in their therapeutic mode. But looming always in the dark background was the unspoken question whether this guru could respect and endorse the use of other treatment techniques? If for whatever reason your overall professional career path put you in a given department in a university or a hospital or even in various professional societies that were largely devoted to a one-and-only psychotherapeutic approach, you would pay a heavy price up to and including a "fatal" end to aspects of your career if you deviated let alone criticized the prevailing god.

❖ I don't know where I got it from but I consider myself very, very fortunate that I enjoy a built-in need to evaluate critically (that does not mean angrily, it means probing for understanding) just about any approach to just about anything in my life and work. When I was in graduate school for my PhD in clinical psychology as well as in psychoanalysis for the first time after I had experienced a breakout of anxiety symptoms, I spent hour after hour in the library of the medical school of our university, whose department of psychiatry at the time was a true haven for psychoanalysis, and after some two years of intensive reading I allowed myself to come to a conclusion to which I subscribe to this day: 60 percent of the literature on psychoanalysis is nonsense and a kind of word masturbation, showing off, or professional competitiveness, but the core of psychoanalysis as a method for accessing the unconscious and the truths of our deep and complex feelings and thoughts, including the techniques of free-association, dream interpretation, and transference-based intervention, are brilliant and enduring breakthroughs to a real (and democratic) psychology—and I love them.

It has been little short of disgusting and dispiriting to have the leaders and devotees of one school of therapy after another insist on purely orthodox ritualistic execution of their conception of their own therapy and aggressively and arrogantly disparage alternative treatment approaches. The examples are endless. In many a psychoanalytic hegemony you were required to do a huge number of almost daily sessions for every patient. And the heavens would roar in anger if you dared to respond to a request let alone yourself initiated meeting with any other member of the family (it took years before a speaker at one psychoanalytic conference dared to ask his audience how many of them also saw other members of the patient's family, and for whatever reason there was an atmosphere of freedom that day that enabled a not small number of brave heretics to raise their hands and tell the truth.)

Similar statements can be made about so many other schools, including more than a few that insist on extensive training and then formal certification of a therapist in their mode. Therefore, much professional learning in the field of psychotherapy becomes in no small part an experience in indoctrination and professional socialization of therapists that turns into a coercive ritual, with heavy sanctions looming for anyone who does not obey the prescribed dicta meticulously.

Try speaking to an imago therapist—a wonderful method of treatment in my judgment—about any other approach to couples therapy, for example, behavioral techniques or a psychodynamic approach to free association of deeper feelings.

Try speaking to an EMDR trauma therapist—a wonderful method of treatment in my judgment—about analyzing the survivor guilt of a soldier suffering post-trauma.

Try speaking to a so-wholesome therapist who bestows positive psychology on patients—a wonderful method of treatment in my judgment—about the legitimacy of anger and the desirability of tapping that anger in one's own mind for one's own energy and for actual interpersonal dialogue with the person who is the object of one's anger.

Try going into many if not most university psychology departments in our times and raising respectful reservations about cognitive behavior therapy (CBT)—a wonderful method of treatment in my judgment; or moving into the emerging science fiction future of what I am sure is going to be a host of chemical and physical manipulations of brain functions in response to the fascinating information that is developing in brain science. In these contexts, try speaking about the real needs of human beings to talk out emotional hurts, angers, ethical dilemmas, and whatever concerns. In all these cases, you have a good chance of finding yourself DOA.

What also deserves special mention is that many of the newer therapies were developed or promoted not as alternative treatments that could better suit given patients, but as entirely superior replacements of psychodynamic treatment, which was now treated as passé, anachronistic, and foolishly ineffective. The derogation of psychodynamic therapy, then, also took on a more scientific face, as it were, when certain treatments, like CBT, were crowned "evidence based," and now ridiculous old-fashioned psychodynamic treatment was treated with snickers as if it were a hoax.

The further tragedy of the above, as we keep pointing out, is that just about every treatment technique that has been developed really has some fine healing power to it. The variety of ways for offering patients help gives us a much richer set of resources that should allow much more matching of styles of treatment to patients' needs and characteristics.

The subject is a powerful one that warrants a book in its own right, but here we want more simply to reestablish not only the facts of so many clinical or case reports by responsible therapists, which have established the effectiveness of psychodynamic therapy, but also an increasing number of scientific studies of its effectiveness. Thus, Jonathan Shedler summarizes a review of the literature:

> Empirical evidence supports the efficacy of psychodynamic psychotherapy. . . . Patients who receive psychodynamic psychotherapy maintain therapeutic gains and appear to continue to improve after treatment ends. . . . The perception that psychodynamic approaches lack empirical support does not accord with available scientific evidence. . . . Non-psychodynamic therapies may be effective in part because the more skilled practitioners utilizes techniques that have long been central to psychodynamic theory and practice.[41]

Psychodynamic Therapy works. There are by now enough studies that report equal to superior outcome for the much aligned dynamic therapy and the duration of the results it gives. Thus see the meta-study by Leichsenring, and Leibing.[42] The study concludes that basic or central assumptions of psychodynamic psychotherapy were confirmed by the empirical studies they reviewed. Intriguingly this study is also cited specifically in an NIMH advisory to the public about various forms of psychotherapy. Although NIMH is obviously biased toward the current in-vogue CBT, it nonetheless concludes on the basis of this study that "23 clinical trials involving psychodynamic therapy found it to be as effective as other established psychotherapies."[43]

Apropos of the biases of researchers and thinkers, I assume the reader knows one of my biases is showing. As a former patient and as a practicing therapist, I really appreciate psychodynamic therapy. However, I am happy to say that in my professional work I combine it integrated with other approaches, especially existential and family systems approaches and also cognitive and behavior therapies. The result is that I feel reasonably equipped for a large number of different psychiatric problems—*though not all by any means.*

Finally, we know that this subject of the effectiveness of psychodynamic therapy also brings us back to a core issue of whether optimally we heal distress and aim for symptom removal or we try as much as possible to treat people to get the best and most out of themselves and their lives. I join wholeheartedly in working toward this goal whenever possible. This is how Shedler concludes his meta-analysis:

> The evidence indicates that the benefits of psychodynamic treatment are lasting and not just transitory and appear to extend well beyond symptoms remission. For many people, psychodynamic therapy may foster inner resource sand capacities that allow richer, freer and more fulfilling lives.[44]

CONCLUSION

For all their sweetness, children are naturally black-and-white thinkers. They do not have the tools for understanding and tolerating nuances. They are thrown completely by contradictions, so that by definition the thinking of children, or what we can call the default original program in the minds of all of us, is a rigid, totalistic, inflexible, tyrannical, threatening insistence on whatever. It is truly sad to see how many ostensible grown-ups who are professionals in our field of psychotherapy behave like such children in flagrant violation of the procedures and rules of scientific thinking that call us to openness and inquiry.

The promise of a mature field of psychotherapy lies precisely in the multiple wisdoms that are contributed by different wonderful thinkers and multiple schools of psychotherapy. So long as each school also respects other techniques and encourages therapists to choose the most appropriate techniques for each patient, we all gain. In many cases a combination of several tools is best, always in a genuinely caring relationship and maturely thoughtful effort to help each patient as well as possible. Sigmund Freud wrote wisely: "All methods are good which produce the aim of the therapy."[45]

> It seems necessary to creatively introduce . . . a science or art of disagreement that could clarify how to disagree *intelligently* rather than do so in a mindless manner requiring some form of violent or repressive reaction to eliminate the disagreement as soon as possible.
>
> —*Encyclopedia of World Problems and Human Potential*[46]

> No difference is less easily overcome than the difference of opinion about semi-abstract questions; they never agreed in any opinion, and had long, indeed, been accustomed to jeer without anger, each at the other's incorrigible aberrations.
>
> —Leo Tolstoy, *Anna Karenina*.[47]

NOTES

1. H. Arkowitz, "Integrative Theories of Therapy," in *History of Psychotherapy: A Century of Change*, ed. Donald K. Freedheim (Washington, DC: American Psychological Association, 1992), 261–303; George Stricker and Jerold R. Gold, eds., *Comprehensive Handbook of Psychotherapy Integration* (New York: Plenum, 1993); Shlomo Ariel, *Culturally Competent Family Therapy* (Westport, CT: Greenwood/Praeger, 1999); Arnold. A. Lazarus, "Multimodal Therapy," in *Handbook of Psychotherapy Integration*, ed. John C. Norcross and Marvin R. Goldfried, second edition (New York: Oxford, 2005), 105–20; Philip Brownell, "The Four Options for Integrative Psychotherapy," *Royal Gazette* (London), May 7, 2013; Paul L. Wachtel, *Cyclical Psychodynamics and the Contextual Self: The Inner World, the Intimate World, and the World of Culture and Society* (New York: Routledge, 2014). Wachtel writes eloquently about "an integrative melding of psychodynamic, cognitive-behavioral, systemic, and experiential points of view, and a focus on the vicious and virtuous circles that perpetuate (or contribute to changing) personality patterns that may have originated in childhood but that persist because they often generate the very feedback from others that is necessary to keep them going" (342).

2. There are a good number of studies that have shown that the relationship between therapist and patient proves more significant than the specific mode or technique of therapy. See an excellent full issue of the journal *Psychotherapy* that is devoted to the subject. Mark J. Hilsenroth, *Special Issue, Therapeutic Relationship*, including a Special Section on Therapeutic Alliance. *Psychotherapy* 51, no. 3 (2014). See among others Paul L. Wachtel, "An Integrative Relational Point of View," 342–49.

3. D. W. Winnicott, "Hate in the Countertransference," *Voices: The Art and Science of Psychotherapy* 1, no. 2 (1965): 102–9. (Originally presented in 1947 and published in *International Journal of Psychoanalysis* 30 (1949): 69–74.

4. William H. Masters, and Virginia C. Johnson, *Human Sexual Inadequacy* (Boston: Little Brown, 1970).

5. Karl Abraham, "Ejaculatio Praecox," in *Selected Papers of Karl Abraham* (New York: Basic Books, 1957 [1917]), 280–98.

6. Following the pioneering work of Masters and Johnson, psychiatrist Helen Kaplan was the outstanding professional who followed with a clear-cut theoretical statement that sex therapy must first address relationship issues and only then advance to the sexual behavior exercises. Helen S. Kaplan, *The New Sex Therapy: Active Treatment of Sexual Dysfunctions* (New York: Brunner/Mazel, 1974).

The following study shows some of the limits of therapy that uses only the sexual behavior tasks: Alexander N. Levay, and Arlene Kagle, "A Study of Treatment Needs Following Sex Therapy," *American Journal Psychiatry*, 134, no. 9 (1977): 970–73. See also A. N. Levay, and A. Kagle, "Interminable Sex Therapy: A Report on Ten Cases of Therapeutic Gridlock," *Journal Marital and Family Therapy* 9, no. 1 (1983): 1–9, 15–17; Alexander N. Levay, "Long-Term Psychodynamic Treatment Needs in Sex Therapy," *American Journal Psychoanalysis* 43, no. 2 (1983): 139–47.

7. Over the years there have developed many structured programs for marital communication—with printed and/or Internet workbooks, instructional groups or

certified individual instructors. The Minnesota Couples Communication Program was perhaps the first such program: Sherod Miller, Elam W. Nunnally, and Daniel B. Wackman, "Minnesota Couples Communication Program (MCCP): Premarital and Marital Groups," in *Treating Relationships* ed. D. H. L. Olson (Lake Mills, IA: Graphic, 1976), 21–40; Sherod Miller, Daniel B. Wackman, and Elam W. Nunnally, "Couple Communication: Equipping Couples to Be Their Own Best Problem Solvers," *Counseling Psychologist* 11, no. 3 (1983): 73–77.

Today there are many variations of worksheets, workbooks, and manuals available on the Internet or to be purchased from professional publishing sources. Two widely promoted programs are *Prepare/Enrich Couple's Workbook* (Minneapolis: Life Innovations), retrieved September 4, 2014, http://www.scacseattle.org/prepare-/couplesworkbook.pdf; and Sherod Miller, Phyllis A. Miller, Daniel B. Wackman, and Elam W. Nunnally, *Collaborative Marriage Skills, the Workbook for Couple Communication I* (Evergreen, CO: Interpersonal Communication Programs). See Sherod L. Miller, P. A. Miller, Elam W. Nunnally, and Daniel B. Wackman, eds., *Talking and Listening Together: Couple Communication* (Denver-Littleton, CO: Interpersonal Communication Programs, 1991). A meaningful guide to such programs which also informs about other programs will be found in Luciano L'Abate, *Using Workbooks in Mental Health: Resources in Prevention, Psychotherapy* (New York: Routledge, 2013).

The following books are well known guides to marital therapy that include strong emphases on marital communication techniques: J. M. Gottman, *The Seven Principles for Making Marriage Work* (New York: Crown, 1999); Lori Gordon, *Passage to Intimacy* (New York: Fireside Books, 1993); Lori Gordon, *If You Really Loved Me* (Palo Alto, CA: Science and Behavior Books, 1997); Harville Hendrix, *Getting the Love You Want: A Guide for Couples* (New York: Holt, 2007).

8. See the discussion later in this chapter, "Deciding Which Therapy Is the Better One for Any Given Condition."

9. An excellent formulation of the contradictory or dialectical aspects of human life and the desirability of our synthesizing them will be found in the works of Roberto Assagioli in the method he called "psychosynthesis": Roberto Assagioli, *Psychosynthesis: A Manual of Principles and Techniques* (London: Turnstone Books, 1965); Roberto Assagioli, *The Act of Will* (Baltimore: Penguin, 1973); Erich Neumann, *Depth Psychology and a New Ethic* (New York: G.P. Putnam, 1969 1949]).

There are many other sources about the naturalness of all feelings, including the ones we naturally tend to identify as bad and therefore undesirable. For one example, Baha'i doctrine accepts all emotions. The Baha'i are a small faith with many beautiful emphases on the sacredness of human life and democracy. Baha'i writings include the concept that "In creation there is no evil, all is good. . . . All the natural qualities of man constitute the capital of life." The trick is how these qualities are used. If they are tapped to advance human life, they are in fulfillment of our God-given potential; but if they are used to destroy life, they constitute evil. "On Good and Evil," Baha'i International Community, retrieved November 14, 2014, http://info.bahai.org/article-1-4-0-9.html.

10. Cerletti and Bini were nominated for a Nobel Prize for Physiology or Medicine in the 1930s.

11. Alessandro Aruta, "Shocking Waves at the Museum: The Bini-Cerletti Electro-Shock Apparatus," *Medical History* 55, no. 3 (2011): 407–12 (quotations on p. 407). For whatever it is worth, the article also tells of a study by a Roberta Passione, who studied Dr. Lucio Bini's notebooks and concluded that the usual description of the breakthrough treatment of the first schizophrenic by ECT is a fiction. Passione writes: "It was an 'electro-shock novel' which was also authored by the self-celebrating Cerletti through the control he exercised over what his students [who were present at the pioneering treatment] could report. It is a self-fashioned heroic science narrative 'that crosses the border of myth.' Omitted is that there had been at least three failed attempts prior to the one described."

12. Masters and Johnson, *Human Sexual Inadequacy*.

13. Kaplan, Helen, *The New Sex Therapy*.

14. Alexander N. Levay, and Arlene Kagle, "A Study of Treatment Needs Following Sex Therapy."

15. Mark D. Rogerson, Michael C. Gottlieb, Mitchell M. Handlesman, Samuel Knapp, and Jeffrey Younggren, "Non-rational Processes in Ethical Decision Making," *American Psychologist* 66, no. 7 (2011): 614–23 (quotations are on p. 617).

16. The following two-volume set teaches very wisely basic interviewing skills for treating psychosomatic illnesses, including asthma: Felix Deutsch, and William F Murphy, *The Clinical Interview: Volume 1, Diagnosis, Volume Two, Therapy: A Method of Teaching Sector Psychotherapy* (New York: International Universities Press, 1955). See also the work of the one of the great fathers of psychosomatic medicine: Franz Alexander, *Psychosomatic Medicine: Its Principles and Applications*, second edition (New York: Norton, 1987); and a specific work on asthma: Thomas M. French and Franz Alexander, *Psychogenic Factors in Bronchial Asthma: Psychosomatic Medicine Monographs IV: Parts 1 and 2* (Washington, DC: National Research Council, 1941). See also Antonio Madrid, R. Ames, S. Skolek, and G. Brown, G. "Does Maternal-Infant Bonding Therapy Improve Breathing in Asthmatic Children?," *Journal Prenatal and Perinatal Psychology and Health* 15, no. 2 (2000): 90–112; See also Antonio Madrid, "Helping Children with Asthma by Repairing Maternal-Infant Bonding Problems," *American Journal Clinical Hypnosis* 48, nos. 2–3 (Oct. 2005, Jan. 2006): 199–211.

I frequently feel a great deal of sadness at how few therapists in our age have been trained to work with the dynamics of psychosomatic conditions—and I also feel quite guilty that as the director of several graduate and postgraduate training programs in my past, I really failed to include such instruction in the curriculum.

17. Joseph C. Rheingold, *The Fear of Being a Woman: A Theory of Maternal Destructiveness* (New York: Grune & Stratton, 1964); and Joseph C. Rheingold, *The Mother, Anxiety and Death: The Catastrophic Death Complex* (New York: Little, Brown, 1967).

18. Deborah L. Cabaniss, Sabrina Cherry, Carolyn Douglas, J. Ruth Graver, and Anna R Schwartz, *Psychodynamic Formulation* (New York: Wiley-Blackwell, 2013) 4. The therapist can also decide to share the key psychodynamic formulation with the

patient. When I was looking for a psychoanalyst years ago, I went to see the dean of an institute in Philadelphia, who was also the editor of the *Psychoanalytic Quarterly*, Leon Saul. He listened to me for twenty-five minutes of the thirty he had agreed to give me and then said, "Now Dr. Charny, I will tell you what your problem is"! He did—in no uncertain words, which were certainly unbecoming of a traditional silent analyst. My metaphor has been that he shot me right through my head, and accurately, damn him. (He himself had no time to treat me and he referred me to one of his students for what developed over the next four years into one of the greatest gifts of my life.) See Leon Joseph Saul, *The Childhood Emotional Pattern and Psychodynamic Therapy* (New York: Van Nostrand Reinhold, 1980).

19. Leo Srole, and Ernest Joel Millman, *Personal History and Health: The Midtown Longitudinal Study, 1954–1974* (Piscatawy, NJ: Transaction, 1998); Assen Jablensky, "The Forest and the Trees," (review of the last volume of the Midtown Study) *Contemporary Psychology, APA Review of Books* 45, no. 2 (2000): 221–23. "As the last volume in the series of reports of this milestone project, this book provides an overview of the design, methods, and results of the entire study." Retrieved from American Psychological Association, PsycINFO Database record 2012.

20. National Institute of Mental Health "Transforming the Understanding and Treatment of Mental Illnesses," retrieved June 1, 2014, www.nimh.nih.gov.. Based on a study published in 2005, NIMH estimates that some 26.2 percent of Americans who are eighteen and older—and itself comments that this means about one in four adults, or 57.7 million people when applied to the US census in 2004—"suffer from a diagnosable mental disorder in a given year." This is a staggering percentage. In fact, the numbers are not that bad—although they are bad enough. What seems to have happened here is that NIMH was following the kind of symptom head counts that we are saying are distorted to begin with, because they do not look at our natural human condition as including a great many "symptoms" as parts of our normal journeys without meaning that we are mentally disturbed. As noted, the NIMH statement goes on to say that, actually, it is "a much smaller proportion—about 6%, or 1 in 17—who suffer from a *serious* mental illness" (italics mine).

See also Derek L. Phillips, "The 'True Prevalence' of Mental Illness in a New England State" *Community Mental Health Journal* 2, no. 1 (1966): 35–40. Retrieved from American Psychological Association, PsycINFO Database record 2012; Ronald C. Kessler, Wai T. Chiu, Olga Demler, and Ellen E. Walters, "Prevalence, Severity, and Comorbidity of Twelve-Month *DSM-IV* Disorders in the National Comorbidity Survey Replication (NCS-R)," *Archives General Psychiatry* 62, no. 6 (2005): 617–27.

21. Florence W. Kaslow, ed., *Handbook of Relational Diagnosis and Other Family Dysfunctions* (New York: Wiley, 1996).

22. PDM Task Force, (*Psychodynamic Diagnostic Manual (PDM)* (Silver Spring, MD: Alliance of Psychoanalytic Organizations, 2006). PDM cites as one of its sources an article in *JAMA*: Paul R. McHugh, "Striving for Coherence: Psychiatry's Efforts Over-Classification," *Journal American Medical Association* 293, no. 20 (2005): 2526–28.

23. *Psychodynamic Diagnostic Manual*, 2.

24. Ibid., 4.

25. Anthony Theuninck, Amazon review, February 9, 2007, http://www.amazon.com/review/RXMOYLCN7G5G0.

26. Birgit Weiz, Amazon review, June 30, 2006, ibid.

27. Israel W. Charny, "The New Psychotherapies and Encounters of the Seventies: Progress or Fads?," *Humanist* 24 no. 3: 1–9, and 24, no. 4: 34–45. Reprinted in I. David Welch, George A. Tate, and Fred Richards, eds., *Humanistic Psychology: A Sourcebook* (New York: Prometheus, 1978), 117–40.

28. This is a direct quotation of the therapist that was told to me by the patient, a Holocaust survivor, who is a very dear colleague and friend.

29. Shamai Davidson, *Holding on to Humanity: The Message of Holocaust Survivors: The Shamai Davidson Papers*, ed. Israel W. Charny, foreword by Robert Jay Lifton (New York: New York University Press, 1992), 16–17.

30. Robert Krell, "Survivors and Their Families: Psychiatric Consequences of the Holocaust," in *Medical and Psychological Effects of Concentration Camps on Holocaust Survivors*, ed. Robert Krell and Marc I. Sherman (New Brunswick, NJ: Transaction, 1997), 24, 25.

31. This quotation of a therapist's instructions to a patient in psychoanalysis, who was a Holocaust survivor and herself also a psychoanalyst, was conveyed to me by my colleague who was the patient.

32. It is my privilege to pay tribute to my late mentor, Richard L. Cohen, MD, who at the time was the director of Oakbourne Hospital, a residential treatment center affiliated with the Philadelphia Child Guidance Clinic and Children's Hospital of Philadelphia, and later was professor of child psychiatry at the University of Pittsburgh, School of Medicine.

33. Alice Miller, *The Drama of the Gifted Child* (New York: Basic Books, 1997).

34. See Israel W. Charny, "Recovering the Lost Art of Naturalistic Family Therapy: Retrospective and Prospective," *Journal of Family Therapy* 25, no. 2 (2014): 99–116.

35. Rollo May, *The Meaning of Anxiety* (New York: W.W. Norton, 1996 [1950])

36. A welcome literature of solid research of outcomes of psychotherapy is growing apace. See a fine old-timer that is still good current reading: Robert Wallerstein, *Forty-Two Lives in Treatment: A Study of Psychoanalysis and Psychotherapy* (New York: Guilford Press, 1986). See also more recent studies: Sherwood Waldron, and Fonya Helm, "Psychodynamic Features of Two Cognitive-Behavioural and One Psychodynamic Treatment Compared Using the Analytic Process Scales," *Canadian Journal Psychoanalysis* 12 (2004): 346–68; Alan S. Gurman, "Couple Therapy Research and the Practice of Couple Therapy: Can We Talk?," *Family Process* 50 (2011): 280–92; Kevin M. Laska, "Expanding the Lens of Evidence-Based Practice in Psychotherapy: A Common Factors Perspective," *Psychotherapy* 51, no. 4 (2013): 467–81; Francesco Gazillo, Sherwood Waldron, Frederica Geneva, Frederica Angeloni, Chiara Ristucci, and Vittorio Lingiardi, "An Empirical Investigation of Analytic Process: Contrasting a Good and Poor Outcome Case," *Psychotherapy* 51, no. 2 (2014): 270–82; Andrew A. McAleavey and Louis G. Castonguay, "Insight as a Common and Specific Impact of Psychotherapy: Therapist-Reported Exploratory, Directive and Common Factor Interventions," *Psychotherapy* 51, no. 2 (2014): 283–84.

37. Here is an example of a comparative study: Jürgen Barth, Thomas Munder et al., *Comparative Efficacy of Seven Psychotherapeutic Interventions for Patients with Depression: A Network Meta-Analysis*, retrieved July 28, 2014, http://www.plosmedicine.org/article/info%3Adoi%2F10.1371%2Fjournal.pmed.1001454. The authors describe "moderate to large effects" in almost all of the therapy modes. An earlier review article about the effectiveness of different therapies will be found in Drew Westen, Catherine M. Novotny, and Heather Thompson-Brenner, "The Empirical Status of Empirically Supported Psychotherapies: Assumptions, Findings, and Reporting in Controlled Clinical Trials," *Psychological Bulletin* 130 (2004): 631–63. The literature of therapy outcome studies and comparative studies of different therapies is, to put it simply, exploding. See for further examples Michael J. Lambert, "The Efficacy and Effectiveness of Psychotherapy," in *Bergin and Garfield's Handbook of Psychotherapy and Behavior Change*, ed. Michael J. Lambert, sixth edition, 169–218 (Hoboken, NJ: Wiley, 2013); Kevin M. Laska, "Expanding the Lens"; Kevin S. McCarthy, and Jacques P. Barber, "The Multitheoretical List of Therapeutic Interventions (Multi): Initial Report," *Psychotherapy Research* 19, no. 1 (2009): 96–113.

38. Marcelo Feijo de Mello, Jair de Jesus Mari, Josue Bacaltchuk, Helen Verdeli, and Richard Neugebauer, "A Systematic Review of Research Findings on the Efficacy of Interpersonal Therapy for Depressive Disorders," *European Archives Psychiatry and Clinical Neuroscience* 255, no. 2 (2005): 75–82.

39. Gazillo, "An Empirical Investigation of Analytic Process."

40. David Brooks, "What Suffering Does," *International New York Times*, April 7, 2014.

41. Jonathan Shedler, "The Effectiveness of Psychodynamic Psychotherapy," *American Psychologist* 65, no. 2: 98–109 (quotation on p. 98).

42. Falk Leichsenring, and Eric Leibing, "Psychodynamic Psychotherapy: A Systematic Review of Techniques, Indications and Empirical Evidence," *Psychology and Psychotherapy* 80 Pt. 2 (2007): 217–28.

43. National Institute Mental Health (NIMH), retrieved April 10, 2014, http://www.nimh.nih.gov/health/topics/psychotherapies.

44. Shedler, "The Efficacy of Psychodynamic Psychotherapy," 107.

45. Sigmund Freud, "On Psychotherapy," in *Selected Papers on Hysteria and Other Psychoneuroses* (New York: The Journal of Nervous and Mental Disease Publishing Company, 1912).

46. Union of International Associations *Encyclopedia of World Problems and Human Potential*, second edition (Munich: K. G. Saur Verlag).

47. Leo Tolstoy, *Anna Karenina*, transl. Constance Garnett (New York: P.F. Collier & Son,1917).

Afterword

Personally—I Am, Yet I Am Not, But I Still Hope to Reach a More Democratic Mind

Needless to say, I pray to achieve (by the end of my life) a substantial degree of democratic mind—expressed both in the ways I treat myself and how I treat others. I do know that I can never "go all the way," and that working toward a goal of becoming a healthy human being is a major lifelong challenge in our journey.

- Neither in allowing myself to be tyrannical to myself such as in an order, "you must win and never fall down"; and not allowing any part of myself to drown and crowd out another vital aspect of living, such as a devotion to parenting but disavowal of adult passions.
- Nor in exercising superiority, totalitarian control, or violence against others—in all the known ways of fascism in society, but also in subtle concealments of exploitation of others in supposed decent functional relationships, for example, parental demands of a child to function for them and not for the child himself or herself.

I am sure and have no doubts whatsoever that I don't want to be blindly devoted to an ideology—including any single psychological theory or mode of therapy, nor totally obedient to an authority, or a stupid conformist to whatever society defines at the time as "politically correct."

I think it is because I know the work is never done that I have continued enjoying deeply doing therapy well into my old age. However difficult, reaching for a democratic mind makes me feel more *alive.*

Appendix

Prescriptions for a Free and Democratic Mind

ORGANIZATION OF DIVERSITY AND COMPLEXITY

Take an active coping position in organizing and running your own mind and life. Search for the best ways to deal with problems, including efforts to overcome problems that can be solved along with being ready to yield to unchangeable adversity. Address life's realities as complex and multifaceted, so that you question from the outset any proposals of total and absolute solutions as possibly offering more than can be fulfilled.

ACCEPTANCE OF UNCERTAINTY, PROCESS, POSSIBILITY, AND CREATIVE ANXIETY

Give up certainty in favor of maps of reality based on scientific evidence of probabilities, including also uncertainty, and concepts of process and change. Accept and enjoy anxiety and uncertainty as spurs to creative thinking and efforts.

OPEN-MINDEDNESS TO INFORMATION, QUESTIONING, AND USE OF SCIENTIFIC METHOD

Keep yourself open to new information, including especially evidence that contradicts your current ways of thinking and doing things. Be prepared to discard tried–and-true and favored ideas in the face of new evidence. Look for solutions that can be tried out, tested, and revised over time.

FREEDOM, RESPECT FOR DISSENT, AND RESPONSIBILITY TO MAKE CHOICES

Keep in touch with your own mind, and exercise your own real choices. Have the courage to be wary of authority and not to be automatically obedient or blindly conformist to the dictates of authority, certainly when your own basic moral principles are deeply violated. Be especially careful not to join a band-wagon or populist mind-set.

SHARING POWER, RESPECT, AND BASIC EQUALITY, WITH CHECKS AND BALANCES AGAINST EXCESSIVE POWER

Be aware in yourself of strivings for superiority and power of one part of your personality over all the rest of you, for example, a demand for pleasure at any cost, and be aware of strivings for superiority and power over others. In both cases, renounce excessive power in favor of cooperative structures and egalitarian relationships. Create checks and balances in your own mind against the absoluteness of any impulse, idea or ideology, and seek an interplay with the critical thinking and critical evaluations of you and your ideas by your own self and by others.

NONVIOLENCE, CONFLICT RESOLUTION, AND SEEKING PEACE

Renounce violence to your own self and/or to other human beings. Commit yourself to the holiness of life, protecting your own and others' lives, and to nurturing health and a good quality of living for yourself and for others.

ACCEPTANCE OF RESPONSIBILITY FOR DOING HARM TO SELF AND OTHERS

When you do end up doing harm to yourself or others, make every effort to acknowledge the harm you are doing. Whenever you are able to do so, take responsibility for the harm you have done to yourself or to others, and makes whatever corrections or compensation possible. Above all, take greater responsibility for stopping further harm and destructiveness.

Bibliography

Abraham, Karl (1957) [written in 1917]. Ejaculatio praecox. In *Selected Papers of Karl Abraham*. New York: Basic Books, pp. 280–298. [London: Karnac Books, 1979].

Aldarondo, Etiony (Ed.) (2007). *Advancing Social Justice through Clinical Practice*. Mahwah, NJ: Lawrence Erlbaum.

Alexander, Franz (1987). *Psychosomatic Medicine: Its Principles and Applications*. Second edition. New York: Norton.

American Psychiatric Association (1980). *DSM-III: Diagnostic and Statistical Manual of Mental Disorders*. Third Edition. Washington, DC: American Psychiatric Association.

American Psychiatric Association (1994). *DSM-IV: Diagnostic and Statistical Manual of Mental Disorders*. Fourth Edition. Washington, DC.

American Psychiatric Association (2013). *DSM-5: Diagnostic and Statistical Manual of Mental Disorders*. Fifth Edition Revised. Washington, DC: American Psychiatric Association.

Angell, Marcia (2011). The epidemic of mental illness: Why? *New York Review of Books*. Part One, June 23. Part Two, July 28.

Ariel, Shlomo (1999). *Culturally Competent Family Therapy*. Westport, CT: Greenwood/Praeger.

Arieti, Silvano (1975). *Will to be Human*. New York: Delacorte.

Arieti, Silvano (1981). *Abraham and the Contemporary Mind*. New York: Basic Books.

Arieti, Silvano (2000). *The Parnas: A Scene from the Holocaust*. Philadelphia: Paul Dry Books.

Arieti, Silvano, and Meth, Johannes M. (1959). Rare, unclassified, collective and exotic psychiatric syndromes. *American Handbook of Psychiatry*. Vol 1. New York: Basic Books, pp. 144–157.

Assagioli, Roberto (1965). *Psychosynthesis: A Manual of Principles and Techniques*. London: Turnstone Books.

Assagioli, Roberto (1973). *The Act of Will.* Baltimore: Penguin.

Baum, Steven K. (2008). *Antisemitism Explained.* Foreword by Shimon Samuels. Lanham, MD: University Press of America.

Baum, Steven K. (2011). *The Psychology of Genocide: Perpetrators, Bystanders, and Rescuers.* New York: Cambridge University Press.

Becker, Ernest (1973). *The Denial of Death.* New York: Free Press.

Bettelheim, Bruno (1967). *The Empty Fortress: Infantile Autism and the Birth of the Self.* New York: Free Press.

Boszormenyi-Nagy, Ivan (1987). *Foundations of Contextual Therapy: Collected Papers of Ivan Boszormenyi-Nagy, MD.* New York: Brunner/Mazel.

Boszormenyi-Nagy, Ivan, and Spark, Geraldine (1973; 1984). *Invisible Loyalties: Reciprocity in Intergenerational Family Therapy.* New York: Harper & Row. (Second edition, New York: Brunner/Mazel).

Bronfenbrenner, Urie (1970). *Two Worlds of Childhood.* New York: Simon and Schuster.

Bugental, James (1956). *The Search for Authenticity.* New York: Holt, Rinehart and Winston.

Burggraeve, Roger (2012). *The Wisdom of Love in the Service of Love: Emmanuel Levinas on Justice, Peace and Human Rights*, trans. Jeffrey Bloechl. Milwaukee: Marquette University Press.

Burggraeve, Roger (Ed.) (2008). *The Awakening to the Other: A Provocative Dialogue with Emmanuel Levinas.* Leuven: Peeters.

Cabaniss, Deborah L., Cherry, Sabrina, Douglas, Carolyn, Graver, J. Ruth, and Schwartz, Anna R. (2013). *Psychodynamic Formulation.* New York: Wiley-Blackwell.

Camus, Albert (1980). *Neither Victims nor Executioners* (original publication 1946). *Combat.*

Carlat, Daniel (2010). *Unhinged: The Trouble with Psychiatry—A Doctor's Revelations about a Profession in Crisis.* New York: Free Press.

Charny, Israel W. (1982). *How Can We Commit the Unthinkable? Genocide, the Human Cancer.* In collaboration with Chanan Rapaport. Foreword by Elie Wiesel. Boulder, CO: Westview Press, 1982. Paperback with title change: *Genocide, the Human Cancer: How Can We Commit the Unthinkable?* New York: Hearst Professional Books [William Morrow], 1983.

Charny, Israel W. (1986). Genocide and mass destruction: Doing harm to others as a missing dimension in psychopathology. *Psychiatry*, 49(2), 144–157.

Charny, Israel W. (Ed.) (1988). *Genocide: A Critical Bibliographic Review.* London: Mansell; and New York: Facts on File. Awarded *Outstanding Academic Book of the Year* by American Library Association.

Charny, Israel W. (1992). *Existential/Dialectical Marital Therapy: Breaking the Secret Code of Marriage.* New York: Brunner/Mazel.

Charny, Israel W. (1996). Evil in human personality. In Kaslow, Florence (1966). Ed. *Handbook of Relational Diagnosis and Dysfunctional Family Patterns.* New York: Wiley, pp. 477–495.

Charny, Israel W. (1997). A personality disorder of excessive power strivings. *Israel Journal Psychiatry*, 34(1), 3–17.

Charny, Israel W., editor-in-chief, (1999). *Encyclopedia of Genocide*. Two Volumes. ABC-Clio Publishers. Santa Barbara, CA and Denver, CO, USA: December, 1999; London, UK: February 2000. Associate Editors: Rouben Paul Adalian, Steven Jacobs, Eric Markusen and Samuel Totten. Bibliographic Editor: Marc I Sherman. Forewords by Bishop Desmond Tutu and Simon Wiesenthal: "Why Is It Important to Learn about the Holocaust and the Genocides of All Peoples?" Awarded *Outstanding Academic Book of the Year* by the American Library Association; Charny, Israel W. (2008).

Charny, Israel W. (2006). *Fascism and Democracy in the Human Mind: A Bridge between Mind and Society*. Lincoln: University of Nebraska Press. Awarded *Outstanding Academic Book of the Year* 2007 by American Library Association.

Charny, Israel W. (2014). Recovering the lost art of naturalistic family therapy: Retrospective and perspective. *Journal Family Psychotherapy*, 25(2), 99–116.

Charny, Israel W. (2016) *The Genocide Contagion: How We Commit and Can Prevent Holocaust and Genocide—a Book for Learning about Ourselves B E F O R E*. Lanham, MD: Rowman & Littlefield.

Charny, I. W. (in press 2017). *Psychotherapy for a Democratic Mind: Intimacy, Tragedy, Violence and Evil*. Lanham, MD: Rowman and Littlefield.

Davidson, Shamai (1992). *Holding on to Humanity—the Message of Holocaust Survivors: The Shamai Davidson Papers*. Edited by Israel W. Charny. Foreword by Robert Jay Lifton. New York: New York University Press.

Deutsch, Felix, and Murphy, William F. (1955). *The Clinical Interview. Volume 1: Diagnosis*. New York: International Universities Press.

Deutsch, Felix, and Murphy, William F. (1955). *The Clinical Interview, Volume Two: Therapy: A Method of Teaching Sector Psychotherapy*. New York: International Universities Press.

Diamond, Stephen A. (1996/2007). *Anger, Madness, and the Daimonic: The Psychological Genesis of Violence, Evil, and Creativity*. Albany: State University New York Press.

Doherty, William J. (1995). *Soul Searching: Why Psychotherapy Must Promote Moral Responsibility*. New York: Basic Books.

Doherty, William J. (2001). Value-sensitive therapy. In Jon Carlson and Diane Kjos (Eds.), *Theories and Strategies of Family Therapy*. Boston, MA: Allyn & Bacon, pp. 98–122.

Ellis, Albert (1987). The impossibility of achieving consistently good mental health. *American Psychologist*, 42, 364–75.

Ellis, Albert (1994). *Reason and Emotion in Psychotherapy* (originally published in 1962). Secaucus, NJ: Carol Publishing Group.

Epstein, Seymour (1994). Integration of the cognitive and the psychodynamic unconscious. *American Psychologist*, 49(8), 709–24.

Festinger, Leon (1957). *A Theory of Cognitive Dissonance*. Evanston: IL: Row-Peterson.

Framo, James L. (1992). *Family-of-Origin Therapy: An Intergenerational Approach*. New York: Brunner/ Mazel.

Framo, James L. (2003). Co-authored with Timothy Weber and his wife Felise Levine) and published posthumously. *Coming Home Again: A Family of Origin Consultation*. New York: Brunner/Routledge.

Frances, Allen (2013). *Essentials of Psychiatric Diagnosis*. New York: Guilford Press.

Frances, Allen (2013). *Saving Normal: An Insider's Revolt against Out-of-Control Psychiatric Diagnosis: DSM-5, Big Pharma, and the Medicalization of Ordinary Life*. New York: William Morrow.

Frankl, Viktor. (1963). *Man's Search for Meaning: An Introduction to Logotherapy*. New York: Pocket Books [New York: Beacon, 2006]

Freedheim, Donald K. (Ed.), *History of Psychotherapy: A Century of Change*. Washington, DC: American Psychological Association.

Fromm, Erich (1966). *Man for Himself: An Inquiry into the Psychology of Ethics*. Originally published in 1947. Austin, TX: Holt Rinehart and Winston

Fromm, Erich (1955). *The Sane Society*. New York: Reinhardt & Co., p. 275.

Fromm, Erich (1964). *The Heart of Man: Its Genius for Good and Evil*. New York: Harper & Row and American Mental Health Foundation Books, November 2010.

Fromm, Eric (1992). *The Anatomy of Human Destructiveness*. New York: Holt Paperbacks. Originally published 1964.

Fromm, Erich (1994). *Escape from Freedom*. New York: Henry Holt. Originally published 1941.

Fromm, Erich (1991). *On Being Human*. London: Bloomsbury.

Goffman, Erving (1961). *Asylums: Essays on the Social Situation of Mental Patients and Other Inmates*. New York: Anchor Books.

Gordon, Lori (1997). *If You Really Loved Me*. Palo Alto: Science and Behavior Books.

Gordon, Lori (1993). *Passage to Intimacy*. New York: Fireside Books.

Gottman, J. M. (1999). *The Seven Principles for Making Marriage Work*. New York: Crown.

Hendrix, Harville (2007). *Getting the Love You Want: A Guide for Couples*. 20th Anniversary Edition, Paperback. New York: Holt.

Hilsenroth, Mark J. (Ed.) (2014). *Special Issue, Therapeutic Relationship,* including a Special Section on Therapeutic Alliance. *Psychotherapy*, 51(3), whole issue.

Horney, Karen (1950). *Neurosis and Human Growth*. New York: Norton.

Horwitz, Allan, V., and Wakefield, Jerome C. (2012). *All We Have to Fear: Psychiatry's Transformation of Natural Anxieties into Mental Disorders*. New York: Oxford University Press.

Horwitz, Allan, V., and Wakefield, Jerome C. (2014). *The Loss of Sadness: How Psychiatry Transformed Normal Sorrow into Depressive Disorder*. New York: Oxford University Press.

Kaffman, Mordecai (1981). Monodeism in psychiatry: theoretical and clinical implications. *American Journal Psychotherapy*, 35(2), 235–243.

Kaffman, Mordecai (1983). Inflexible belief-constructs in families of paranoid patient. *International Journal Family Therapy*, 3(4), 487–500.

Kaffman, Mordecai (1984). Paranoid disorders: The core of truth behind the delusional system. *International Journal Family Therapy*, 4(6), 220–232.

Kaplan, Helen S. (1974). *The New Sex Therapy: Active Treatment of Sexual Dysfunctions*. New York: Brunner/Mazel.

Kaslow, Florence W. (Ed.) (1996). *Handbook of Relational Diagnosis and Dysfunctional Family Patterns*. New York: John Wiley and Sons.

Kelly, George (1963). *A Theory of Personality: The Psychology of Personal Constructs*. New York: Norton.

Kelman, Herbert C., and Hamilton, V. Lee (1989). *Crimes of Obedience: Towards a Social Psychology of Authority and Responsibility*. New Haven, CT: Yale University Press.

Kesey, Ken (1962). *One Flew over the Cuckoo's Nest*. New York: Viking.

Kirsch, Irving (2009). *The Emperor's New Drugs: Exploding the Antidepressant Myth*, New York: Basic Books.

Krell, Robert, and Sherman, Marc I. (Eds.) (1997). *Medical and Psychological Effects of Concentration Camps on Holocaust Survivors*. New Brunswick, NJ: Transaction.

L'Abate, Luciano (2013). *Using Workbooks in Mental Health: Resources in Prevention, Psychotherapy*. New York: Routledge.

Lazarus, Arnold. A. (2005). Multimodal therapy. In John C. Norcross and Marvin R. Goldfried (Eds.), *Handbook of Psychotherapy Integration*. Second edition. New York: Oxford, pp. 105–120.

Lifton, Robert Jay (1968). *Death in Life: Survivors of Hiroshima*. New York: Random House.

Lifton, Robert Jay (1973). *Home from the War: Vietnam Veterans—Neither Victims nor Executioners*. New York: Simon & Schuster.

Lifton, Robert Jay, and Markusen, Eric (1990). *The Genocidal Mentality: Nazi Holocaust and Nuclear Threat*. New York: Basic Books.

Lifton, Robert Jay (2000). *The Nazi Doctors: Medical Killing and the Psychology of Genocide*. New York: Basic Books.

Maslach, Christina (2000). An outsider's view of the underside of the Stanford Prison Experiment. My role in the Stanford Prison Experiment. Section in chapter by Zimbardo, Maslach, and Haney. In Thomas Blass (2000) (Ed.) *Obedience to Authority: Current Perspectives on the Milgram Paradigm*. Mahwah N J: Lawrence Erlbaum.

Masters, William H., and Johnson, Virginia C. (1970). *Human Sexual Inadequacy*. Boston: Little Brown.

May, Rollo (1972). *Power and Innocence: A Search for the Sources of Violence*. New York: Norton.

May, Rollo (1983/86). *The Discovery of Being: Writings in Existential Psychology*. New York: Norton.

May, Rollo (1996). *The Meaning of Anxiety*. New York: Ronald Press (original publication 1950).

May, Rollo (1998). *Power and Innocence: A Search for the Sources of Violence*. New York: Norton. Originally published in 1972.

Menninger, Karl, Mayman, Markus, and Pruyser, Paul (1963). *The Vital Balance: The Life Process in Mental Health and Illness*. New York: Viking Press.

Milgram, Stanley (1965). *Obedience* (A Film). University Park: Pennsylvania State Audio Visual Services [distributor].

Milgram, Stanley (1965). Some conditions of obedience and disobedience to authority. *Human Relations*, 18, 57–76.

Milgram, Stanley (1974). *Obedience to Authority: An Experimental View*. New York: Harper & Row.

Miller, Alice (1997). *The Drama of the Gifted Child*. New York: Basic Books.

Mowrer, O. Hobart (1972). Integrity Groups: Principles and procedures. *Counseling Psychologist*, 3(2), 7–33.

Mowrer, O. Hobart (2013). *The Crisis in Psychiatry and Religion*. London: Forgotten Books. Originally published in 1961.

Neumann, Erich (1969). *Depth Psychology and a New Ethic*. New York: G.P. Putnam [originally published in German in 1949].

PDM Task Force (2006). *Psychodynamic Diagnostic Manual (PDM)*. Silver Spring, MD: Alliance of Psychoanalytic Organizations.

Pilisuk, Marc, and Ober, Lyn (1976). Torture and genocide as public health problems. *American Journal Orthopsychiatry*, 46(3), 388–392.

Porter, Roy (1999). *The Greatest Benefit to Mankind: A Medical History of Humanity from Antiquity to the Present*. Waukegan, IL: Fontana Press.

Resnick, H. L. P. (Ed.) (1968). *Suicidal Behaviors: Diagnosis and Management*. Boston: Little Brown & Co.

Rheingold, Joseph C. (1964). *The Fear of Being a Woman: A Theory of Maternal Destructiveness*. New York: Grune & Stratton.

Rheingold, Joseph C. (1967), *The Mother, Anxiety and Death: The Catastrophic Death Complex*. New York: Little Brown.

Rogerson, Mark D., Gottlieb, Michael C., Handlesman, Mitchell M., Knapp, Samuel, and Younggren, Jeffrey (2011). Non-rational processes in ethical decision making. *American Psychologist*, 66(7), 614–623.

Rosenhan, David (1973), On being same in insane places. *Science*, 179 (no. 4070), 250–58.

Rosenhan, David L., and Seligman, Martin E. P. (1984). *Abnormal Psychology*. New York: Norton.

Saul, Leon Joseph (1980), *The Childhood Emotional Pattern and Psychodynamic Therapy*. New York: Van Nostrand Reinhold.

Schneider, Kirk, and May, Rollo (1995). *The Psychology of Existence*. New York: McGraw-Hill.

Scull, Andrew (2005). *Madhouse: A Tragic Tale of Megalomania and Modern Medicine*. New Haven: Yale University Press.

Searles, Harold F. (1960). The desire to become nonhuman as a defense against various feeling-states. In *The Nonhuman Environment in Normal Development and in Schizophrenia*. New York International Universities Press, pp. 223–249.

Sharkey, Joe (1994). *Bedlam: Greed, Profiteering and Fraud in a Mental System Gone Crazy*. New York: St. Martin's Press.

Shedler, J., Mayman, M., and Manis, M. (1993). The illusion of mental health. *American Psychologist*, 48(11), 1117–31.

Shedler, Jonathan (2010). The effectiveness of psychodynamic psychotherapy. *American Psychologist*, 65 (2), 98–109.

Sheehy, Gail (1976). *Passages: Predictable Crises of Adult Life*. New York: E.P. Dutton.

Srole, Leo, and Millman, Ernest Joel (1998). *Personal History and Health: The Midtown Longitudinal Study, 1954–1974.* Piscatawy, NJ: Transaction.

Staub, Ervin (1989). *The Roots of Evil: The Origins of Genocide and Other Group Violence.* New York: Cambridge University Press.

Staub, Ervin (2011). *Overcoming Evil: Genocide, Violent Conflict, and Terrorism.* New York: Oxford University Press.

Stricker, George, and Gold, Jerold R. (Eds.) (1993). *Comprehensive Handbook of Psychotherapy Integration.* New York: Plenum.

Tustin, Frances (1973). *Autism and Childhood Psychosis.* London: Hogarth.

Tversky, Amos, and Kahneman, Daniel (1974, September 27). Judgment under uncertainty: Heuristics and biases. *Science*, 185(4157), 1124–31.

Wachtel, Paul L. (2014). *Cyclical Psychodynamics and the Contextual Self: The Inner World, the Intimate World, and the World of Culture and Society.* New York: Routledge.

Waller, James (2002). *Becoming Evil: How Ordinary People Commit Genocide and Mass Killing*. New York: Oxford University Press.

Wallerstein, Robert (1986). *Forty-Two Lives in Treatment: A Study of Psychoanalysis and Psychotherapy.* New York, NY: Guilford Press.

Watts, Alan W. (1951). *The Wisdom of Insecurity: A Message for an Age of Anxiety.* New York: Vintage. (Second edition 2011)

Whitaker, Robert (2010). *Anatomy of an Epidemic: Magic Bullets, Psychiatric Drugs, and the Astonishing Rise of Mental Illness in America.* New York: Crown.

Winnicott, D. W. (1965). Hate in the countertransference. *Voices: The Art and Science of Psychotherapy*, 1(2), 102–109. [Originally presented in 1947 and published in *International Journal Psychoanalysis,* 1949, 30, 69–74.]

Yalom, Irvin D. (1980). *Existential Psychotherapy*. New York: Basic Books.

Yalom, Irvin D. (1989). *Love's Executioner and Other Tales of Psychotherapy*. New York: Basic Books.

Yalom, Irvin D. (2002). *The Gift of Therapy*. New York: HarperCollins.

Yalom, Irvin D. (2005). *The Schopenhauer Cure*. New York: HarperCollins.

Yalom, Irvin D. (2008). *The Spinoza Problem*. New York: Basic Books.

Zimbardo, Philip G.; Haney, Craig; Banks, W. Curtis; and Jaffe, David. (1974). The psychology of imprisonment: Privation, power, and pathology. In Zick Rubin (Ed.), *Doing unto Others: Joining, Melding, Conforming, Helping, Loving.* Englewood Cliffs, NJ: Prentice-Hall, pp. 61–73.

Zimbardo, Philip G., Maslach, Christina, and Haney, Craig. (2000). Reflections on the Stanford Prison Experiment: Genesis, transformations, consequences. In Thomas Blass (2000).(Ed.) *Obedience to Authority: Current Perspectives on the Milgram Paradigm*. Mahwah N J: Lawrence Erlbaum, pp. 193–237.

Zimbardo. Philip G., and Funt, Alan (1992). *Candid Camera Classics in Social Psychology: Viewer's Guide and Instructor's Manual.* New York: McGraw-Hill.

Index

About the Author

I. W. Charny is an American and Israeli who is widely known in the United States, Europe, and Israel as a leader in both family therapy and genocide studies and prevention. In both cases his work is anchored in his continuing clinical practice and professional leadership as a clinical psychologist and family therapist. He is well known as founder and first president of the Israel Family Therapy Association, a past president of the International Family Therapy Association, and a cofounder and past president of the International Association of Genocide Scholars. In 2011 he was honored with a Presidential Prize by the president of Armenia "in recognition of his decades-long academic work and activities contributing to international recognition of the Armenian Genocide and his researches of denials of genocides." He has written a good deal about marriage and family therapy, including two books, *Marital Love and Hate*, 1972, and *Existential Dialectical Marital Therapy: Breaking the Secret Code of Marriage*, 1992. Three of his previous books have been awarded "Outstanding Academic Book of the Year" by the American Library Association: Editor, *Genocide: A Critical Bibliographic Review*, 1988; Editor, *Encyclopedia of Genocide*, 1999; and *Fascism and Democracy in the Human Mind*, 2006. A recent book, *The Genocide Contagion: How We Commit and Confront Genocide*, 2016 has won the "Spirituality and Practice Book Award."

www.ingramcontent.com/pod-product-compliance
Lightning Source LLC
Chambersburg PA
CBHW031414220926
51612CB00004B/21